REDHANDED

REDHANDED

Inside the Spy Ring that Changed the World

Gordon Lunan

Optimum Publishing International
Maxville Montreal Ottawa

Redhanded: Inside the Spy Ring that Changed the World
By Gordon Lunan

Published by Optimum Publishing International Inc.
10 Highland Drive, Box 524
Maxville, ON
K0C 1T0
Michael S. Baxendale, Publisher
www.optimumbooks.com

National Library of Canada Cataloguing in Publication
Lunan, Gordon, 1915-
Redhanded : Igor Gouzenko, Paul Martin Sr., Winston Churchill, Kingston Penitentiary; Inside the spy ring that changed the world / Gordon Lunan.

Originally Published under title: The making of a spy
Includes bibliographical references and Index
ISBN 0-88890-243-3

1.Lunan, Gordon, 1915-. 2. Gouzenko, Igor, 1919-1982. 3. Defectors—Soviet Union—Biography. 4. Espionage, Soviet-Canada. 5. Spies—Canada—Biography. 1. Title

UB271.C32L85 2004 327.12'092 C2004-900789-0
Cover Design: Optimum Publishing International Inc.
Editor: Craig MacLaine

Printed and bound in Canada on acid free, recycled paper.

Table of Contents

Part One – "Roots"

Part Two – "Life Under the Padlock Law"

Part Three – "From Ally to Enemy"

Part Four – "Home on the Range"

Epilogue

Foreword

On September 5th 1945, Igor Gouzenko – a cipher clerk at the Soviet legation in Ottawa – walked out of the building never to return. Hidden inside his shirt were 109 documents he had accumulated while sending and receiving messages between Moscow and the diplomatic mission. The secrets they contained would be his ticket to a new life of freedom in the West. At first, the Canadian authorities refused to take his defection seriously. But that changed two days later when military officials at the Soviet diplomatic mission launched a failed attempt to capture Gouzenko and drag him back to Soviet soil. Why would Moscow risk the diplomatic consequences of such a blatant violation of international law? The Royal Canadian Mounted Police decided to take a closer look at the documents. What they found would lead to one of the great spy scandals of modern times – one that would transform the Soviet Union from Second World War ally to dangerous and deadly Cold War foe.

The documents showed the Soviets had built an extensive espionage ring in the West. Dozens of arrests in the United States, Britain and Canada would follow. Among those who would be exposed were Alger Hiss, Harry Gold, Klaus Fuchs and Sir Anthony Blunt. They were just some of those accused of helping the Soviets to acquire the technology to build nuclear bombs. The Gouzenko documents made it clear that the Western democracies were under attack from a repressive and ruthless enemy – and that there were traitors deep within the hearts of the bureaucracies in Washington, London and Ottawa.

Or did they? Gordon Lunan was one of those arrested following the Gouzenko defection. An officer in the Canadian military and a speechwriter for Paul Martin (father of the future prime minister of Canada), Lunan was tried and convicted of helping the Soviets. For his crimes, he would spend five years in one of Canada's toughest prisons. But were Lunan and the others really traitors working for a sophisticated and frightening enemy?

No, says Lunan, and it is time to set the record straight.

Years before Senator Joe McCarthy launched his anti-communist campaign in the U.S., Canadian officials were hunting down real and imagined communist sympathizers at home. Basic democratic rights were ignored, legal principles were overridden – all in the name of defending the free world from the red menace.

Gouzenko would live his life in hiding under the false name "Krysac," always afraid of retribution from Soviet agents. He died – a blind diabetic – in 1982 after suffering a massive heart attack. In June 2003, the Canadian government would unveil a monument in Ottawa honoring Gouzenko for his contribution to the preservation of democracy.

It was a different tale for Lunan. After a series of trials in which his photograph and name were splashed across newspaper front pages throughout Canada and around the world, Lunan was sent to Kingston Penitentiary to serve his sentence. Today, he is a largely forgotten figure in the spy story that so shook the world.

But he never forgot. This is his story.

CM, Optimum Publishing

In loving memory of Miriam Magee

PART ONE
ROOTS

One
The Interrogation

The Date: Feb 20th, 1946
The Place: Justice Building, Ottawa
Subject: Capt Gordon Lunan
Interrogator: Inspector Clifford W. Harvison

The inspector seated opposite me at a narrow desk looked at me with cold eyes. He was a tall, thin, almost cadaverous man with a long, bony face. The eyebrows and unshaven tufts on his cheekbones gave him somewhat the appearance of a raccoon.

So this was Inspector Harvison of the Royal Canadian Mounted Police, the scourge of the labour movement. He reached out and touched a small desk clock.

Immediately I thought to myself, "Aha, a microphone, no doubt!"

"Well," he began, "We've tangled with you reds before. And you scream your heads off. But there's no way you're going to wiggle out of this one. You know why you're here. Are you ready to tell us what you know?"

"I do not know why I am here and I don't know what you're talking about."

"I see. The name 'Igor Gouzenko' means nothing to you?"

"Never heard of it." (Which was absolutely true).

"And the name Fred Rose?"

"Yes, I know that name. He's a member of Parliament I believe," I replied cautiously.

He paused a long moment before continuing. "I have reason to believe that you know a whole lot about Fred Rose, and that you were deeply involved with him and others in an espionage conspiracy. You would save us a great deal of time if you would simply answer my questions."

"I am being held here incommunicado. I want to know what are my rights. I want to see my wife and my lawyer."

"All in due course," he said before adding ominously, "At the moment you have no rights. You are being legally detained under an Order in Council and you are obliged by law to answer my questions."

"I have nothing to say."

The inspector pressed a button and a stocky man appeared in the doorway. His face was expressionless, but the lack of expression only made him more menacing.

My God, I thought, here comes the third degree.

Instead, Harvison said simply, "Take him away, Corporal Smith."

I was to see a good deal more of Corporal Smith (if that was, in fact, his real name and not his *nom de guerre*.) He popped up outside the Royal Commission hearing rooms, in the courtroom corridors, any place where subsequent proceedings unfolded.

Months later during a trial at which I had been subpoenaed, I went to the courthouse washroom and was standing at the urinal when three men came in. As I turned to look they stopped in their tracks. Between Corporal Smith and his clone stood a frightened Gouzenko, the cipher clerk whose defection from the Soviet Embassy in Ottawa with a shirtful of documents had sparked the spy probe.

I recognized him from his court appearances, as he must have recognized me. He probably thought he had walked into an assassination ambush. His escorts hustled him to a urinal and the three of them crowded up to one stall.

"My God, do you actually have to pull it out for him?" I asked.

But that first encounter with Gouzenko was still in the future. On this occasion, Smith's assignment was merely to conduct me through the labyrinth of elevators, staircases and passages to the unmarked car which drove me back from the Justice Building to RCMP Rockcliffe barracks where I had been locked up incommunicado since February 16th. I had been brought to the barracks a couple of days earlier by car from Dorval airport, arriving late at night. Just two days before that I had been sitting in an over-sized office at Canada House in London enjoying my position as acting Information Officer.

Two
Canada House

It was January 1946. I had been seconded from the army to the Wartime Information Board in Ottawa where, with half a dozen other servicemen from all branches, I was producing *Canadian Affairs*. The publication was designed for Canadian servicemen overseas. Our job was to inform them on current affairs, to encourage discussion and to prepare them for the return to "Civvy Street." The first meeting of the General Assembly of the United Nations Organization was about to take place at Westminster Central Hall in London. I was re-assigned from the Wartime Information Board to duty in Canada House to help with publicity.

Commercial trans-Atlantic flights were just resuming, using hastily converted Lancaster bombers. It was a long, perishingly cold flight from Ottawa to London, there being no heat on the planes. After what seemed an eternity, our plane flew over Ireland which glinted like emeralds in the dawn light. Minutes later we bounced down at Prestwick airport in Scotland where the human cost of war suddenly became all too real. A cheerful RAF flight lieutenant, his face one huge burn scar, met the plane.

"Anyone for London? Okay, pull the rag out. We're leaving right away."

We followed him to a nearby Dakota, the wartime version of the DC3, found a seat on the metal benches and without further formality zoomed off for London. There we landed RAF style, powering down to the end of the runway followed by a tight U-turn and panic-stop at a Quonset hut.

The Canadian delegation to the United Nations General Assembly was put up at the Dorchester Hotel on Park Lane but I opted to stay with my parents whom I had not seen for eight years. The reliable London tube got me to work at Canada House or at the hotel as needed.

The cream of Canadian political and diplomatic circles was assembled for the occasion, including Minister of Justice Louis St. Laurent, cabinet ministers Paul Martin and Jimmy Gardiner, and CCF Member of Parliament Stanley Knowles. External Affairs personnel included Escott Reid, Charles Ritchie, John Holmes, Hume Wrong and Louis Rasminsky – men whose distinguished careers would soon flower and later be recalled in best-selling memoirs. War correspondent Ross Munro was covering the event for the Canadian Press news agency. Who would not have been impressed at mixing with such luminaries in hotel rooms, receptions and cocktail parties?

I was installed at a barricade of a desk in a huge office on the ground floor of Canada House where I was expected to field the enquiries of all who came seeking information on Canada. On my second day I was escorted upstairs by a liveried footman and ushered into the High Commissioner's office, a room the size of a tennis court. Somewhere in the gloomy middle distance stood a little man waiting for me to traverse the yards of deep pile carpet. Vincent Massey greeted me without the slightest trace of bonhomie, real or assumed.

After a few perfunctory questions he motioned me to an armchair and took another chair opposite me. The footman appeared with tea in a silver pot and the usual afternoon tea selection of dainty sandwiches and cakes.

(It was a process with which I was not unfamiliar. At Mill Hill School the new boys had been invited in small groups to take tea with the Headmaster's wife. After tea we were required to play Spillikins, a table game in which you took turns using an ivory wand to extricate slivers of ivory one by one from a pile without moving any but the one you were after. Even at age fourteen we weren't dumb enough to think we had been invited for the pleasure of our company. It was, we knew, an elaborate device to test our manners, social poise, cleanliness of hands and fingernails, sense of fairness and sportsmanship, chivalry and ability to steer clear of contentious conversation – in other words, whether we were suitable for inclusion amongst the chosen.)

Massey began to assess me, beginning with my school history. Only when he realized that I was a genuine product of an English public school did he slightly unbend. The interview ended, if not affably, at least civilly.

One of the people who came to my office looking for information on Canada was a middle-aged man who was an academic planning to apply for a University position in Saskatchewan. He had one overriding concern:

"Tell me honestly, is there anti-Semitism in Canada?"

I answered him honestly: "Yes, there is."

He looked so stricken at my blunt answer that I was immediately sorry I had not used some circumlocution more appropriate to my temporary diplomatic status. I was answering him out of my own experience in business, in the army and as someone married to a Jew. Of course there was widespread anti-Semitism in Canada. What I did not realize at the time was how official and institutionalized it was, nor the part which High Commissioner Vincent Massey upstairs had played, together with prominent bureaucrats, politicians and churchmen, in stirring up what Anthony Burgess was to call "the fetid brew of hatred and ignorance on which anti-Semitism is based."

One morning, I was asked to attend an 8 a.m. breakfast meeting in Paul Martin's suite at which Canada's particular concern in relation to the developing United Nations agenda was to be discussed – namely, our unique ability to supply wheat to war-battered nations. I arrived early to find Paul still in boxer shorts negotiating with a salesman the purchase of a piece of jewellery for his wife, Nell. The best that the Dorchester, in the grip of rationing and shortages, could do for breakfast was two or three mushrooms and a piece of fried bread which the eight or so of us around the table quickly despatched before getting down to business.

"Well, who has it?" Paul began, snapping his fingers impatiently.

One of the External Affairs crew handed him a typewritten script. Paul picked up a pencil and began to read. He read maybe half a page then quickly leafed through the rest. Suddenly he sent the pencil flying across the room.

"Who," he demanded glaring around the table, "wrote this shit?"

Nobody stirred. His glance came to rest on me.

"You're supposed to be a writer," he said.

"That's right, sir," I answered somewhat hesitantly.

He threw me the draft of what turned out to be the speech he was to give over CBC International Radio that same evening.

"Stay after the meeting and we'll talk about it."

In spite of his outburst, I found Paul Martin easy to work with. I had always admired his apparent commitment to small "l" liberalism. He represented the best days of Liberal Party rule, out of which ultimately grew much of the social legislation Canadians enjoy today. I appreciate also that, whereas he might have blasted me when recalling the occasion in his memoirs, on the contrary, he recorded his impression of me as a capable and co-operative co-worker and went out of his way to try to explain subsequent developments in as kind a way as possible to my parents.

I holed up for the day with a typewriter and met Paul that evening as arranged. He read the draft without comment.

"Okay, let's go," was all he said afterward.

We taxied to the BBC studios where he delivered the speech – very well, too, I thought – into a big round microphone.

My euphoria was unfounded. What I did not know was that St. Laurent, if not other members of the delegation, knew exactly who I was. He had been responsible for the secret orders-in-council which would result in me and eleven others named by Soviet defector Igor Gouzenko being held incommunicado in police barracks with no access to legal counsel, to wives or next-of-kin or to any of the time-honoured civil rights of accused persons, and for our subsequent appearance before the secret Taschereau-Kellock Royal Commission investigating Soviet espionage. As we now know from Paul Martin's memoirs, *A Very Public Life*, St. Laurent, upon leaving London on January 25th to return to Canada, indicated to him that something important was afoot and that he might receive "one or two rather peculiar requests."

It was clear that I had been sent to London for a purpose other than the officially-stated one. But what purpose? The answer would only come to me later during my interrogation at the hands of Harvison.

On the eve of my departure for London I had looked up an old friend, Cam Ballantyne, who was with the International Labour Office and was about to be transferred to Geneva. We discussed the names of people I might get in touch with in London.

"I think Alan Nunn May is in London," Cam said. "You might like to look him up."

The name meant nothing to me but I entered it in my little black book anyway. This book, of course, eventually fell into the hands of the RCMP. The name undoubtedly accounted for the repeated questioning by Harvison about my allegedly meeting someone in front of the British Museum in London whom I supposedly identified by the copy of *The Times* under his arm. In spite of my repeated denials, Harvison appeared unconvinced. It was clear he had arranged to have me sent to London in the hope that I would lead MI5 to a meeting in *flagrante delicto* with Nunn May who was already under surveillance and who was subsequently found guilty of the charge of passing information to the Russians. The fact that I disappeared each evening to the suburbs instead of staying put at the hotel must further have aroused their suspicions.

Three
Arrest

The summons to return to Ottawa for "an important assignment" after only a month at Canada House came without warning. Within hours I was on the night train to Prestwick accompanied by Geoff Andrews, ostensibly my Wartime Information boss for the new assignment, but in reality my guard. The few other passengers on the Trans Canada Airlines converted-Lancaster bomber were assorted business types, except for one James Bond look-alike in a green tweed suit who took the seat immediately behind me.

According to the navigator, who welcomed passengers to his office up front, we were bucking unusually strong head winds which reduced our forward progress to less than a hundred miles an hour. Poor weather made it necessary to put down for refuelling at Reykjavik in Iceland where we were delayed for more than a day. James Bond disappeared, to attend – he said – to his business of peddling fishing nets, but no doubt to inform Ottawa of the delay. This must have caused some anxious moments at RCMP headquarters because they were on the brink of making arrests in Canada. They evidently decided to stick to their timetable because at our next stop at Goose Bay, where crew and passengers crowded into the terminal hut to warm up with a coffee, the news of a sensational spy case and the arrests of a number of well-placed Canadians was blaring from the radio. There were also reports that an army officer was being returned to Canada from England. This set off some good-natured joshing by the others who found what they took to be just a coincidence too good to pass up. My smile became more frozen and my responses less and less jocular as the miles wound down to Montreal.

It was dark when the plane landed at Dorval Airport and taxied up close to the building, leaving only a short gauntlet of tarmac leading to the arrival lounge doors. The moment I passed through the doors I heard my name being called on the loudspeakers. Who, me? I had the impression of being fingered by Geoff Andrews and being pointed in the direction of an office in which all the window blinds had been drawn. Here I was surrounded and restrained by three plainclothes men, frisked and told to empty my pockets. Gut-wrenching an experience as it was, I felt like laughing at their extreme nervousness. They jumped at my slightest gesture. What kind of stories had they been fed? Did they expect a poisoned stiletto in my shoe? Or that I would suddenly bite down on a cyanide capsule, depriving them of their prey? I would have to get used to my alter ego – not the real me but the portrait, unrecognizable at times, that would now be circulated world-wide – and to steel myself for the months of knotted intestines, shaky knees, dry mouth and rebellious stomach that lay ahead.

My nervous guards refused every request – to communicate with my wife who was somewhere in the building in the expectation of meeting me; to cite their authority for the arrest; even to divulge our destination after I had been put in the rear seat of a car.

The destination turned out to be the RCMP barracks, a huge floodlit brick block in Rockcliffe, a suburb of Ottawa. The building inside was compulsively clean and smelled faintly of carbolic acid.

A flabby uniformed Mountie was waiting in the lobby.

"We've brought Lunan," he was told.

He looked me up and down appraisingly. Then he motioned with his head for me to climb the stairs. He followed behind issuing instructions: "Another floor up…Left…Stop there."

We had come to a large dormitory of what seemed like twenty beds one of which was made up presumably for me. I was given pyjamas and toilet articles which had been removed from my confiscated suitcase – but no razor, which would be issued for use only under supervision. Dog-tired and drained by stress, I was only too glad to get to bed. All the ceiling lights were on in the dormitory. My bed was directly under one of them. When I asked for the lights to be put out, the guard refused, explaining that orders were that they were to be on at all times.

I slept anyway, but was awakened during the night by the Mountie pulling the sheet back from my face where I had put it to shield the worst of the light. He, too, believed in the suicide theory.

By the time I had seen thc end of this man I had almost begun to feel sorry for him. He was the lowest kind of gumshoe, assigned to stomp around government buildings. The force, it seemed, had scraped the bottom of the barrel to staff the operation. But for him it was the chance of a lifetime to merit the spurs which clanked manfully as he strode up and down the dormitory.

He set about to make friends by sympathizing with my plight, deploring the methods being used, criticizing the RCMP brass and trying to establish solidarity with me as a couple of guys being taken advantage of by the big shots. He told me harrowing stories about his problems with his wife and his young daughter's accidental injuries. From time to time he would lift a leg and break wind with a trumpeting sound. He was proud of the fact that he could modulate the sound by manipulating his sphincter muscle. Having thus gained my confidence, he evidently reasoned, he could begin slyly to question me and relay my unsuspecting answers to his grateful superiors.

He could have saved his wind. A couple of days later I was back in front of Harvison.

"Unfortunately for you," he said, "Mazerall has made a clean breast of it and has confirmed what we already knew in any case. Perhaps you think this is just a fishing expedition."

He then produced a ledger of large yellow sheets with column after column of typewritten entries.

"In 1939 while you were living at 3610 Oxenden Avenue you provided a secret distribution point for the communist newspaper the *Clarion*."

Silence. Then, with a theatrical sweep, he turned the page.

"On August 30, 1940 while you were living at 2048 Union Avenue in Montreal, you were visited by Fred Rose and Emery Samuel who stayed from 1700 until 2210 hours."

Like anyone active in the left wing or labour movement in Montreal during those years I knew that, under the terms of the infamous Padlock Law, every public (and sometimes even private) action or statement was susceptible to secret surveillance. Taking appropriate precautions became second nature. Yet as Harvison read out item after item from the yellow sheets, I was shocked at the extent of the detailed information the Red Squads had assembled. There had evidently been more informers in our ranks than we had imagined. And of course, any entry in a police file, no matter how innocent or unfounded, automatically assumes presumptions of guilt.

He opened a drawer and pulled out a sheaf of papers which he spread out in front of me. All too plainly, they were documents from my typewriter, some of them in my handwriting, which had arrived on his desk via the Soviet embassy.

To deny such overwhelming evidence seemed to me to be not only pointless but stupid, hardly the reaction of an intelligent man. Lacking the wits or the legal sophistication to say nothing further and throw the onus of proof on the accusers, I began to answer Harvison's questions. As anyone who has been through the process knows, a good interrogator wants more than anything else to start you talking, even about banalities, confident that as long as you are talking he will sooner or later get the answers he wants. The more one talks, the more difficult it becomes to stop. And Harvison was certainly a highly skilled interrogator. It seems likely that he had approached Mazerall the same way – telling him that I had talked – an elementary technique which succeeded if only by inducing me to explain my motives.

When the session was over, Harvison looked at me with scorn.

"How could someone with your background and education get mixed up with people like this?" He read off some names. "Rosenberg, Kogan, Gerson, Mazerall."

How do we account for our attitudes? How do we explain our convictions, our ethics, our beliefs, and how do we come to house them? Is it in our genes? If so, how do we explain why amongst siblings, sharing the same heritage, there can be such violently-held opposite views? Is it nature or nurture? What gives some the ability to step over a homeless reject with averted eyes while others bleed inwardly? Is it as random as the flick of a thumb which sent some to slave labour and others to the gas chamber? Some see the jug half-full; others see it half-empty. A pilot light of compassion burns in us all but why is it that in many it remains on standby while in others it ignites a fury of anger and protest.

I shall try to supply some of the answers to Harvison's question. Other answers he unwittingly supplied himself in his revealing memoir *The Horsemen* about more of which later.

Four
Golden Rule Days

Back in the custody of my flatulent guard in the RCMP dormitory I pondered Harvison's question. What indeed had set me on a path which, amongst other things, made me reject the anti-labour and anti-Semitic viewpoints held by Harvison and so many people in positions of power at that time?

My mind went all the way back to Leeds, a Yorkshire town where I had lived from the age of four to nine, and where I spent my first school days. Leeds had for centuries been linked to the Low Countries in the wool trade. It had a large Jewish population engaged in the worsted and clothing industries. We lived in a terrace of brick houses. To one side our immediate neighbours were the Cohens while a few doors on the other side lived the Goldbergs.

I don't think my mother, always occupied with the strategy of upward mobility, ever exchanged a word with the Cohens. Mr. Cohen could be seen leaving the house at irregular hours with a sackful of something over his shoulder. Perhaps he was a custom pedlar or perhaps a cottage manufacturer. Mrs. Cohen seemed to me like a grey, shrivelled witch although always kind and friendly. She would sometimes beckon to me, inviting me to enter her house, but I was terrified of this territory, partly because of the viciously barking black dog which ran up and down the high wall separating the two yards. One day she succeeded in getting me to go into her house. I was overwhelmed not only by the exotic and unfamiliar cooking smells but also by the almost palpable affectionate attention she showered on me, something I had rarely experienced at home. I suppose it must have been Passover because I left with a big packet of matzos. We never saw any people going to the house, young or old, and hindsight tells me that she sought me out as a surrogate grandchild on whom to pour her love.

The Goldberg boy was my age and we were in the same class at Cowper Street Elementary School. I can still see him clearly – swarthy skin, black eyes, crinkly black hair – dressed in short pants (you didn't move into long trousers until roughly the time your voice broke) and a tattered bright blue jersey. He always seemed to have a crumb at the corner of his mouth. One day he suddenly broke down in class and began to sob out of control. Our teacher tried without success to comfort him and then sent him to the cloakroom to weep alone. (Only when I returned home did I find out what had happened. His father was a receiver of stolen goods and had been arrested. My mother delivered the news with evident satisfaction. "Serves him right. What can you expect from people like that?" or words to that effect.)

We were in a class of about thirty boys and girls presided over by Miss McGregor, a sandy-haired lady wearing a tartan woolen skirt down to her ankles. There were two other teachers who occasionally took the class – Mr. Joy and Mr. Noble. We endured Mr. Noble who was too remote and wimpy for us after the bracing presence of Miss McGregor, but we feared and hated Mr. Joy who was a bully and a sadist. The muscles of his jaw would stand out like walnuts and spittle would spill from his mouth as he delivered slashing cuts with a cane to the outstretched hand of some unlucky boy or girl. I remember getting three on each hand for being a few seconds late for class. I suppose he wanted to teach me punctuality but instead he opened my eyes to the irrationality of authority.

Miss McGregor, on the other hand, made school almost a pleasure. We learned our "times tables" from two to twelve until we were figure perfect. She would draw a large chalk circle on the blackboard, numbered like a clock from one to twelve. Then she would chalk in at random any number from two to twelve. We had to rattle off the answers in quick succession around the class. Then she challenged us to master our sixteen-times table. To this day I have no trouble remembering – thirty-two, forty-eight, sixty-four, eighty, ninety-six and so on. We learned the rudiments of grammar and we learned to spell – or else!

Miss McGregor cared only peripherally about our juvenile psyches – not that she would knowingly have bruised them, but her concentration was on teaching, not on psychology. She taught us how to make change which nobody knew how to do – except Eric Levy whose father owned a store and who was roundly praised for his expert demonstration.

Miss McGregor leavened her no-nonsense teaching with other classroom diversions, the sights and sounds of which linger even after eighty years – the white whorls of hyacinth roots coiled in the wasp-waisted glasses; the overpowering hyacinth smell; sticky horse chestnut buds bursting into leaf; the orange and purple cocoons of silk worms fed on mulberry leaves stuffed into jam jars; the hand-painted Valentine and Christmas cards; the paper lanterns and chains. And always the exhortation to learn, to enjoy, to excel.

I took readily to schooling and became one of Miss McGregor's favourites, entrusted with a few coppers to fetch her a bun or some biscuits from the corner store with a ha'penny left over for myself. It gave me a feeling of importance and self-esteem which I had rarely felt at home. At home I was made to feel that I was wicked and perverse. Sin, or perhaps just my innate bloody-mindedness, made me do everything wrong including those things over which I had no conscious control. I was too pale. I walked funny, and funnier still as I tried to follow the directions to "turn your feet in, mon" or "ho'd yer head back" or "pit yer knees together." I later realized that my problem arose from being bow-legged and having a mild scoliosis, as diagnosed by the school doctor in a routine examination.

My mother was furious. He doesn't know what he's talking about, she thought. How dare he say that about my boy?

Worse still, sin paralysed my colon, making it impossible for me to move my bowels for days on end. In a home where open bowels were more important than an open mind, faeces were under constant scrutiny. I seemed to have spent hours in enforced, usually unproductive sessions, first on a china chamber pot before graduating to the W.C. Perversely, my anal sphincter, inoperative when on the pot, would loosen up unexpectedly at other times making me mess my pants.

It is hardly surprising that I wet the bed, I blushed at the mention of my name, I bit my nails, my larynx froze when required to say anything in company, even to answer to roll call in first grade.

At home, the words "mummy" and "daddy" were never uttered. It was always a formal "mother" and "father." I don't remember being hugged or cooed at or made an approving fuss of, although I possibly was in infancy. The words I most remember are "If I'd done that at your age I'd have been thrashed to within an inch of my life."

My mother was probably stating the truth. She was one of seven children of small shopkeepers in a small Scottish town. An irascible, domineering father (he died in his early sixties of a so-called apoplectic fit), the constraints of narrow-minded Calvinistic society; and the demands of a barely surviving family draper shop warped her spirit. What choice did she have but to pass on the defective emotional gene to me? It is not surprising that she took the earliest possible escape into marriage.

My father was ten years older, one of the few surviving children of a stonemason turned failed fruit farmer. Until the age of thirty a large part of his earnings had gone to help his younger siblings who were dying from infectious diseases including tuberculosis of the bone. He was a correspondence clerk when he married my mother, which meant that he copied business letters in pen and ink in a beautiful copperplate hand which he retained all his life. He stayed with the company until he retired in his seventies, winding up as managing director of one of its subsidiaries and a member of the board of directors.

My brothers were no help. At the time of my birth in 1915 my older brother, Douglas, was four years old. Within a few months my mother would be pregnant again, and soon after my father would be called up for service in the trenches. Big brother was far enough removed in age to rate more as a surrogate critic and disciplinarian than as a fraternal ally and protector. The younger one, John, was too close in age to be anything but a rival for whatever crumbs of approval dropped from the parental table. It is not hard to see how the middle kid would be lost in the shuffle. Justifiably or not, I had the perception of being unloved. I felt alone and vulnerable.

And yet, despite all the shame and anger, an inner voice told me I was something special. The hell with them, it said. I'd show them what I was made of and how far I would go. Just let's get this childhood bit over with as soon as possible. Meanwhile I could escape into an inner life of heroic fantasies.

Our house was in a Victorian terrace that had been built to accommodate animals as well as humans. Ours had the remains of a stable, complete with cast iron manger, untouchable by me because of the Jesus connection. Next to it was a wooden ladder leading to a loft still stuffed with straw. I would imagine taking up residence there, hidden in the straw, where I could listen undetected to the family's belated anguish and remorse at their heartless treatment. In recalling this, I am shocked at the intensity of the emotion and the photographic clarity of remembered scenes after so many years. My memories would probably be equally shocking to family friends, who would think them unfounded, spiteful, even malicious. They no doubt saw a more or less normal family – one of the boys being a bit odd, it's true – but didn't they look nice, polished and polite, sitting in a row in the family pew on Sunday mornings!

As I grew up, fear and anger changed to indifference and, too late, to understanding and compassion. The lack of love was probably more perceived than real. My parents had no doubt suffered themselves from a lack of overt affection and had really never learned how to express love. They had been taught that there was something unhealthy and "soppy" about showing emotion, even in the presence of the austere Presbyterian God before whom they might condescend to bow their heads but never to go on their knees.

Retrospectively I suppose the germ of love was there. Otherwise, why would my father sometimes burden himself with my eight-year-old presence as a passenger in his Morris Oxford open touring car as he made his commercial traveller's rounds calling on furniture stores, careening at thirty-five miles an hour from town to town. And why would he unknowingly forfeit the credit for his gesture, in my eyes, to the effusive store owners – Jewish for the most part – who made much of me and rewarded me with little presents just for being me.

My father was an untalented driver with no mechanical aptitude. On one trip he thought he smelt kerosene instead of petrol in the fuel line and wondered aloud if the car might explode. I spent the next hour in a catatonic expectation of doom. Going for a "run" in the car was a favourite family diversion in the '20s and '30s when the relatively uncluttered rolling English roads made the countryside easily accessible together with its bonus of tea rooms offering watercress sandwiches, scones, strawberry jam and clotted cream. Understandably, a carload of backseat drivers did nothing to improve my father's judgment or skill. He twice put us into avoidable accidents, producing frightening quantities of blood because these were the days before safety glass when windshields were made of ordinary plate glass. But...he did let me drive at the age of fifteen and freely lent the car thereafter.

Only twice do I remember my father's disciplined, buttoned-up demeanour breaking down. Once, when I was eighteen or nineteen, I happened to be present as an argument developed between him and my mother. She had become friendly with a young priest she had met at the golf club and was taunting my father with the spiritual and intellectual rewards of the relationship that, she implied, weren't to be enjoyed with her husband. My father was clearly furious at the thought of this young Papist upstart, and doubly so when my mother accused him of being jealous.

"Jealous? He can suck my arse!" my father blurted out.

The outburst was so uncharacteristic that my mother and I both burst out laughing and the quarrel went up in smoke.

The second incident I only heard about from my brother in Scotland who had had the unpleasant job of persuading the old man, now nearing ninety and living precariously alone, to go most reluctantly into a home for the elderly. Almost immediately his mind backed up two generations and he took refuge in imagined youth. He flirted with the nurses and scandalized the elderly ladies by singing dirty army songs at the top of his voice. He very soon died, not from any specific ailment but just from having worn out.

Five
Go South, Young Man

Another humiliation my parents unwittingly inflicted on my brothers and me was insisting that we parade our privileged ancestry by wearing our kilts and sporrans to church on Sunday mornings. Church itself was bad enough, an eternity of squirming on a hard pew while the minister stuttered his way through a lengthy, mournful sermon. Even worse was the three-block walk to church, exposed to the derision of our peers. The requests to lift our kilts and show what was beneath and the patronizing smiles of the grown-ups did little to convince me of the joys of church-going.

Our kilts, which marked the graduation from infancy to boyhood, were expected to serve for several years. The wrap-around design of the kilt accommodated itself to expanding waists. To provide for vertical growth the original kilt was made with a hem that was almost as deep at the kilt itself and could be let out as growth dictated. Living in Yorkshire, surrounded by people who spoke the broad Yorkshire dialect, and speaking it myself – except at home where it seemed unnatural to speak anything but family Scotch – I was pleased when we finally ran out of hem and I could discard that alienating symbol for good.

This happened to coincide with my father's first important promotion. His company, the inventors and near monopolists of linoleum, chose him to manage a new subsidiary they had formed to handle the sales of Congoleum, for which they had bought the sterling block rights.

Their idea was to nip this upstart competition for linoleum in the bud and they thought my father would be a suitably compliant employee. They put him on commission, thinking this would hold his earnings down while still providing the carrot he was used to as a salesman.

They badly miscalculated. The public quickly responded to this cheap, garish substitute and before long the cart began to pull the horse. My father began to make far more money than the titled, top-hatted owners thought appropriate. For three consecutive years they unilaterally renegotiated his contract to up the ante and better the odds in their favour.

My father, who had still not fully outgrown his forelock-pulling upbringing, allowed himself to be victimized until my outraged mother finally insisted he fight back.

This piece of exploitation by his bosses was not lost on me. Looking back on it, however, I realize that money was only part of the motivation. The owners, Sir Michael Nairn, his relatives and descendants, were minor aristocrats who simply could not allow an outsider from a lower social order to rise too far above his station.

My father had been sent to Philadelphia and Montreal, the two principal Congoleum centres, to be briefed before moving to London to set up headquarters for the new business. In both places he had evidently been warmly received, entertained and made to feel at home from top to bottom of the Congoleum world. His accounts made real to me the myth of this free-and-easy, egalitarian, rich and beckoning land which I had gleaned from the silent movies and the comics. He had brought back little presents – dollar Ingersoll watches and shiny dimes – and also an Indian wall-hanging consisting of a tasseled deerskin with a pokerwork design of a brave with feathered head-dress, smoking a peace pipe. This was probably a piece of tourist kitsch, but when I took it to school for a show-and-tell session, Miss McGregor praised it as a genuine Indian artifact. It helped me to form a mental picture of Montreal as a real place of wigwams and peace pipes and not just a spot on the map. The French presence was never mentioned.

Soon after my father's return from America, the family walked with mixed excitement and anxiety in a tight knot down the front path of 81 Spencer Place, Leeds, to the cast iron gate which my father carefully wired shut before we set out for London – the very centre of the Universe.

There are times in life when the present suddenly becomes the frozen past, distant, alien, filed and almost forgotten. Departure for London was such a time. It was as though my father had wired up the past along with the garden gate.

London, 1925: How was I to know that Hitler was out on parole after serving time for the "beer hall putsch"? Or that W. L. Mackenzie King in Canada had gambled on a snap election and had lost seventeen seats including his own? Or that Al Capone, a committed free-enterpriser, alarmed at the growing militancy of working men's union demands had declared "Bolshevism is knocking at our gates"?

The tide of political events had not yet washed over my feet making it necessary for me to choose between getting really wet or scurrying for dry ground. But an event a year later set me thinking. I was nine years old. My mother uncovered a distant relative who was a schoolmaster at Mill Hill, a non-conformist public school. Consistent with the parental attitude the Scots share with the Jews –namely, to give their children, if nothing else, the best possible education – she managed to arrange for our names to leap-frog to the head of the school waiting-list. That still meant a wait of a year which I spent in a local school run with uncompromising discipline by an Oxford-educated Indian and his son.

During that year of 1926, the British General Strike took place. The country immediately divided into two camps – them and us. Our headmaster made it plain to us which side we were on. As responsible, patriotic citizens, we must unanimously resolve to put up uncomplainingly with the withdrawal of the goods and services to which we were accustomed and wherever possible to act as strike-breakers. Most of us envied the thousands of young white-collar workers who thought it a great lark to drive buses, parade with armbands as special constables and generally show their disdain for the striking workers with whom, had they known it, they had a good deal more in common than with their employers.

One of our teachers, a sour young man with a mouthful of rotted teeth, became a train driver during the strike and had the commuters scrambling down the tracks to where he had managed to stop the train a hundred yards past the platform. It may have been that my dislike of this teacher was transferred to his position as strikebreaker. In any case, I began to question the motives of "our" side, perhaps not from any rational analysis but rather from the feeling of not really belonging, being already twice *déraciné*, and without any compelling tribal or class loyalty.

Instinctively, I felt far more sympathy for the clumps of picketing strikers in the streets than for my scab teacher. My newspaper reading didn't extend much beyond following the misadventures of the cartoon cat, Felix. And even if it had, it would have been difficult to get the real story from the popular press.

For the whole of that spring, the coal miners and the Coal Commission had been at loggerheads over wages. The Coal Commission, acting for the Tory Government and the mine owners, who included the Church of England, had made recommendations that would have reduced the miners' standard of living to 30 per cent below that of 1914. What had been a miners' quarrel suddenly exploded into a national labour union revolt, fueled by the traditional May Day rhetoric. On May 4th, when the Trades Union Council called for a general strike, Labour's support was total. Even *The Times* compositors and printers walked out, causing the defiant editors to publish on May 5th the newspaper's first and only typewritten edition before hastily-recruited scab labour could take over.

More and more my instinct was to side with the underdog, not because I felt myself to be an underdog but, rather, an outsider distrustful of authority in all its forms, skeptical of its motives and jargon. It would be a long time, however, before this attitude would congeal into a committed political position. First would come seven years of exposure to the ways of the "haves" of society in prep and public schools, during which I would acquire the accent, the manners and quite a few of the prejudices and attitudes of the majority of my schoolmates.

Six
Prep School

The preparatory school, Belmont, and the senior school, Mill Hill School, were separate but loosely associated establishments. Boys graduating from Belmont would normally go on to Mill Hill, although there were times when a *nouveau riche* parent whose fortunes had zoomed would break ranks and send his son to Harrow or some other school considered to be more prestigious.

"Public Schools" were the creation of the monasteries, designed to educate deserving children of the poor. Only after the dissolution of the monasteries did they gradually metamorphose into preserves of the rich and privileged. The popular idea of such boarding schools as advanced by magazines like *Boy's Own Paper* and *Chums* was that bullying was rife and "newbugs" faced a year or two of "fagging," random cruelties and ostracism or being "sent to Coventry."

It was not only the penny dreadfuls that spread this notion. English writers through the years, probably because the schools tended to put gentlemanly conduct ahead of intellectual or artistic ability, found the schools hard to endure and later let fly at them with sardonic barbs. Henry Fielding called them "the nurseries of all vice and immorality." Saki wrote: "You can't expect a boy to be depraved until he has been to a good school." Douglas Reed, one of the very few English writers of lowly birth to crash the Old Boy's network to become a *Times* foreign correspondent and best-selling author quotes, with a *soupçon* of malice, a distinguished churchman who said that the first public school man was born in Nazareth and his name was Jesus Christ.

I doubt if my mother ever read either *Chums* or Saki. But she evidently believed all of this to be true and she described the horrors in detail well in advance to prepare me for my fate, succeeding in making me steadily more apprehensive as my imagination went to work.

The experience, when the day arrived, was as new for my parents as it was for me. They deposited me at the school as arranged, to join the other "newbugs" a day in advance of the 1926 autumn term. I was ten years old. My father gave me two shillings as pocket money (to last me, I suppose, for the next thirteen weeks!) then, avoiding eye contact, admonished me not to play with myself "down there," indicating my crotch. This was the first and only sex education I had received up till then. It gave me a new idea of the significance of "down there." Before long my knowledge would be greatly expanded as I tapped the rich lode of sexual knowledge of ten-to-fourteen- year-old boys, including the fact that each time you did it meant a baby, so you could only do it at the most three times every nine months unless, of course, the woman was standing up, in which case she couldn't make a baby.

My mother's predictions did not come true. I had a good time at the school and did well. In my first interview with the headmaster, Rooker Roberts, he liberated my suppressed confidence and self-esteem, probably without being aware of it. Like convicts and servicemen, we were allotted numbers that identified us and our belongings all the way through school. Rooker Roberts, who was held in almost God-like reverence, bestowed on me the number 86 as though it were the Holy Grail. Number 86 was the one he had held himself all the way through his own schooldays. He was quite confident, he said, that I would be worthy of it. The therapy, conscious or not, worked for the three years I was at the school where I wound up one of the two head boys.

At Belmont I came under the influence of some excellent if kinky teachers who kindled my interest in literature and writing. This was only a few years after the end of World War I. The masters were drawn from the survivors of the trenches or from the generation too young to have served. One of them held us spellbound as he hinted at, rather than related, in a husky whisper after first going to the classroom door and furtively looking up and down the corridor, incidents from his secret service career. Sometimes he would turn up in class wearing dark glasses and a long white silk scarf with the end flung carelessly over his shoulder. He had the air of a man about to be shot who was gallantly refusing the blindfold, though not the cigarette. He littered his teaching with French phrases – *alors mes chers amis...voilà tout pour la journée...*– delivered in an authentic plummy French accent. It was the first time I had heard an Englishman speak an unaccented foreign tongue and it gave me a better feeling about the schoolboy French we were ploddingly beginning to learn.

Another master, Bertie Ricks, was a manic-depressive, although we were ignorant of the term at the time. He alternated between wildly dramatic behaviour and frightening depressions. Lanky and loose limbed, he could move like a marionette, eyes rolling and head flopping from side to side, or he could mount such a convincing performance of a man choking to death that, even if you had seen it all before, you still felt compelled to call for medical aid. In his depressions he was a man to avoid rather than become the butt of his hostile, sneering assaults.

In spite of this, he was a memorable influence on me. He ran the school lending library and I became his helper. In this capacity I was occasionally allowed to accompany him on trips to London. These were held to be essential to his librarian duties, but I believe he just wanted to have the excuse to prowl around the West End and wind up with a sumptuous and expensive tea at the Savoy Hotel. The ambivalence of his behaviour – pedagogue at war with iconoclast and often losing – put him on my side...the outsider's side. It confirmed to me that it wasn't all that important to conform; there was room in society for the eccentric as long as you were prepared to settle for being tolerated rather than loved.

Rooker Roberts was a mountain climber, birder and nature photographer who made it seem that a love of nature was an essential part of the educated, literate man. I got good marks for composition, writing about nature events and situations which I either invented or loosely adapted from the headmaster's favourite essayists. On Sunday evenings after the inevitable chapel service he read to us for two hours. In this way I came to know Rider Haggard's *She*, Anthony Hope's *Rupert of Hentzau*, Rudyard Kipling's *Gunga Din* and Ralph Connor's *Sky Pilot* with its crippled young heroine of the Canadian Wild West, never dreaming that I would wind up living just a short distance from the Glengarry County village of St. Elmo, birthplace of the Reverend Charles Gordon, a. k. a. Ralph Connor.

The school occupied a former country house set in seventy-five acres of woods and lawns. Georgian brick extensions had been added as often as the non-stop appeals to the old boys for funds made possible. We were encouraged to climb the centuries-old oaks, burrow into the rhododendron thickets, locate and identify the bird nests and even take egg samples as long as we could justify it as the act of a serious collector and not just a thoughtless theft.

Stoicism – stiff upper lip and all that – was a much admired attribute, and one that was essential if you were to survive the hunger, lack of privacy, occasional loneliness and, especially, any contact with the school doctor and his able co-conspirator, Miss Campion, the school Matron.

I had the misfortune to suffer from a plague of boils which caused me much pain and humiliation. Boils were thought to be caused by rich blood or bad blood; infection was never mentioned. Treatment consisted of the matron poulticing the developing boil with a dressing straight out of boiling water, then bandaging it up in the hope that it would stay in place till the next torture session the following day. When in the matron's judgment the boil had softened up enough, she went to work with her bony thumbs to squeeze out the contents. As often as not she did not succeed, which she seemed to take as an affront. She would keep on squeezing until at last I came to the end of my manliness and with tears rolling down my face I would beg her to stop. It was the root she was after. When at last the boil ejaculated she would display the yellow worm of the root triumphantly for all to see – because the whole performance had been witnessed by other boys waiting in line in her sanctum. One boil, however, had her beaten from the start. It was in the funnel of my ear where she couldn't get her thumbs on it. She reluctantly turned me over to the doctor for it to be lanced. The doctor sat me on a stepladder with my ear at his eye level. He then put into my hand a strange bottle with a trigger device and positioned his hand at my ear.

"Now, hold that position and when I tell you, pull the trigger for the count of three," he commanded.

I did as he said and felt a freezing jet in the ear. A moment later he displayed to me the entire boil sitting like a miniature volcano on the blade of his scalpel.

Seven
Going Public

Graduation from Belmont coincided with puberty, somewhat akin to being *bar mitzvoth*. Our cherubic chins began to sprout hairs, proudly counted; our scraped and weather-beaten knees would fade to suety white inside our first long trousers; our trebles and altos would break uncertainly before deciding between tenor, bass or baritone, and the pressure would be on to "be a man, my son."

Being a "newbug" at the big school was closer to my mother's prediction. Far from finding it an advantage to have come from Belmont I quickly found out that Old Belmontians were not only in a minority but were considered to have an unwarranted sense of their superiority about which they badly needed to be disabused.

Mill Hill School was a paradox. Founded by non-conformists who rejected the authority of the established Church of England, it nevertheless shared with other public schools the aim of providing an elitist education and philosophical base to prepare its privileged students for leadership, originally in the service of the Empire.

An important part of the process was to teach aspiring leaders that to give orders effectively you first had to learn to take orders, and, by extension, that to feel comfortable handing out corporal punishment you had to have endured it yourself. Thus, from your first day at school you were on the very bottom rung of a punishment hierarchy which made you liable to beatings on the behind with the heel of a shoe by prefects; with a short cane by monitors, the student aristocracy; and with a lethally long cane by house masters and the Head himself.

Sixty years later this no doubt sounds barbaric and in violation of all humane, pedagogical principles, but I do not think we were harmed by it. At least, we resented the punishments less than we did that of some sadistic master who handed out "lines" for infractions. The "line," which had to be written all on one line of the ruled paper fifty or a hundred times, was: "Few things are more distressing to the well-regulated mind than to see boys who ought to know better disporting themselves on improper occasions."

For the first two years, the pressure was on to matriculate. This you did not by sitting for the standard government examination for common-or-garden students but by passing the School Certificate of the Oxford and Cambridge Examining Board with sufficiently high marks. At this stage the curriculum was broad and eclectic. Thereafter you had to decide between specializing in the classics, mathematics, modern languages or science. The curriculum shrank to three or four subjects, classes became much smaller and half your class time was in the form of free periods studying on your own in the well-stocked school library. It was up to you whether you daydreamed, looked up dirty words in the Complete Oxford Dictionary or even did some studying. It was an ideal milieu in which to take the first wobbly steps in creative writing.

This university-style approach produced some outstanding students – mathematicians who outstripped their teachers, poets and doctors-to-be who had done all the anatomy, biology and fish and animal dissection to earn their pre-MD bachelor degrees before leaving school at the age of seventeen or eighteen.

Ideally, the school looked for a blend of scholarship and manly sportsmanship, but in reality it turned out very few intellectual jocks. One in particular I remember: Peter Howard. Howard had suffered from what was then known only as infantile paralysis, as a result of which one leg was just a stick of skin-covered bone, giving him a pronounced limp. He was an otherwise powerfully built young man. He competed in all school sports, even high-jumping off his muscular good leg. In his final year he made the "lst Fifteen" school rugby team and went on to play on the Oxford University and English International teams. After university he applied his great energy and intellectual resources to the Oxford Movement or Moral Re-Armament.

At school we admired him for his athletic ability and his contemptuous disregard for his physical disability. The public schools were prime recruiting pools for Moral Re-Armament, but being neither a jock nor a "Christian" I did not fall under Howard's spell – unlike many of my schoolmates.

I was not surprised to see the Oxford Group unveiled as being less of a religious movement than a right-wing political organization, bordering on fascism. This became clear in 1936 when the founder, Dr. Buchman, on a visit to New York, told his audience in the Waldorf Astoria hotel: "We thank God for a man like Adolf Hitler." German industrialist Fritz Thyssen, writing shortly after the outbreak of war, revealed that Gestapo Chief Heinrich Himmler was also an Oxford Group devotee, as was Henry Ford, who was generous with cash transfusions.

Except for a deep bow to Chaucer, Shakespeare and the Lake poets, the arts in general got short shrift at the school. You had to discover painting for yourself. I shall never forget my excitement at accidentally stumbling upon Van Gogh's *Cypresses* in a gallery window in London on one of my outings with Bertie Ricks.

We had our noses rubbed in music by being forced to attend a class given by a visiting Doctor of Music who was hopelessly inept as a teacher and had no control over a class whose idea of good music was the Colonel Bogey March, popularly known as "Bollocks and the same to you." Somehow, through the pandemonium, I received and retained a basic course in musical instruments, learning to recognize the *cor anglais*, the bassoon, the oboe and all the other instruments of the orchestra which he displayed and demonstrated, ignoring the competition from the farts of his disgusting pupils.

Although Mill Hill was a non-conformist school, the chapel services were considerably fancier than the dreary Presbyterian routines of my earlier childhood. The singing of anthems, responses and hymns made daily chapel attendance (twice on Sundays) somewhat less onerous. In fact, I even had a brief hormonal fling with religion at the age of fifteen, bellowing out anthems in the burnished mahogany glow of the summer-lit pews. The chapel also served an instructive purpose other than religion: the top echelon of senior boys was required to take turns reading the lesson from the Bible. Who could tell in what corner of the Empire, remote battlefield or even boardroom they might be called on to provide Christian leadership and feel comfortable in doing so?

Surprisingly, the school excelled in theatrics. There was never a problem to find enough actors and singers for a Gilbert and Sullivan opera or a full-length Shakespeare play. If an alto voice could not be found amongst the pupils, some master's wife would always step into the breach. We willingly suspended disbelief as much for a stout, middle-aged lady playing sweet little Buttercup as we did for an adolescent "Captain of the Queen's Navee." A popular player in these shows was Richard Dimbleby who went on to achieve fame and adulation as a BBC celebrity during and after the war.

The school provided space and facilities for hobbies of all sorts, from model railways to chess, giving an outlet for endless disparate interests. But in the class sense the school was unified.

There was a scattering of well-born black and brown skins as well as Dutch, Spanish and Belgian boys and even one American, all of whom were readily assimilated into the school life as "one of us." Unhappily this did not always work for the handful of Jews. The latent anti-Semitism was aroused by one boy in particular who was quickly given the nickname "Ratty." His home was in Vienna where, by his own account, he spent the holidays luxuriating in bed with willing young boys. He was physically unbecoming – plump, puffy-eyed, flat-footed, given to screaming if threatened by words or physical force. He was no closet homosexual; he made overt advances to all who took his fancy.

Quite the opposite was a good-looking boy named Salinger. He was unusually small but made up for it by exuberance and sunny good nature, also guts disproportionate to his size. He was in my class along with a lout who loved to torment him with words and by occasional vicious punches. The lout was performing as usual one day while we waited for the master, Mr. Forster, a powerful Irish international rugby player, to arrive. Appearing suddenly and seeing what was happening, Forster addressed not the lout but Salinger.

"That's no way to behave, for heaven's sake. If you let the scum get away with that, he'll be on your back forever. Here, I'll show you what to do."

He stood behind Salinger, enclosed the boy's small fists in his own meaty paws and landed a series of hard blows on the lout's face and body.

"That's how it's done...see? Now hit him again." Bam. "And again." Bam...bam. "I'll bet you he'll never lay a hand on you again now that he knows that you fight back."

Those days were uncomplicated by psychologists, behaviourists and prying parents. In fact, had the parents on both sides known of the incident they would probably have approved, as we did, of this summary justice.

When Ratty and Salinger had acquired enough seniority to move out of the hurly-burly of the common room into the relative privacy of a study, the school authorities put them together, probably thinking that two Jews would be more comfortable in each other's company.

However, it was not long before Ratty's libido boiled over and he was caught trying to rape Salinger. The following day he was packed off to Vienna and was never seen again.

Eight
The Pits

One of my friends, Jimmy Brass, came from Durham County where his father, I gathered, had something to do with coal mines. We were drawn together because of our love of cars. He owned a Morgan three-wheeler and had access to his father's Buick saloon, as sedans were called, and an SS coupe, the forerunner of the Jaguar. He was an only child, always looking for company during the school holidays. So when he invited me to his home for the summer, I accepted with pleasure.

I was not prepared for the manorial splendour of the Brass residence sitting high up on the beautiful Durham moors which, except for the pithead gantries dotting the landscape, gave no clue to the black business going on below. Jimmy's father clearly sat at the apex of the mining enterprise but Jimmy had been brought up in the district and knew the miners and their families intimately...was in some respects one of them. They surprised me by their friendliness and complete lack of obsequiousness. It was hard to understand how men who spent their days at one of the dirtiest, most dangerous and underpaid jobs in the world could survive with such good humour, pride and quiet courtesy.

I found it difficult to respond with the same spontaneity. It caused much soul searching. What was the matter? At home we always had a maid, usually from the impoverished Tyneside, not so far from these Durham people, for whom the chance to be a slavey down south was a godsend. The hard work and long hours must have seemed a small price to pay for hot baths, healthy meals, the hand-me-downs of clean clothing from my mother and the chance to get their teeth fixed. How they were able to sniff out a beau on their two half-days off a week is a mystery, but as often as not their association with the family ended in marriage to a milk deliveryman or a policeman. And yet, even living under the same roof with them, I do not recall ever having a genuine one-on-one human relationship or being able to switch out of the employer/servant mode. (Now I think of it, there was one exception. When I was fourteen, we briefly employed a nubile Cockney teenager. She was fired after being caught showing me a dirty postcard with a drawing of a rabbi in the act of circumcising an infant, with the caption: "There is a divinity that shapes our ends".)

This depressing flaw in my character, as I perceived it, got me into trouble with Jimmy. A travelling fair, one of the big events of the summer, came to the village. Jimmy arranged a date with a village girl and a blind date for me. I could see that he expected the excitement of the swings and roundabouts to lead to stimulating body contact and who knows what dénouement. When we met our dates I was dismayed to find that mine was, to put it charitably, unattractive, not too clean and without compensating wit or personality. I simply could not respond in the way she clearly expected. We spent a miserable time whirling around on the rides with my arm limply draped around her. Jimmy was furious with me. The girls were hurt by what they took to be a snobbish put-down and Jimmy wanted no part of the blame. There could be many a slip, I realized, between the cup of egalitarian theory and the lip of social practice. Being an outsider from your own class didn't necessarily make you an insider with another.

The miners were housed in cramped, early nineteenth-century row houses without bathrooms. They came home filthy from the pits to bathe in a tin tub in the kitchen. All the washing in the world, however, could not keep pace with the daily dose of coal dust that penetrated the skin and left their faces etched in blue as though they had been tattooed. They were short but powerfully built from the buttocks up, the result of spending their days crouched in the shallow seams swinging picks at the coal face. They maintained this crouch in their spare time, hunkered down outside their homes, backs to the brick walls, often with their beloved whippets or greyhounds.

The pit, even by the standards of the thirties, was close to obsolescence. The workable seams were as far as a mile underground from the shaft. Since the men were on piecework, paid not by the hour but by the actual amount of coal hewn, they travelled this distance underground to and from work on their own time.

The engine that powered the cages carrying coal and men up and down the three-thousand-foot shaft was a Victorian relic. A single-cylinder horizontal steam engine some thirty feet long, it was enclosed in polished mahogany. Its stroke was so long that the inlet and exhaust valves were activated by hand by means of strings held by the operator who sat in a cabin above. He would let the cage dial on the wall tell him it had reached a certain point. He would then juggle his valves so that the cage would be braked against the cushion of incoming steam in the huge cylinder and gently bring it to a halt. As far as I could see, he had no other braking device.

On the day when Jimmy and I were invited to go down the pit, we reported in our oldest clothes and were issued with hard hats, lamps and short stout sticks about two feet long. The purpose of these sticks became clear as soon as we were loaded into the double-decker cage. There was so little headroom that you had to squeeze in in a deep crouch. By holding the stick between your legs you gained the stability of a tripod. Underground, as I discovered, the men could travel at an incredible speed in a reptilian waddle, pulling themselves ahead with the stick.

The cage dropped with a force which pressed us against the ceiling. I prayed that the elderly engine operator would not have a sneezing fit or a heart attack. But for the hundred-thousandth time he slowed us down at the last moment and we emerged from the cage that bobbed gently like an obedient yo-yo within inches of the loading platform.

We came out into what could have been a well-lit subway station but soon ran out of light and headroom as we travelled in ever-smaller passages to the work face. At times we had to scurry for the safety of niches cut in the rock face to avoid being run over by the loads of coal drawn by pit ponies, those unlucky beasts who spent their lives deep underground, blinded by the dark. For an hour we travelled bent over, up and down slopes as steep as thirty degrees, through foot-deep water and, once, crawling on our bellies under an eighteen-inch fault in the rock. At one stage our guide had us put our lamps out so that we could experience the crushing, almost palpable, total darkness. How many thousands of miners world-wide, accidentally trapped in this black purgatory, had slowly perished, sustained only by the solidarity born of shared danger and a belief in God's inscrutable will?

The experience left me with a respect for these Durham men which extends to miners everywhere – in Cape Breton, the Donetz basin, the hymn-filled valleys of Wales. How appropriate it would be, I sometimes thought, if a month of work below ground could be made a prerequisite for employment as a politician, lawyer (which would automatically take care of judges), bureaucrat, police – even doctor, journalist and preacher...especially preacher, as I later found out that the Church of England owned many coal fields, along with much of Britain's slum property.

Nine
Fix Bayonets

Like most schools of its kind, Mill Hill included Officer Training in its compulsory extra-curricular program. Having fed an endless supply of officer cannon fodder into the military mill, the school had no intention of breaking with this patriotic tradition. Each of the half dozen "Houses" at the school competed with each other at sports, including OTC (Officers Training Corps) proficiency. Once a year, in June, some visiting General would inspect the sweltering troops and name the winner.

This was only a dozen years after the end of World War I but the pacifist reaction had already set in. Even the masters who had survived the war with reserve rank and still had their uniform hanging in the closet had little enthusiasm for the charade of parade-ground drill, and the boys had even less. But the school took the training seriously enough to maintain a permanent orderly room staffed by a retired officer – a fierce walking-moustache called Slim who looked as though he had stepped out of a Lord Kitchener recruiting poster.

The young masters were nominally in charge of the platoons and companies while Slim provided the requisite bumpf to keep the whole farce on sacred military track. Since none of them wanted any part of controlling a reluctant and, to the extent they could get away with it, insolent bunch of cadets on the parade ground, they turned this chore over to a permanent army sergeant-major from the nearby barracks of the Middlesex Regiment. This immaculate, bristling Cockney had perfected the class art of delivering the most scathing abuse in the most respectful of tones, disarming his insults with the frequent use of "gentlemen."

He drilled us remorselessly as we sweated, sometimes fainted, in our Great War heavy serge uniforms, buttoned up tight under our ears, our Ross rifles getting heavier and slippery with sweat as we sloped, presented, ordered and trailed arms.

He liked to treat us effete, privileged boys as though we were girls: "Stan' hat hize…cummon, put yer legs apart…you won't drop nuff'n."

But at other times, where his little joke required it, he had to treat us like grown men. For example, one of the most frustrating drill operations was fixing and unfixing bayonets which were still the immense blades of the First World War. It was eyes ahead; no looking at what you were doing. Fixing was bad enough, but at least it was up front where you might sneak a look. But unfixing required you to support your rifle between your knees, unfix the bayonet, reach behind where you knew there had to be a scabbard somewhere on your web belt, then somehow blindly shove the bayonet into it. Invariably there would be two or three in the platoon who, unable to find the hole in the scabbard, would become the butt of the sergeant-major's predictable wit.

"Gor blimey, what a bunch. Mebbe we should put some 'air on it. You'd bloody quick find it then."

When the time came for me to volunteer for service in the Canadian Army, I mentioned this OTC training to the recruiting officer. He immediately decided that I did not need any further basic training in spite of the fact the army was now forming threes instead of fours and had changed beyond recognition in the intervening twelve years. He pulled all the right strings and within forty-eight hours I found myself in a cadet platoon at Brockville Officers Training Centre still feverish from needles in both arms, ready to take my ignorant and uneasy place with seasoned troops.

Ten

Pen Pal

Mill Hill School encouraged international intercourse, although in practice this meant corresponding with or visiting your social counterparts in other countries. In 1932, partly in the spirit of universal brotherhood but mostly because it gave me points in my German class, I acquired a German pen pal, Horst, in Torgau am Elbe. The arrangement was that each would write in the other's language.

Horst, I quickly discovered, was an enthusiastic Nazi whose command of English and powers of rhetoric far outstripped my stumbling German. To prop up my shortcoming I took to sending him tearsheets taken at random from newspapers and magazines which had anything to do with Germany, including the occasional cartoon. Inevitably some of this material was not very flattering to Herr Hitler. Before long Horst interpreted my choice of material as a deliberately hostile act. Our penpalship ended in a furious burst of Nazi polemics. How much better it might have been if I had had the good sense to hold on to this pipeline into the Nazi mind and reinforce my growing anti-fascist stance with facts, as it were, from the Horst's mouth. Ironically, it was at Torgau am Elbe that the Red and American armies came together, severing North and South Germany and sealing Hitler's fate. I cannot help wondering if Horst survived to taste this bitter conclusion and see the Iron Curtain slam down on his hometown.

My experience with Horst was not unique. A whole generation of Hitler Jugend beamed its paranoia at every possible target including, unlikely as it sounds, the Rock and Fell Champion of the English Lake District. I fell in with this chap during one of my solitary scrambles in the mountains – a cross between walking and climbing. I came upon him while descending a boulder-strewn slope on Scafell – or rather, he came upon me, because he was bounding like a goat from rock to rock while I was slowly picking my way down. Seeing me, he stopped. I noticed that he was wearing open leather sandals on bare feet.

"Why in God's name are you wearing those boots?" he asked.

The boots were stout Alpine leather ones, heavy with Tricouni nails, which I had always considered de rigueur for the consecrated scrambler.

"That's a sure way to ruin your feet," he said. "You should always go as near to barefoot as possible…strengthen your feet. You don't do that by giving them a crutch."

He slowed down to my pace and began to tell me how the Rock and Fell Championship went to the one who got to the top of the most mountains in the Lake District in a twenty-four hour period. This was done non-stop, mostly on the double.

My companion told me he was the president of his association that had traditionally enjoyed fraternal relationships with its counterparts abroad, especially in Germany. This year, however, in preparation for a meet in Germany, Horst's *Kamaraden* in the Hitler *Jugend* had put such conditions on the get-together, including an embargo on Jews, that he withdrew his group in protest. The idea of taking a principled stand which involved some self-sacrifice was new to me. It impressed me. Clearly these meets were important to him. He was itching to beat the young Germans fair and square – but never on their imposed terms.

"And they call themselves sportsmen," he said with disdain.

This was a typical British reaction to Hitler – based less on political or deeply-held philosophical beliefs than on a feeling of fair play abused. It would be a while yet before the comic little man with the music hall moustache and the ridiculous gestures became more than just a figure of fun to the average man in the street.

Eleven
Widening Horizons

Britain in the early 1930s was still a tight little island. The rich, the aristocracy and the intelligentsia travelled to Italy, France and Greece as they had been doing for a century or more, but the middle class generally stayed put at home, safely protected from greasy, garlic-laden foreign food, unsafe drinking water, embarrassing plumbing and the constant fear of being cheated and short-changed. The working class certainly did not travel abroad, except as servants. You would never have heard what a young clerk in a clothing store in Scotland said to me in 1969 before the breakup of Yugoslavia: "Yer goin' to Dubrovnik? I was there last year. I didna like it. I think I'll try Spa-a-in this year."

My first venture abroad was a tightly chaperoned affair – a student exchange visit to Denmark, where I stayed with a kind and agreeable family in the little town of Skaelskor, sailed on the Kattegat and discovered that foreigners not only did things differently from the vaunted British but often did them much better (eating, to mention only one).

I arrived from a rough North Sea crossing with a case of delayed seasickness. There was nothing wrong with me; it was *terra firma* that would not stay *firma*. My concerned hostess put me to bed and called a doctor. As the two of them peered at me as though I were a beached whale, the doctor produced a thermometer from a jar of liquid, wiped it with a cotton swab and handed it to me. I thought it was rather large but stuck it under my tongue where, as everyone knows, temperatures are taken. My hostess gave a little scream of shock, bent her portly frame and stabbed a finger to her rear end. I immediately realized my mistake but pride prevented me from admitting it. To save face I shook my head and pointed confidently to my mouth. They both seemed surprised to find that the thermometer was capable of registering in either orifice.

Since I spoke no Danish, I tried out my schoolboy German only to find that, although several of the family and neighbours understood the language, they were loath to speak it. Separated from Germany by only a few miles of common border and the strategic Kiel Canal, the Danes appeared to be always looking distrustfully over their shoulders at their bellicose neighbour to the south. I was aware of a tension in Denmark wherever I went, quite different from the almost smug disassociation from Continental politics which prevailed in England. It came as no surprise half a dozen years later that the Danes, in a national display of dumb insolence, closed ranks against the contemptible Nazi occupation, even their king defiantly wearing the yellow Star of David.

There were, of course, no TV antennae or satellite dishes to beam instant news to every living room, but the general pattern of Hitler terror was known even in idyllic Skaelskor. People were still speaking with disgust of the book burning orgy a few months earlier in May when the Hitler Youth had raided libraries and put twenty thousand books to the torch – cremating not just the works of Marx but also *All Quiet on the Western Front* and books by such subversives as Ernest Hemingway, Jack London, H. G. Wells and Albert Einstein.

Of course, I was still wandering in the political wilderness, as yet without the compass which would help me through the maze, the needle pointing always in the direction of power and greed.

In Denmark I was cut off from Lord Rothermere's *Daily Mail* and Lord Beaverbrook's *Daily Express*, meagre and biased sources of information though they were. And anyway, political thoughts had difficulty competing with the smörrebröd, Tuborg lager, visits to Hans Andersen's house at Roskilde, to Tivoli pleasure gardens in Copenhagen (what a clean and civilized contrast to the British fun-fairs) and to Hamlet's stamping ground at Helsingor.

Back home I tried to stay abreast of the news by reading a broader range of newspapers – including *The Times* and the Labourite *Daily*

Herald. I hadn't yet come to the *Daily Worker*. If I had started on the *Daily Herald* sooner I would have known that the probable ultimate fate of the Jews, their wholesale massacre by the Nazis, was well known to the Western democracies in 1933. A report from the newspaper's correspondent in Berlin predicted as much and said that the policy was being considered "in the highest quarters." The Nazis threw him in jail, thus taking the heat off genocide and shifting it, in the eyes of the British Establishment, to unwarranted interference with the freedom of the foreign press.

Another school friend helped broaden my outlook on life, although not in a political sense. François Cammaerts was a Belgian, son of the Belgian poet laureate of the day, and of course, he spoke fluent French. This was not good enough for our French teacher "Camel" – brilliantly nick-named because he did indeed make you think of a camel with his small head perched haughtily above a long neck. Camel usually avoided asking Cammaerts questions, knowing that he was the only one in the room with an honest claim on the language, but when he did he would always correct the answer, rephrasing it in his own pedantic Scottish-accented French. I thought Cammaerts bore these insults with uncalled-for patience but he had his own rationale.

"No point arguing with an idiot."

During our last school holiday, when we were seventeen and for some reason he had not gone home to Belgium, he suggested we have an evening on the town in London. Under his guidance, this turned out to be dinner at a French restaurant followed by good seats at Noel Coward's smash hit "Cavalcade." At the restaurant, Cammaerts casually ordered a bottle of Pommard. It was the first wine I had tasted other than Wincarnis, a British pseudo-wine (the carnis part presumably meant to imply beef) advertised as a tonic to allay any puritanical prejudice against alcohol. One sip of the Elysian burgundy enrolled me as a lifelong wine lover. We paid, if I recall, not more than the equivalent of $1.50 for that magnificent bottle and about the same again for the four-course dinner.

Twelve
Working Stiff

For some reason, perhaps responding to the manufacturer's slogan "Keep your boys at home" and hence out of trouble, my father had installed a billiard table in our house at Leeds. It stayed there, being too expensive to move with us to London, but the same spirit seemed to be still at work because, as soon as we were eligible, he made us junior members of Crews Hill Golf Club. It was here, in my last year at school, that I met Teddy Linstead. Teddy, probably without wanting to, became my cultural guru and an important influence in my life.

He was writing poetry and was at work on a novel. When I timidly showed him some of my school essays, he lavishly praised the good parts and matter-of-factly shot down the clichés and the juvenile posturing, as one professional to another. I learned more from that first critique than from all my English masters to date.

Teddy, the youngest of three sons, was a fellow outsider. His older brothers were already launched on careers that would take them to great distinction – Hugh to the House of Commons, Patrick to the crest of the British chemical industry, and both to knighthoods.

Teddy's parents decided that pharmaceutics would be a suitable profession for him and arranged for him to be articled to a West End London pharmacist. Although fascinated by the inhabitants of the demimonde of drugs and prostitution that drifted through the shop, Teddy felt trapped in a dead-end career. When the time came for him to sit for the final examination, he waited for a seemly fifteen minutes at his desk before handing in a completely blank paper. He found a job with an advertising agency writing copy for Aspro, simple acetyl salicylic acid which, like Bayer's Aspirin, had been elevated to the mystery and efficacy, and the price, of a patent medicine, for which Britishers seemed to have an insatiable appetite.

Teddy's family environment was strongly conservative, both small and big "C." His mother was active in the Primrose League, the Conservative Party's women's auxiliary. His two brothers rose steadily in the Establishment, but Teddy was an iconoclast in all things, including politics. He was impartially cynical about all parties and movements, left or right. At the same time he was, in my eyes, spectacularly well informed. He exuded historical facts, including backroom and boudoir gossip, and could spontaneously weave together the threads of an international power conspiracy that made sense, at least to me, of the tangled past.

Teddy brushed aside my literary idols like Shaw, Belloc and Chesterton as either charlatans or opportunists and replaced them with names I had not heard before – names like C.E. Montagu, Kafka, Norman Douglas and Aldous Huxley. I would spend many an evening in Teddy's room while he read to me from his novel in progress or played Strauss waltzes by ear on a battered push-pull accordion. Coming and going I had to pass his parents who, while cordial, clearly disapproved of this whole writing business and anyone associated with it and mourned the loss of a respectable pharmacist. My own parents shared this view of Teddy – too much of an egghead and an aesthete (he writes poetry!!) for their liking. Although I was living at home when not at school, I used it more as a boarding house, skipping meals and coming in at all hours, showing them, with some malice it has to be said, that I preferred the bohemian atmosphere of Teddy's den to that of the family living room – or "lounge" as it was called.

It must have pleased Teddy to have such a loyal acolyte. On weekends we walked countless miles in each other's company, that admirable English pastime which so civilly exercises mind and body, once even walking twelve miles via Hampstead Heath to the Tate Gallery for my first real look at paintings through the eyes of a knowing critic.

At seventeen I did not think of myself as a youth, far less a boy. I was on the threshold of manhood, independence and self-determination. It astonished me later in Canada to hear men in their twenties being described as youths, as though they were not yet expected to behave as responsible adults.

I left school with no regrets and sidetracked the expected procedure of formally joining the Old Boys Club. The sacred old boy's tie seemed to me to be more of a shackle than a fraternal bond. With the wide world waiting for me in London I could not picture myself spending my Saturdays playing rugger and downing beers with the same people I had lived with in a sometimes-edgy relationship for the last four years.

One night my older brother Douglas who, although not a jock, had a more conventional and dutiful social attitude, persuaded me to go to an old boys' dinner. The institutionalized jollity was not for me. The last bond was severed at the end of the evening when the club president was kindly driving us to the tube station. He told of his efforts to intervene with the bench on behalf of a disreputable fellow old boy whose drunkenness had led him into a theft.

"Can't let the side down, what? One of us, you know, poor sod."

It would be nice to be able to claim that high moral principles lay behind my disaffection, but I was not naive enough to think that people did not look out for their own kind, nor did I condemn them for it. Rather, my friendship with Teddy plus my random encounters with "outsiders" – both in the national and class sense – told me that there was a richer and more interesting life lurking somewhere to be discovered.

The idea of working to achieve this life hadn't really occurred to me. I thought of myself as a writer, building my aspirations on the slender foundation of a few school essays and the short stories I was beginning to turn out. Doubtless my association with Teddy and the fact that I had the free family roof over my head encouraged my illusions. My brother Douglas, now close enough to his Chartered Accountant degree to become engaged, and methodically planning each step of his future, challenged me to declare my plans.

"I want to be free to do absolutely nothing," I told him.

Ironically he was shocked not at my lack of career ambition but my lack of idealism, a failure to devote myself to service to my fellow man. This in his view meant following the principle of "Charity begins at home." To give of your best to society you had first to make sure you had the best yourself.

What I was really expressing was my dismay at the thought of a nine-to-six job (plus nine-to-one on Saturdays), the season ticket, the umbrella and the bowler hat. It was my father who resolved the situation without consulting me. He was a client of the exalted advertising agency, S. H. Benson Ltd. He told them I was good at writing and was looking for a job. The Creative Director, a brilliant Oxford-educated English scholar, agreed to see me and sent me a message: Read the essays of Montaigne. They hired me – after all, I was a client's son – but hedged their bet by paying me only seventeen and sixpence a week. That worked out to about $3.50 at the time – not enough for tube fare, cigarettes and lunches. It took me two years to rise to the copy department. I first had to do my time learning the ropes in every other department.

My first boss was a gnome-like Cockney appropriately called Sparrow. His department checked the papers for clients' ads and tore them out, my job being to type the covering letter forwarding the tearsheets to the client. "Dear Sirs: Please find enclosed voucher copies of the following...." over and over and over again. My three or four confrères had all started life with the company as uniformed messenger boys at the age of fourteen when it took courage to ride a heavy three-wheeled delivery bike in all weathers through London streets to meet tight deadlines at printers, engravers and publications. They were glad to have someone to save them from the typing job but otherwise treated me as completely incompetent, without a clue to real life.

They were not far wrong, as I discovered when I was moved to the next department – the so-called Control which converted the brilliant thoughts from upstairs into lead and copper plates to be distributed to newspapers and periodicals in time for the scheduled insertions.

The job required a thorough knowledge of all the technical aspects of printing and the chutzpah to drive suppliers often to do the impossible. My new boss, R.A. Hughes, immediately recognized my deficiency in both areas but did nothing to instruct me, preferring to let me hang myself with my own mistakes. He was a working-class Londoner on his way up, nauseatingly obsequious to anyone above him and cruel to his subordinates. In keeping with his recent promotion, he had acquired a tailored suit, probably his first, which he patted and smoothed admiringly when he thought we were not looking, and he affected a black Homburg like Sir Nevile Henderson's. Unfortunately, his manners trailed behind. He had been given a secretary, a very young woman on her first job. She badly needed the money, he discovered, because she was supporting a "crippled" sister. Hughes never let her forget it. At the slightest mistake he would remind her about her crippled sister and how close she was sailing to disaster until he finally had her reduced to a sobbing heap.

I owed my survival to Al Bowyer, another working-class Londoner but of a totally different cut. Only a year or two older than me, he was expert not only in the technical aspects of the job but in the critical-path management of a half dozen complicated advertising schedules. He made it plain that he couldn't understand why a supposedly educated person should be such a nitwit, but he patiently taught me what I needed to know and shepherded me through many a crisis. We became friends. He began to confide in me, even telling me of his problems in his love life, mostly premature ejaculation. I had already discovered some cheap, interesting bistros in the district and I repeatedly asked Al to have lunch with me but he invariably found a reason not to. I found it odd that someone who so openly discussed his most intimate affairs would balk at eating with me. I did eventually persuade him to have a meal with me one evening when we had been working late, hoping to get him hooked on Italian food. He felt so miserable, out of place and out of class in the unfamiliar surroundings that I gave up trying to close the social gap. Al had the intelligence, energy and character to shoot to the top in Canada but he had the wrong accent and lived at the wrong time in pre-war Britain.

In many ways the agency was run like a factory. We had to sign in each morning and, if we were more than a few minutes late, face the displeasure of the Dingbat, the forbidding female who kept the time sheets. Mac, the uniformed doorman, was an ex-serviceman with a wooden leg like a pirate and a friendly nature. From the beginning he was curious about me – I suppose because I had started at the agency without having worked my way up from messenger and certainly had not been hired because of my expertise. One day after work he asked me to have a beer with him at a pub just a few doors from the agency.

True to my desire to broaden my class connections I accepted. I quickly realized I was far out-classed as a beer drinker, managing to swallow one to Mac's four, mostly at my expense. It was not long before he was revolving on his peg leg, grabbing me – his pal, his mate – for physical support, and more and more for moral support as he became increasingly belligerent and insulting towards the other men in the pub. Soon fists were up as the inevitable donnybrook began to shape up. Seeing myself involved in a scandalous situation almost on the doorstep of the agency, losing my job, maybe winding up in a police cell – not to mention the thought of being the recipient of one of those gnarled fists in my nose – I sidled off to the lavatory where I made a dishonourable exit by the window.

The next day Mac was more interested in an explanation of my magical disappearance than in blasting me for my cowardice for abandoning a mate in distress. But cowardice I knew it to be, a burden I bore secretly for a long time and one that coloured many of my subsequent decisions in life as I strove to exorcise the gnawing demon.

Thirteen
Gathering Storm

Nineteen-thirty-four. It was a rather desperate year during which I was largely self-absorbed in trying to grasp the ground rules for survival in a world of unremitting multiple deadlines. Yet there was no escaping an awareness of the gathering storm in Europe. Teddy had steered me to the *New Statesman & Nation*, a socialist weekly in the polite, literate Fabian tradition, which helped me lift the curtain somewhat on the skulduggery behind the one-dimensional news of the popular press.

The year got off to a bloody start in Austria. Englebert Dollfuss, the fascist "Pocket Chancellor," who made up in vindictiveness what he lacked in physical stature, called out the artillery to destroy the famous public housing blocks in Vienna which had been hailed by left-wingers everywhere as shining achievements of socialism. I followed this story up because I had a special affection for the country as a result of a skiing holiday in the Tirol. By the time Dollfuss was finished with the socialists he had hanged ten people, including a half-wit whose crime had been to set fire to a haystack, and handed thirty-one others a total of four hundred years in prison. There was no mistaking where "my" government stood on the socialist question. Conservative Party spokesman Leopold Amery said that Dollfuss had done the right thing; there had been a socialist revolution, the housing units were "fortresses" and therefore fair game.

During this year Hitler was capitalizing on his stunning victory at the polls the previous November when over ninety per cent of the voters in a record turnout had registered their approval. The Germans were no different from electorates the world over in voting for charlatans, frauds and megalomaniacs.

Lest his readers, including my father, should be misled into thinking this was anything but a most desirable development, Lord Rothermere set the record straight in the *Daily Mail*. In a year-end summary of Hitler's achievements he praised the Nazi labour camps that provided "the finest imaginable physical and social discipline," their road building programs, their growing self-sufficiency through the development of synthetics and their success in cutting unemployment. He had little to say about how unemployment had been cut – by putting women back in the *Küche* where they belonged, by amputating Jews from the labour force, by herding unemployed youths into labour camps and by hauling anyone who got in Hitler's way in front of Nazi-appointed judges in secret People's Courts.

Rothermere summed up the Jewish question as follows: "Nearly all the news regarding the Nazi regime…is pure moonshine. Not true that Jews lead an almost hunted existence…In German hotels and restaurants I have seen merry and festive parties of German Jews who showed no symptoms of insecurity or suffering."

His Lordship could not have lunched at any of the small bistros in Bloomsbury run by German anti-fascist refugees and catering to students and thrifty customers like me. I stumbled on them in my search for cheap lunch places and found them a welcome change from the egg-and-cress sandwiches and currant buns of English fare. Many of the patrons were anti-Nazi refugees, Jews and non-Jews, who had sought haven in London, people who had got out of Germany early, some because of anti-Semitism, others because their left-wing politics made them able to see clearly what lay ahead, unlike so many of their more sanguine, unpoliticized countrymen who would, within the year, be overwhelmed by an avalanche of Nazi repression, Rothermere's moonshine notwithstanding. Just mingling with them as a customer gave me a pleasant glow of international solidarity.

There was a curious lack of revulsion on the part of the general public against the growing violence against the Jews in Germany. This was hard to explain because even if you took your line straight from the *Daily Mail* there were still newsreel scenes of Jewish doctors and professionals made to scrub streets on their hands and knees by the Nazi thugs, to the jeers of bystanders. My recollection of anti-Semitism in England at the time is that it was prevalent amongst the middle class but discreetly practised. It was understood that Jews could not live in certain neighbourhoods, join certain clubs or hold certain jobs. People used terms like "Jew-boy" unashamedly, but only amongst themselves, of course. It would have been "infra dig" to be overheard using the term in the wrong quarters. Until the domestic fascist Oswald Mosley came along there was little overt, violent anti-Semitism.

(My mother who, paradoxically, had a closet Jew as her close friend, was upset at my marriage years later to a Jewish wife because she believed that our daughter would be legally barred from inheriting. And I was shocked later to find that Montrealers displayed their anti-Semitism much more openly than the British. Legally binding property deeds rather than gentlemen's agreements prevented the sale of property to Jewish buyers. Bluebird signs in Montreal store windows assured customers that none of the merchandise had been obtained from Jewish sources. And then there were the signs outside Laurentian resort hotels: No Jews or Dogs.)

The year had still more violence and gore to offer. In October I watched the assassination of King Alexander of Yugoslavia in Marseille – on Movie-tone News, it is true, but brutal and immediate enough to send shivers of fear through Europe as people remembered 1914 and Sarajevo. And in the very same month Spain popped into the news.

I knew probably more about Spain than ninety-five per cent of Britons simply because I had been at Belmont School with a boy whose home was in Spain, his father being an executive with the British-controlled Rio Tinto mining company, and I was the only one who enjoyed sharing the olives which his family sent to him by the barrel. He represented to me the sunlit, languorous, luxurious life of this improbable country – a view which was much modified later when I read *As I Walked Out One Mid-Summer Morning*, Laurie Lee's moving account of walking through Spain in the twenties playing his violin, telling of his love and respect for the poverty-stricken peasants who were reduced to eating earth to eke out a starvation diet.

Crowned heads fascinated the British public, so everyone knew that another of their diminishing number had fallen with the abdication of King Alfonso of Spain a few years earlier under pressure from a democratic republican coalition. The monarchists and their army friends soon regained power, however, and established a military dictatorship. By 1934 the workers had had enough and went on strike. This culminated in the appearance on the international scene of Francisco Franco who put down a strike of miners in the Asturias using notoriously brutal Moorish troops in a storm of rape, torture and murder that sickened not only the scorned bleeding hearts, idealists and pinkos like me, but also decent conservatives, including members of the Spanish army itself. Of course, it took time for the truth of the Asturias butchery to filter through the fine mesh of the British press. The Asturias miners cannot have been that much different from the Durham ones I had learned to admire. I felt not only horror at the brutality and inhumanity of Franco, a self-proclaimed defender of Christianity, but also the shiver of fear which his tactics were no doubt designed to generate in those who might be foolhardy enough to oppose him – and, commensurate with the fear, a growing hatred of our own domestic apologists who sprang to the defence of the world's Francos and Dollfusses.

I paint here a picture of a developing political dissident, socialist, ultimately communist. So where is the Soviet Union in all of this? Where are the ubiquitous Bolshevik brainwashers? Surely Great Britain, with its tolerance of free speech and assembly, in contrast to the Canada of those years, must have been riddled with them. The fact is that up until then I had been only marginally aware of the USSR. But 1934 was also the year when it finally came out of the closet, joined the League of Nations and became a potent piece in the fascist/anti-fascist chess game. From now on its policies and actions would be impossible to ignore.

Fourteen
Guinness Is Good For You

When at last I ascended to the copy department – literally...it was on the top floor – to become the agency's youngest copywriter at the age of twenty, the feeling of release and rebirth was akin to being sprung from jail, a simile that would not, of course, have occurred to me at the time. Here, class warfare and the desperate need to mark out and defend your turf were irrelevant. Wits were what counted.

The department was staffed mostly by talented writers or would-be writers of books, plays and radio scripts who were gladly selling their brains to mammon to support their serious creative work. Dorothy Sayers was one. She had left the agency shortly before I joined. I became intimately acquainted with the spiral iron staircase and other features of the agency which she used as the setting for her novel *Murder Must Advertise*, and thought I could recognize some of the employees on whom she had modeled her characters. She was admiringly remembered by Mac, the doorman, for refusing his help to wheel the heavy motorcycle on which she came to work up the steep ramp to its parking place; and by the copy department secretary for her ability to dictate a piece of copy loaded with mild expletives and asides which, when edited out, left a perfect text.

I found myself in the company of a sophisticated, knowledgeable group, some of whom were far better briefed on politics and world affairs than I was. Amongst others it included I. I. Milne, nephew of Winnie the Pooh author A. A.; a former actor with the Old Vic company and sidekick to Lawrence Olivier; an East End Londoner who played international soccer and later became a popular song writer; a former editor of a Cambridge University magazine and BBC script writer; and, because there is always a need for a literal-minded writer for manuals and brochures, a middle-aged man who had fought the Soviets in 1919 and had permanently scarred his esophagus by drinking bootleg vodka.

The other old man of our group, all of thirty-seven years old, had been vacationing in Berlin in the twenties when snowballing inflation buried him in wealth. He suddenly found himself a millionaire, going to the bank twice a day to withdraw money by the suitcase, followed wherever he went by a waiter with a bucket of iced champagne and blind to the poverty and degradation he was exploiting and which would erupt into the Nazi euphoria now filling our newspapers.

It is hardly surprising that creative people, trained to exploit the gullibility of the man in the street for profit motives, should be equally cynical about politics and public life. Between endless debates on literature, politics, sex and current scandals this happy gang churned out the slogans and posters that would persuade a gullible public that drinking Guinness stout was good for their health and would put lead in their pencils; that Bovril meat extract would buoy them up physically and emotionally; that they could beat their stomach ulcers and persistent heartburn by swallowing a patented chalky powder; that they could put an end once and for all to that low back pain which virtually every adult suffers from by introducing their kidneys to these fantastic pills with their secret ingredient – soap. As the department neophyte I got the less glamorous assignments and was initiated in such esoterica as advising nursing mothers to rub a little brand name malt extract on their nipples to promote good suction.

A portion of some clients' advertising budgets was allotted to "class" media directed to a literate and sophisticated readership. This resulted in creative jam sessions with the entire copy department clustered around the chief at his stand-up desk, the more liquid-lunched of the group nodding in the back row. Outrageous puns and plays on words were the fashion. For a new Kodak camera: "It's magnifique but it's not Daguerre and that's no hocus-focus." We were all aware that our offerings were expected to be of a very high standard because the Kodak advertising manager was Julian Yeatman whose classic *1066 and All That* had just been published. The department in committee rewrote Lewis Carroll's poems and Alice books to serve the commercial ends of Guinness stout. This was the heyday of the "My Goodness, my Guinness" animal posters by John Gilroy which were to be seen on every tube and railway station platform – seals balancing Guinnesses on their noses, ostriches with the outlines of glasses of Guinness stuck in their throats and toucans sheltering a couple of Guinnesses under their huge beaks. ("If one Guinness is good for you, just think what toucan do!")

A few years later in Montreal I was to see some of the S.H. Benson slogans surface as original ideas ("Where's Joe? Gone for a Dow!").

Fifteen
Hoare-Laval Pact

In October of 1935 Mussolini added another ingredient to the international slumgullion by invading Abyssinia from the adjoining Italian territory of Somaliland. Mussolini up till then had tended to be a figure of fun to the British newspaper reader – all chin and bluff and fancy uniform. Now he had to be taken seriously as someone with troops and planes, and prepared to use them. This is not to suggest that everyone found the attack abhorrent. After all, it was only golliwogs – black Africans – who were being bombed. Mussolini's son, Vittorio, a bomber pilot, rhapsodized about the bomb bursts in the desert below, likening them to flowers, "the quintessence of beauty." The London Stock Exchange wits responded as always with topical jokes lampooning Emperor Haile Selassie of Ethiopia, the Lion of Judah. A stockbroker member of the golf club had an elaborate X-rated toy depicting Haile Selassie carrying Mussolini pick-a-back. When you pulled a string Mussolini swivelled downwards to reveal what he was really up to behind the Emperor's back. One of the copywriters at the agency passed around propaganda photos circulated by the Italians showing "innocent" fascist corpses lying in the desert with their trousers around their knees and their genitals ripped off by the savage Ethiopians. Nobody had taken shots of the corpses of spear-toting Ethiopian tribesmen who had died under the Italian poison gas attacks.

The League, as might be expected, condemned Mussolini's rape of Abyssinia but proved unable to rally a sufficient number of its member states to support effective sanctions. Britain and France, in particular, secretly worked behind the League's back to appease Mussolini, resulting in the so-called Hoare-Laval Pact, named after the British Foreign Secretary, Sir Samuel Hoare, and the French Premier, Pierre Laval. This effectively handed over to Italy most of the conquered Ethiopian territory. Hoare managed to survive his appeasing past, but not so Laval. Condemned to death as a traitor and Nazi collaborator he was taken from his prison cell in sackcloth and chains and executed by his countrymen in October 1945.

Sir Samuel Hoare has been immortalized in song, at least in left wing circles, along with another Tory cabinet member:

Belisha-Hore is Minister of War
And then we have Sir Samuel Hoare
Oh, can we save the country yet
With two whores in the cabinet?

This was a time of disillusionment for many Britons, not only young idealistic intellectuals. Few southerners with jobs saw with their own eyes the miserable living conditions of the unemployed workers of the Tyneside, Merseyside, Southern Wales or the battered Midlands, but they could not avoid seeing the groups of Welsh miners shuffling slowly in lockstep along the gutters of London streets, singing for pennies in magnificent harmony. More and more non-working-class people broke class ranks to subscribe to socialist journals, attend left-wing lectures and support left-wing causes. Victor Gollancz, the publisher, founded the popular paperback Left Book Club which popularized the works of middle-class dissidents like Harold Laski and George Orwell. The latter's *Road to Wigan Pier*, shocking as it was in the depiction of British slum squalor, came as no surprise to me, having spent a short time in the Durham coal fields.

The era of appeasement and disillusionment was well underway. But the disillusionment was tempered by the sense of a growing international solidarity, a united front of progressive people catalyzed by the upsurge of fascism. This was especially true of people my own age, typified by the motion passed in the Oxford University Debating Society to the effect that the undergraduate members would on no account bear arms for King and Country.

Why such disaffection? What was going on? Could it be true that the government through its apparent disinterest and hands-off policy towards Hitler was actually rooting for him? Could it really be true that high-placed Britons like Lady Astor's so-called Cliveden Set, named after their country estate hangout, and even including the then Prince of Wales, were all in cahoots with the Nazis?

We at the agency got a glimpse of how the Establishment could manipulate the news to suit its own end. Nineteen thirty-six was the year when the Prince of Wales somewhat reluctantly ascended the throne to become Edward VIII. It was also the year his lover Wally Simpson moved to centre stage. In the eyes of the British Establishment, Simpson was an unspeakable, twice-divorced American gold-digger. It was more than they could stomach.

A cabal made up of Queen Mary, Prime Minister Stanley Baldwin, Archbishop of Canterbury Cosmo Lang and the press barons quietly censored all news of the disgraceful liaison even while it was widely known in the United States. When *Time* newsmagazine wrote about it the British censors tore out the offending pages from the relatively few copies available on British newsstands. However, at the agency our copy came direct by mail, uncensored, so we were amongst the minority outside the King's circle of cronies who knew what was going on. We looked on Edward as a confused and spoiled little man who showed his sympathy for the working poor on visits to the Welsh mining towns and elsewhere but saw the solution to their problems in the sort of discipline and tough leadership shown by the Nazis, whom he much admired. Nevertheless, the left wing sympathized with him over his treatment by the pillars of Church and State – especially Church, as personified by Cosmo Lang. The New Statesman & Nation summed it up in typical fashion:

My Lord Archbishop, what a scold you are,
And when your man is down, how bold you are;
Of Christian charity how scant you are.
*You old Lang swine, how full of Cantuar.***

*** Latin for "Canterbury."*

Sixteen
Inside Spain

At the advertising agency I had become friendly with Chris Brackenbury, a blasé, somewhat supercilious man my own age who opened up fascinating new vistas and avenues. His father was an inventor who had had a hand in the development of television; his mother had been an actress; and his young sister was an aspiring actress, still a student at the Royal Academy of Dramatic Art. He was a product of Westminster School which, while a dayschool, was a cut above good old Mill Hill from a social point of view. The family lived on Cheyne Walk, Chelsea, a fashionably Bohemian address. There was not a shred of deference about Chris. He acted as though the world was indeed his oyster and he went fearlessly about doing whatever took his fancy.

My friendship with him took me into situations I would never have dreamed of on my own. Neither of us had any money to speak of. But whereas I dressed carefully and, of necessity, conventionally, he wore elegantly tailored Austin Reed suits, a rakish Tirolean hat with a badger brush, and an avant-garde camel hair wrap-around overcoat with a loosely tied sash like a film star. His mother unwittingly fed me a line one day that made me feel better about my own plebeian overcoat. "Isn't that original of Gordon," she said, "to wear a coat like that." My only piece of one-upmanship over him was that I was a copywriter and he was still slaving in the agency slums.

Under Chris' influence, I learned to play squash, go to the Café Royale, squander a week's wages on Friday night dinner and drinks at Scott's Restaurant in Leicester Square, take winter instead of summer holidays and reappear in the office in February deeply tanned from a fortnight's skiing in Austria. We had a plan to rent a Rolls Royce Silver Cloud – theoretically possible – and to show up in it at the agency's annual picnic, but this fell through because the renting company insisted we also hire a chauffeur which put the whole antic beyond our budget. Through Chris I met famous people (like romance novelist Denise Robbins, the Barbara Cartland of her day), stayed in their country cottages, swam in their pools. Standing in for Chris's sister at her request, I took Pamela Brown to lunch. She was still a student actress at the time. Little did I know to what heights in the theatre she would rise.

Sometimes Chris cynically used me to help in some outrage, as when he got me included on the guest list for a formal society ball that his aunt was hosting. It was the first time I had been exposed to all the protocol and hoopla of receiving lines and dance programs. His aunt, of course, was delighted to have another young male for her seraglio of maidens. How could she have known that Chris had planned that neither of us would do what was expected of us but instead engage in some noisy and unsociable drinking, thumbing our noses at high society.

It was through Chris that I came to know Spain at first hand. Chris had a girlfriend, Gloria, a señorita from Barcelona. I first met her at the Gare d'Orsay in Paris where we had arranged a rendez-vous en route to a skiing holiday à *trois* in Austria. With the shameless arrogance of young Brits abroad, we managed to get a compartment on the Orient Express to ourselves by claiming that Gloria was *enceinte* and might imminently miscarry. Even the conductor fell for it. Gloria, all of nineteen, was an able co-conspirator. She had already made this plain on the platform at the Gare d'Orsay when the French porter had contemptuously complained about his miserly tip. "Oh, you don't want a *pourboire*?" she said sweetly, picking the money off his palm and putting it back in her purse.

Gloria came from a wealthy, highborn Catalan family. However, her mother had suffered for many years in an arranged marriage from which under Spanish law there was not the remotest possibility of escape by divorce, not until the first republican government came to power and made divorce legal for the first time. Gloria's mother was one of the first Spanish women to take advantage of the new law and from then on was one of the minority of well-to-do republican supporters.

In April of 1936, Chris proposed that we visit Gloria in Barcelona over the Easter holiday, which in England was a four-day break. Chris had a cousin Charles with the same family name who was a well-known racecar and rally driver. Chris figured that if he wrote to the Sunbeam Motor Company asking for the loan of a car for a weekend for test purposes, and signed the letter using the initial "C" there was a good chance that the company would mistake him for his cousin and lend him the car. The company responded with a stinging letter to his cousin asking him if he had taken leave of his senses. We had to try another tack. There was no way in which we could have raised the money for boat and train fares, so it was decided to ask two other friends to join us in renting a car for the trip. Once in Barcelona, we would be living free of charge – and higher on the hog than we had ever imagined, as it turned out.

One of our foursome was already in Paris, where he succeeded in renting a car. By using the cheapest and most inconvenient route to Paris, we arrived sleepless shortly after five a.m. at the Gare du Nord where our friend was waiting for us with the car – an early Ford V-8 painted a head-turning shocking pink with turquoise accents. He insisted that one of us would have to drive because he had been up all night getting the car ready. Unfortunately none of the three of us had had any sleep either, having travelled third class from London to Newhaven, wallowed across the Channel to Dieppe the long and nauseating way, then on to Paris on fourth class wooden benches over the noisy steel-tied tracks of the French railways.

We decided to spell each other in the driver's seat at half-hour intervals and hope for the best. The route we had chosen seemed to be the straightest to the Spanish border – straightest, yes; shortest, no. All went well for a while as we bowled down the hypnotically straight Route Nationale side by side with the railroad tracks. Unnoticed by us on the map, the road suddenly took a right angle turn and crossed the railroad tracks to proceed down the other side. Since all four of us were sound asleep, we failed to make the turn and woke up in a field, still bouncing southwards in a straight line. From then on, sleeping was confined to the rear seat.

Our ill-chosen route led us through the highest part of the Massif Central so that by nightfall we were hairpinning endlessly up mountain roads and down on the other side. It was not until six o'clock on Saturday morning that we reached the Spanish border at La Junquera. There appeared to be no sign of life and neither was there a barrier, so we decided to drive on. Moments later we heard sirens and gunshots and realized we were being chased. We stopped, hauled out our British passports, those documents which we trusted to be an antidote to whatever poisonous foreign behaviour was aimed our way, waved them in the air and shouted: "Inglese…Inglese." Looking back, I am surprised that the frontier guard refrained from shooting at least one of us in token disgust, which he could probably have got away with.

With great restraint he told us that the border was closed until eight o'clock, escorted us back to the frontier, took the car keys and had us sit on the sidewalk under his surveillance for the next two hours.

Barcelona was garlanded for Easter. The centre strip of the Ramblas, the city's Fifth Avenue, was ablaze with flowers. The people, even the buildings, smiled under the bright Easter sky. Fatigue forgotten, we found Gloria's home – an impressive penthouse, much of it *al fresco* in the shape of sheltered tiled balconies and terraces, one of which was assigned to me as a bedroom. Gloria's mother treated the invasion of four grubby young men as an everyday event. She suggested we bathe before having luncheon, for which she apologized in advance as being a meagre offering, unworthy of such welcome guests but the best she had been able to do on such short notice.

The plumbing arrangements were *fin de siècle*, of a luxury so decadent and indulgent as to put Jacuzzi to shame – a huge, deep tub you could snorkel in, rococo fixtures with sprays and jets of water coming from every direction at any desired velocity to caress or flagellate. Dried by pre-heated towels the size of billiard tables and slightly aromatic from sampling the free eau de Cologne, we presented ourselves for lunch.

Gloria, uncharacteristically demure on her home turf, escorted us to the dining room where her mother was putting the finishing touches to bowls of flowers on a table glittering with silver and crystal. Once again she apologized for the meagre meal we would eat. It proved to be a four-course feast, not including the olives, tapas, cheeses and baskets of fruit, served by a white-gloved liveried footman. After lunch our hostess diffidently suggested a program of activities for the weekend. This included a bull fight, an evening of flamenco dancing at a night club and some sightseeing – clearly all carefully organized in advance but made to seem like our idea.

This blissful atmosphere was shattered in the early hours of Easter Sunday by a series of explosions, the last of which seemed to be very close to the house. At breakfast we learned that these bombings, for that was what they were, were becoming more frequent and were, as everyone took for granted, the work of Franco's Falangist fifth column.

Incredibly, in an effort to appear legal and above reproach, the Republican government had kept General Francisco Franco on as Chief of Staff. Three months to the day after our little jaunt he invaded Spain from Spanish Morocco, where the government had belatedly banished him, again using Moorish troops because he had no confidence that Spaniards would so willingly murder their own. He did so after carefully seeding the country with his own Falangist followers, the same people who had set off the bombs we had heard at Easter.

Propaganda against the Spanish Republican government, both then and now, was so bitter and full of misinformation that the myth persists that Franco was a knight in shining Christian armour saving Spain from an atheistic communist dictatorship. The pro-Loyalist and pro-Franco supporters split into two camps as bitterly divided and irreconcilable as in today's abortion debate – and divided along much the same lines. In fact, the popular front government, a coalition of all parties democratically elected on February 16, 1936, declared itself as standing for "mild liberal reform." The British Establishment saw things differently. Reporting the results of the Spanish election, *The Times* of London, under a heading "Reverses for the Right," quoted Gil Robles, leader of the clerical, monarchist and conservative parties, as calling on every voter "to take a place in the trenches in the defence against hordes bent on assassination and arson captained by foreigners with Mongolian (sic) faces." Right Honourable Lord Lloyd, a Tory peer bursting with Christian rectitude, saw the Franco revolt as a "national uprising against the godless."

Gloria could not be reached by telephone, but a couple of weeks later a long letter arrived describing the scene in the Ramblas with "deads lying everywhere in the streets." I happened to know the editor of the *Daily Mirror* who was a fellow golf club member and I took Chris to see him and show him the letter. We got a surprisingly hostile reception and were accused of just wanting to profit from Gloria's misfortunes. There was some truth in this, but it was also true that the press with very few exceptions was already solidly behind Franco and was in no mood to help the republican government by printing heart-wrenching stories like Gloria's.

The Spanish civil war did more than any other event to clarify the political issues of the day and to push people into taking a stand – laissez-faire or militantly anti-fascist. It gave rise to the biggest Popular Front ever seen – embracing people of all political persuasions and nationalities. For me, as for many of my age group, it was the catalyst that determined my political future.

Spain began to dominate our thoughts. We switched our restaurant patronage to the España, a small bistro just opened by republican refugees. (We never considered that they might have shown greater loyalty to the cause by staying to fight.) We drank our wine out of a *porron*, the glass version of a wine skin, mastering the art of catching the stream of wine on our tonsils and swallowing with our mouths open. We learned this from the restaurant owner before catching on that for each demonstration he gave he drank a good part of our porron.

Communist ripples were reaching out in ever-increasing circles as voluntary international brigades began to be recruited for service with the Loyalist armies. Neither of us had any contact with the communists, nor for that matter with any left-wing organization, although there were undoubtedly some undeclared members in our orbit. But the popular front enthusiasm was so pervasive that the thought of "doing something for Spain" was always there.

One evening Chris asked me to meet him at the Holborn Hotel bar, our neighbourhood pub, to have a sherry and meet a friend. The friend, Esmond Romilly, was about to leave for Spain to fight against Franco. This incident typified the spread within families in political thinking and loyalties, crossing class lines, common in Britain during this festering decade, a credit to the ingrained respect for individual freedom of thought, including freedom of dissent, in contrast to what I later saw in Canada. For Romilly's uncle was Winston Churchill. His wife, Jessica Mitford, was a committed left-wing activist, while one of her sisters was married to British fascist Oswald Mosley and another was an intimate friend of Adolf Hitler.

We occasionally discussed following Romilly to Spain but now Chris began to talk about learning to fly. He was motivated by a sense of adventure rather than political conviction. He could picture himself cutting heroic figures in the sky but hardly slugging it out in mud and misery as a rifleman. He never did go to Spain, although I later heard that he had fought with distinction with the RAF. Romilly survived Spain only to be killed with the RAF in the bigger war to come. Gloria, I was told, married a Luftwaffe pilot.

I did not return to Spain either, but I realized that I had seen General Franco in person. He had passed on foot at a snail's pace before my eyes on the streets of London on January 20th, 1936 along with the four royal princes; Marshall Pétain of France; Maxim Litvinoff and Marshal Tukhachevsky of the Soviet Union; Jan Masaryk of Czechoslovakia; Baron Mannerheim of Finland; Nazi Baron von Neurath; and most of the crowned heads of Europe – Leopold of Belgium, Boris of Bulgaria, Christian of Denmark, Carol of Rumania, Haakon of Norway; Princes Farouk of Egypt, Paul of Yugoslavia, George of Greece, and Piedmont, heir to the Italian throne – as they followed the gun carriage bearing the flag-draped remains of King George V. For most of them, buffeted by history, it would be their last big scene before conquest, abdication or exile swept them off the world stage, but not from my mind's eye.

Seventeen
Tightening of the Screw

I now belonged to the amorphous, unofficial popular front which had coalesced around the appeasement issue. At least I had learned to distinguish between what the powers-that-be said had happened or would happen, and what had actually happened or was likely to happen.

I was becoming "political," whether by instinct, prejudice or intuition, drawing conclusions that are sometimes difficult to prop up with facts. But facts or no facts, the political compass needle points insistently towards one's personal magnetic north. The facts that justify these conclusions are often elusive, deliberately concealed. You have to wait for time to unlock the archives, for old age and retirement to loosen the memories of diplomats and politicians who have outlived the threats to their careers and reputations that telling the truth incurs – the secret bombings, the assassinations, the perjuries, the cover-ups.

So, when Hitler publicly renounced the Versailles Treaty in January 1937, it was clear to me that this was a German call to arms. Thanks to the secret German files produced at the Nuremberg trials of the Nazi leaders, their preparations for war during this period have been fully documented together with their confidence that the British would not stand in the way of their drive for Lebensraum or "living space." The German Foreign Office put its seal of approval on Prime Minister Neville Chamberlain because he was already known as an appeaser served by super-appeasers like Sir Nevile Henderson, his ambassador in Berlin who worked to have England love Hitler and called Nazism "a great social experiment."

The most cynical manifestation of the non-intervention policy (an ingenious swindle, according to G.E.R. Gedye) was the attitude to the war in Spain. While the British Navy blockaded Russian relief ships from entering Spanish ports, German planes were freely bombing Spanish towns and villages, as Goering would later admit with pride from the dock at Nuremberg.

Mussolini was also doing his bit for Franco. While assuring the British that he had no part in the war, he was at the same time cabling Franco: "I am particularly proud that the Italian legionaries have, during ten days of hard fighting, contributed mightily to the splendid victory at Santander…This brotherhood of arms…guarantees the final victory which will liberate Spain and the Mediterranean from any menace to our common civilization."

Winston Churchill, a laughable maverick barely on the fringes of power at the time, was one of the very few not to give Franco whole-hearted endorsement. He declared himself neutral and non-partisan in the civil war, but said that if he had to choose between communism and fascism, he would choose communism. Lloyd George, another frayed statesman, was more forthright in the House of Commons: "…if its [non-intervention's] object was to give a definite and what might be a decisive advantage to the insurgents over the legitimate government of Spain, then it had been a triumphant success." But it was Anthony Eden who voiced official policy when he said that he did not think Franco would be unfriendly to England and that there are countries that hold communism to be the real culprit.

I did not need to look only abroad to see the gathering clouds. Guided by my built-in political compass, which was becoming ever more sensitive, I could detect war in the wings – not the war that actually happened, but a war that would do to socialism in general and the Soviet

Union in particular what Franco was doing to Spain. Much of the evidence was out in the open for all who had eyes to see. Some would be documented later when the people involved had written about it. (Some still remains to be resolved – for example, the precise participation of the Duke of Windsor and the truth about Rudolph Hess' flight to Scotland.)

One inescapable facet of domestic fascism was the rise of the British Union of Fascists under Sir Oswald Mosley. They made a specialty of taking their marches and meetings into the heart of Labour and especially Jewish territory, provoking confrontations that were often made to appear the fault of the very people they had set out to provoke. I particularly remember one of the worst of these – a Blackshirt procession to, as *The Times* put it, "invade" a largely Jewish area of southeast London. One of my copywriter colleagues happened to live on the route of the procession so he and his family were eyewitnesses to the affair. Mosley's thugs had the way cleared for them by thirty-two mounted police followed by police vans and cars. Not surprisingly the fascists got a hostile reception, but after the skin and hair had settled, of the one hundred and five people arrested only a handful were fascists. Among those charged was one Louis Karbitz, tailor, of Whitechapel. He was fined ten pounds for "using insulting language with intent to cause a breach of the peace" directed at a fascist who had made remarks about the size of his nose. Another of the arrested, Anne Lipscombe, was asked by the magistrate if her name was Jewish. She said it was not, denied throwing a brick at a mounted policeman, and was acquitted. There was not a single mention of anti-Semitism in *The Times* report.

For a brief moment in the spring of 1938 we Popular Fronters thought the tide might yet turn against the appeasers. When German troops streamed into Austria, Foreign Minister Anthony Eden resigned in protest. This gesture of a popular and respected Tory was of no avail. Chamberlain appointed Lord Halifax, a true appeaser, to replace him. An exasperated MP, referring to "Chamberlain and his fascist friends" said in the House: "What need of coloured shirts when we have the old school tie?"

At this point the USSR proposed a meeting of the powers to discuss ways of stopping further Nazi aggression. Chamberlain rejected the proposal out of hand. "Forming exclusive groups of nations," he said, "would be inimical to the prospects of European peace."

In the same speech he said the United Kingdom would not help Czechoslovakia nor would it support France if the French should promise to defend Czechoslovakia from Nazi aggression. A gleeful Hitler, poised to swallow Czechoslovakia, could hardly believe how easy they were making it for him. Chamberlain, in what were supposed to be off-the-record remarks to his "fascist friends" at a luncheon party at Cliveden, apparently said that he favoured the break-up of Czechoslovakia and the formation of a 4-power pact between Britain, France, Germany and Italy from which the USSR would be excluded.

The story was broken by U. S. correspondent Joseph Driscoll. Chamberlain made the expected denials in the House. But no doubt Hitler got the message, which was further emphasized by anti-Czech editorials in *The Times* and by Nevile Henderson's assurances in Berlin that Britain would never go to Czechoslovakia's rescue even if France did.

Even during the last stages of appeasement, when Chamberlain was shuttling between Downing Street and Hitler's Bavarian mountain retreat at Berchtesgaden, the Soviet Union insisted it was ready to meet its treaty to stand by Czechoslovakia provided France did likewise. It is hardly surprising that the policies and actions of the Soviet Union during these appeasement days should have appeared to me as to many of my contemporaries as statesmanlike and enlightened when compared with those of our own Government.

Eighteen
Now or Never

During this year I had quarreled with Chris over some triviality and we were ignoring each other, even peeing in silence side by side in the agency washroom. My social life was as erratic as the flight of a dandelion seed, landing in the strangest, unrelated places but never taking root. I had a brief affair with a young West End hairdresser who I discovered had to submit to her boss on the stairs leading to their sub-basement salon as part of the terms of her employment.

One of the other girls had an all-in wrestler for a boyfriend and we had some fascinating times together patronizing East End London dives until the foursome broke up when the wrestler playfully tossed the boy helper at the beauty parlour over his shoulder and cracked his skull on the low ceiling. On another occasion I went skating at the Harringay arena, equipped like everyone else with elegantly curved figure skates, and picked up a girl. She seemed to be impressed with my courtly, rather constipated manner and my interest in politics and with some hesitation agreed to a further date. Her reluctance, it turned out, was due to her being Jewish and wary of any liaison with a non-Jew. But she did pay me the compliment that I wasn't too bad considering I wasn't Jewish. She had taken me to be a communist, which I think she must have been, so evidently I had begun to wear my political heart on my sleeve.

At the agency my wages and productivity were both at a standstill. The wide world I had hoped for was proving to be more and more narrow and confining. I was still living at home, guilty and unhappy at being alienated from the family yet taking advantage of their generosity. I was twenty-two years old. My youth was draining away. It was clearly time to move on. But was I really capable of striking out alone into the world? To shed my outsider status? To find the like-minded people who must surely exist somewhere?

Why I had not sought these like-minded people in the flourishing left-wing movements in Great Britain I find difficult to explain. Obviously, my emotional reaction to events had not gelled into an intellectual resolve to take the pledge, so to speak. Yet there was no doubt another reason. After more than half a century in Canada with its relatively egalitarian society, the ever-present class-consciousness of those days in Great Britain seems remote, almost bizarre. Yet it must have been a factor. I remember not only the Durham blind date and Al Bowyer, but also the marriage of one of our maids at which I represented the family and was the only male not to kiss the bride. Class-consciousness worked in both directions – up and down – and I suppose I felt unsure of my welcome.

The day of decision came on May Day, Britain's traditional Labour holiday. It is, incidentally, also the day on which London bus drivers switched to their white summer coats and cap covers. On this spring day in 1938 the bus drivers were in high spirits, having come out the winners in a lengthy labour dispute, and were in the place of honour, leading the parade in a river of white. I stood at the corner of Hyde Park near Marble Arch for what seemed like hours as group after group streamed by, each holding aloft its banner, some proudly, some defiantly, some sheepishly, as they marched and sang labour songs in the bright Spring sunshine. Everyone was there – not just the miners and brewery workers and pants pressers, but also the communists, Trotskyites and anarchists – and barely a policeman in sight. Was that, perhaps, why the Blackshirts sniped at the procession and tried to shout down the speakers, including Herbert Morrison, M.P., who charged that the Chamberlain government "…now cynically recognizes and almost encourages the continuance of the Italian and German invasion of Spain"? According to press estimates 200,000 people marched that day. I think it was then that I finally decided that war would surely come and that I had better see more of the world before the sword of Damocles dropped, or forget it forever.

I must admit there was another less noble incentive to nail down the decision to leave. I had begun going out with one of the secretaries at the agency. In those days casual sex was not so easy to come by, even between a consenting couple. The owners of rooming houses, at least the respectable ones, protected their premises like eunuchs guarding a seraglio. There were no motels. Most hotels would not knowingly register unmarried couples, and in any case were too expensive. There was always a rumble seat if you were athletic and had or could borrow a jalopy for the occasion. And, depending on the season, hay ricks, wheat fields or beds of bracken.

My friend Connie and I were compatible. We enjoyed each other's company although we had not made love. It wasn't long before I could see she thought she was heading for a diamond ring, a wedding dress and a family.

One evening after having a meal together I walked her home to her rooming house and was surprised to be invited unchallenged up to her tiny room. Clearly she had set the scene for a seduction which, it seemed to me, would be the equivalent of a proposal of marriage. I froze. I could see my imminent freedom snatched from me. Braving her shocked disbelief turning to humiliation and anger, and my own sense of shame and betrayal, I slunk out of her life.

When I casually leaked my plans to the family, my father thought that I had finally taken leave of my senses. He had reprimanded me earlier for talking disrespectfully about Hitler – a head of state – and now I was going to throw up a respectable job! For what?

"There's going to be a war," I told him, "and I'd just like to see a bit of the world before it comes."

"You're crazy" he said.

I found one ally in Derek Putnam, a golfing friend who for his own reasons wanted to get away. Canada seemed to be the logical first destination. We began to look for the cheapest way to get there and before long we had booked passage on a grain boat due to call at the Yorkshire port of Hull on its next round trip to Montreal some weeks ahead. There was no turning back.

Nineteen
The Immigrant

When it became clear that I was serious about going to Canada there was an abrupt change in the attitude of friends. All of a sudden, it seemed, everyone envied me my imminent freedom…if only they had the opportunity, the guts, the lack of family responsibility or whatever, they'd be with me like a shot. I could have led a posse of adventurers *manqués* for the second conquest of Canada. Our boarding party, however, stayed at the original two – Derek and myself. I never quite understood Derek's motives for making such an important change in his life. He had a job on the London Stock Exchange where he had the aptitude and the opportunity to become rich. He was the only son of Roman Catholic parents who had separated long before I met him and, of course, considered divorce out of the question. He never spoke of his mother; I gather he rarely if ever saw her. He lived in "rooms" with his father, an embittered and militantly Catholic man whom I tried to avoid because of his hatred for the Spanish Loyalists and obvious disapproval of my friendship with Derek. Still, one had to feel sorry for him, eating a solitary supper from a tray in a dismal sitting room on the increasing number of evenings when Derek was about his own social life.

I suppose Derek saw no future except complete escape. My father's attitude changed, too – from refusal to take my plan seriously to concern for my future welfare. When he discovered that the fifteen pounds I had paid for my passage to Montreal almost cleaned me out, he wisely and generously gave me fifty pounds in letters of credit on a Montreal bank. He then arranged with a fellow director of his company, Sir John Wallace, who was also a Conservative MP, to provide me with letters of introduction to executives of their Canadian associated company, Dominion Oilcloth Co., including one to the future Air Vice Marshall Frank McGill.

Thus armed, I set out with a light heart to join the good ship *Bassano* at the port of Hull on July 1st, 1938.

The *Bassano* was a small coal-fired grain boat plying between Montreal, Hull and Aberdeen. She carried six passengers, who slept two to a cabin and ate with the ship's officers. The crew was all from Yorkshire except the Chief Engineer who, of course, like Chiefs the world over, was a Scot.

We left Hull for Aberdeen where the last of the cargo of grain was discharged. Since we took nothing on, I realized that we would be making the trans-Atlantic trip in ballast, bobbing like a bottle. On leaving

Aberdeen and hitting open water, the captain, a fat but far from jolly individual, was sick – not a good sign, but according to one of the crew a routine occurrence – after which he settled down to enjoying the gigantic meals which issued three times a day from the galley. At breakfast the first day out, he polished off a couple of mutton (not lamb) chops before settling down to bacon and eggs.

We were making a "north about" passage that took us through the Pentland Firth between the Orkneys and the Scottish mainland and then north of the Hebrides out into the broad Atlantic. At midnight at this latitude in mid-summer there is still enough reflected sunlight to give a pearly luminescence to land and seascape. It could not have been a more romantic start to a voyage.

The other passengers were a young Scottish doctor and a couple of Americans; a spoiled-rotten high-school student returning from the grand tour of Europe with his guardian – a somewhat older, cynical college boy earning his way through school the hard way. It was my first taste of adolescent arrogance *à l'Américaine.* The rest of us – passengers and officers – found it hard to take. By contrast, the young Scot, all of twenty-four, was already an MD with a year's internship behind him. He was on his way to Medicine Hat to claim an inheritance.

The second day out we hit the North Atlantic swells – row on row of parallel waves that we took at right-angles, rising and falling like a roller coaster. It became clear why everything in the saloon was bolted down, and why there were holes in the table tops to hold the cups and plates in place. But after a couple of days of this, boredom set in. We were given the run of the ship, so we began to explore.

The *Bassano* was equipped with a device that took the exhaust steam from the conventional piston engine and fed it to a turbine flexibly coupled to the drive shaft, supposedly giving it much greater efficiency and economy. The Chief was especially proud of his state-of-the-art turbine drive and liked to show it off. Hi-tech as this was, the coal was still fed to boilers the old-fashioned way, shovel by shovel into the hellish fires. The stokers, stripped to the waist, loaded the big coal scoops and stood poised at the open grates waiting to co-ordinate their actions with the motion of the ship. At exactly the right moment, the merest thrust would send the coal flying deep onto the fire. No amount of strength would persuade the coal to leave the scoop until the ship was in sync. There was also the possibility that, if your timing was off, you could pitch yourself into the fire along with the coal. I tried it, to much laughter and good-natured Yorkshire mockery. The temperature in the stokehold was unbelievably hot. Whenever possible between stokings, the men would stand directly in the blast of frigid Atlantic air which was scooped up by the deck ventilators and funnelled below. When the long shift was over, they would go on deck, still half naked, and stand for an hour or so in the wind.

Periodically, ash and clinker from the fires would be collected and thrown overboard, a procedure known as "dumping your dirty ashes." This expression took on another meaning as I found out later in Montreal when the crew, after a violent soccer game and a few beers went off to "dump their dirty ashes" at a handy whorehouse.

These men, gnarled, bandy-legged, bony and yet muscular, reminded me of the Durham miners. They had the same quiet pride in their competence, the same fatalistic acceptance of their lot and, as it turned out, the same ferocious competitiveness at sports. This was a time when the British still operated a large fleet of merchant ships under their own registry and with British crews. They were able to do this by keeping the crews in abysmally poor, underpaid, tightly-disciplined conditions. The *Bassano* crew told me of conditions on board a P & 0 liner where their only toilet facilities were in a narrow hut on a deck in full view of the passengers. They had to back into the hut with their trousers unbuttoned at the ready. On one occasion, so they said, a whole pan of chicken Marengo from the passengers' galley (giving verisimilitude to the story; this was a favourite P & O dish) was left on a hatch cover, presumably for them to help themselves. This they declined to do, reasoning that if it was left for them it must be inedible.

I remembered these Yorkshiremen when not long after I came to Canada I met Blackie Myers, vice-president of the National Maritime Union of the United States who was on a visit to Montreal. He told me how disgusted the American seamen were with the British crews docking in New York when they found out the conditions the "Limeys" were tolerating – no sheets, no hot showers, lousy food, no laundry facilities, no crew committee to handle complaints and so on, all of which the NMU had won from the owners.

I made friends also with the deck crew. Their main job was to clean out the grain holds in readiness for the next trip. They were skeptical about my offer to work but agreed to let me try. It meant descending to the very bottom of the ship by means of two vertical steel ladders bolted to the bulkheads – not an easy manoeuvre in a pitching vessel – then sweeping and shovelling three inches of fine wheat dust which flew in the air at a touch to clog eyes and lungs. Anyone with the choice would have avoided all contact with that dust. I suppose, not really knowing what means of livelihood lay ahead, I wanted to prove to myself that a "constipated Peter Pan" (to borrow Cedric Belfrage's inspired description from *Away from It All*) could hack it no matter what.

I was naturally pleased when the crew, who had been puzzled why anyone should want to leave what seemed to be a comfortable existence to venture into the unknown, delivered their verdict. "We ain't worried about you. You're gonna be all right. It's that other bloke [meaning Derek] we ain't so sure of."

They need not have worried. Derek soon left Canada for the United States, got a job as a salesman, married, raised a family and became a prosperous and law-abiding member of the community.

On July 11th, we docked in Montreal. Here I was somewhat surprised to be prevented from disembarking until seen by an immigration official and a doctor. After all, I had a valid British passport. And anyway, didn't we own the place? Far from raising any objections, however, the immigration officer was most helpful. After satisfying himself that I was white, educated and well connected, as witness my letters of introduction, he confided that it would not look good in my file to be recorded as having arrived on a freighter. "I'll put you down as cabin class," he said. "Then nobody will know the difference."

The medical examination was even more cursory. The doctor took my word that I was not suffering from syphilis, gonorrhea or tuberculosis, then leaned to put his ear briefly on my chest before signing my acceptance papers. I was issued with a wallet-sized blue immigration identification card which was all I needed for legal immigrant status leading to automatic citizenship.

PART TWO

LIFE UNDER THE PADLOCK LAW

Twenty
Instant Canadian

The *Bassano* had docked close to the foot of St. Lawrence Boulevard – The Main – which was my entrée to Montreal. The first impression was that it consisted of cheap greasy spoons where trays of ten- or fifteen-cent meals of beans, macaroni and cabbage rolls were displayed in the windows to tempt, surely, only the very hungry. Almost every other door had a quack's sign advertising venereal disease treatment – "discrete and guaranteed, one floor up." A gauntlet of Gallic-looking girls with hollow cheeks and mocking or appraising eyes monitored our progress uptown. The mediaeval-habited nuns and the young black-suited seminarists walking in safely unconspiratorial threes, whom we later saw everywhere uptown, evidently steered clear of the Lower Main.

Derek and I took a room for the first night at the Ford Hotel on Dorchester Street for four dollars – the hotel that later became the headquarters of Radio Canada – and woke up in the middle of the night to find a girl trying to get into bed with us. Apparently the desk clerk was moonlighting as a pimp, supplying his girls with keys and likely room numbers. (On the second night we moved to the YMCA for five dollars a week, where the problem was of a different sexual nature, particularly in the common shower room.)

Early the following morning I moved to present my letters of introduction at Dominion Oilcloth where I was cordially received and made aware of the Canadian habit of deferring important decisions until after Labour Day, an annual feast day I had never heard of. The message seemed to be to forget about employment for several weeks, until at least the first week of September. However, there was a message for me to meet Frank McGill at the United Services Club that afternoon at five o'clock. Here, too, I was made to feel at ease amid the gleaming brass, Turkish carpets, bum-polished leather sofas and copies of *Punch*, and was graciously offered a Scotch and soda.

My conversation with McGill went well until he asked me my opinion of "things in England." I replied at some length about the menace of fascism, the Mosley Blackshirts and their anti-Semitic raids in London's East End, the disgraceful behaviour of the British and French governments towards the Spanish republicans, the anti-war sentiment of the British, particularly amongst the young – unaware until too late of McGill's increasingly glazed eyes and tightening jaw. When I had finished, he excused himself without further comment and left. It was the last I saw of him.

This was the first of many encounters with business and professional people whose seemingly parochial and crutch-bound approach to politics and current affairs struck me, fresh from the stewpot of cosmopolitan London, as being as anachronistic as their Argyle socks and their fuzzy fedoras. I was yet to learn of R.B.Bennett, Section 98 of the Canadian Criminal Code, Maurice Duplessis, the Padlock Law and other symbols of hard-line conservative, union-busting control.

Luckily, there was one aspect of my "Limeyness" in demand – my certificate as an Associate of the Institute of Practitioners in Advertising, proof of five solid years of apprenticeship in all aspects of advertising. It eventually got me a job as an advertising copywriter with the A. McKim advertising agency, but not until after the sacred Labour Day date.

Excruciating loneliness set in. For the lonely, time creeps along at the slowest of paces. Great stretches of arid desert separate the oases of meals and bed. I walked hundreds of miles of Montreal streets and saw every acre of surrounding territory from the windows of the two-dollar "Nowhere" bus trips. The *Bassano* was still in port and I was always welcome aboard to visit and to go with the men on their savage soccer encounters with crews from all over the world in the Seamen's League. These matches took place down-river near the Vickers plant. Few of the players had proper equipment. They played bare-shinned, without pads. There was more blood and skin flying around than you would see in a whole NHL play-off series. After the game we would go to a nearby seaman's pub and sit down at a table covered with ten-cent draft beers. These would be downed, bottoms up, without talk, and with very short pauses between each glass, until the table was cleared, whereupon the group left in a body – presumably to dump their dirty ashes.

Twenty-one
Mac-Paps

Canadian advertising agency life turned out to be different from what I had been used to in London, where the writers and art directors had been the most cosseted employees. At McKim's the copywriters were herded together in a bullpen waiting to be briefed by the privileged account men in the private offices down the hall on what the clients said they wanted. I joined Bill Casey, Bob Campbell and a stenographer in a cement-floored, glassed-in cubicle in full view of the constant traffic in the passageway. There were no creative jam sessions, no bouncing around of ideas. Casey gave me assignments in isolation from the account executives until he judged me capable of talking to them myself.

I soon realized that the agency business was based not so much on creative excellence as on political and corporate connections. This meant that the job was sometimes not how to get publicity but how to *avoid* it, as in the case of Imperial Tobacco Company. The company and its sales subsidiary had fallen afoul of the Combines Investigation Act and were involved in court proceedings which could prove to be embarrassing. This accounted for the appearance in the bullpen from time to time of a small man wearing a soiled raincoat and a derby hat to consult with Bob Campbell. This was the agency's PR hit man who specialized in keeping things out of print in the days before the Newspaper Guild, when reporters supplemented their wages with handouts from politicians, police chiefs, bureaucrats and corporation executives.

While struggling to shed my British idiom and shift into Canadian advertising jargon I had also been doing my best to follow the news from Europe in the unfamiliar Montreal newspapers with the feeling of watching a play from the upper gallery. Chamberlain on one of his many trips to Berchtesgaden to see Hitler reported to the British people reassuringly: "In spite of the hardness and ruthlessness I saw in his face, I got the impression that here was a man who could be relied on to keep his word."

Well, he was not alone. Prime Minister Mackenzie King, I discovered, had also found Hitler to be gentlemanly and trustworthy. Hitler's old friend, Viscount Rothermere, was even more effusive: "Herr Hitler…is simple, unaffected and obviously sincere…He is a man of rare culture."

None of this background to Munich seemed to be of much interest to my colleagues in the bullpen. When Neville Chamberlain soon afterwards signed the Munich agreement that legitimized the rape of Czechoslovakia and pulled the pin on the inevitable war to follow, they seemed pleased at what they saw as an example of British one-upmanship.

My predictions of disaster in the making established me as a "pinko" with Bob Campbell. He had his own political compass, whose polarity was just the reverse of mine.

A month later, the Spanish government, faced with almost certain defeat, (thanks in part to the same Mr. Chamberlain's non-interventionist policies which had given Mussolini and Hitler *carte blanche* to try out their war toys against the Spanish people) decided to repatriate the units of the International Brigade. These had come from all over the world as volunteers to fight with the Loyalist armies.

With this reminder of Spain I looked around for anyone, anyone at all, who was remotely connected with the Spanish Civil War. To my surprise I found a small group of people in a dingy office organizing for the return home and rehabilitation of the 727 survivors of the original 1448-strong Mackenzie-Papineau battalion, Canada's fighting contribution to Spanish democracy. The Mackenzie and Papineau names meant nothing to me. My knowledge of Canada was largely pictorial, consisting of the extensive red-coloured area on the school-room map of the world which was proudly ours. I was even surprised, in the light of my Canadian contacts thus far, to discover that there were any Canadians at all who had heard of the Spanish war, and even more so that they had been prepared to put their lives on the line for it. I offered to help in any way possible.

This contact quickly led me to a group of young men and women mostly in or around the commercial art field, with whom I shared both occupational and political interests. I soon realized that I had, perhaps not altogether accidentally, flown into the communist orbit where I was no doubt considered to be quite a catch. I was drawn towards two in particular with whom I soon formed an inseparable trio.

One was Ron Clark, a free-lance commercial artist who had been raised on a farm. He was thirty-five at the time we met. The suicide of a brother had affected him deeply, causing him to adopt a Spartan regimen of exercise, diet and cold baths, none of which spoiled his appreciation of a bottle of beer. In all the time I knew him he never owned an overcoat. In sub-zero weather he would keep warm by jogging whatever distance he had to go. He slept under a sheet with the window open in the coldest weather. He faithfully followed a diet that forbade the eating of protein and carbohydrate at the same meal. He was one of the healthiest and most cheerful people I have ever known.

The other member of our triumvirate was Dick Hersey, a commercial artist who actually had a steady job with a printing company. Dick hailed from Vancouver from where during the Depression he had shipped out, in his late teens, unqualified, as a fourth class engineer on freighters all over the world. He had come east to Montreal during the Depression riding a bicycle and sleeping under the stars – all the way across the Rockies, the Prairies and around the Great Lakes, with no money in his pocket except what he was able to earn or beg along the way. (Many years later, Hersey would become Art Director at Canada's largest-circulated national weekly, Weekend Magazine. Under Hersey, such talents as Harold Town, Ed MacNally, Doug Wright, and Duncan Macpherson got their first broad public exposure. They were just some of the many Canadian artists Hersey helped keep afloat until their careers were established.) The three of us took a sub-lease on a large flat at 3610 Oxenden (now Aylmer) Avenue.

The French and British authorities treated the returning Mac-Paps like lepers, holding them for days in concentration camps, locking them in trains removed from welcoming committees until they were safely stowed aboard ship for the passage home. The Canadians authorities were no exception. Word leaked out that a trainload would be arriving at Windsor Station where as many as possible of us were asked to form a welcoming committee. The RCMP were out in swarms when the train bearing the Mac-Paps pulled in. Flashbulbs popped as they photographed all in sight, including me giving the clenched fist salute in the excitement of the occasion. The first such salute I had ever given in my life no doubt put me into police records for all eternity. I was no longer merely a sympathizer – now I was an activist.

Inspector Harvison at this time was top man for the RCMP in Montreal. He must have learned about 3610 from the beginning because we volunteered its use as a sleeping-over point for a group of repatriated

Mac-Pap veterans on their way through to the west. For ten days our living room floor was carpeted with snoring comrades who woke only to eat. They seemed dazed and withdrawn, with none of the joy or bravado of conquering heroes. And small wonder. It is one of the ironies of Canadian democracy that the very first Canadians to risk their lives fighting the German Nazis and Italian Fascists had to do so illegally and run the risk of arrest as criminals upon their return. They would be damned by successive governments long after anti-fascist activities had become not just acceptable but indeed praiseworthy. Even Dr. Norman Bethune's blood transfusion activities were made technically illegal on the grounds that they were not offered equally to the opposing fascists. The Canadian authorities had little sympathy for the idea of ordinary people taking it upon themselves to fight, regardless of the justness of the cause. RCMP Commissioner S.T. Wood warned the government that these volunteers were likely to return to Canada to put their guerrilla-warfare skills to use on the barricades of Canadian streets, seemingly unaware that this put him on the same side of the so-called barricades as Mussolini and Hitler. (The British authorities, by contrast, were glad to have Spanish War veteran George Orwell teach these very same skills to the Home Guard.)

Gregory Clark (the popular *Toronto Daily Star* writer who won the Military Cross at Vimy Ridge and got Ernest Hemingway a job at the Star) made a prediction: "Some day it will be remembered to their glory that they served in Spain with the international brigades of many men from many lands." But few of those who went to Spain would live to see that day. It wouldn't be until 2001 that a monument to the Canadian veterans of the Spanish Civil War would be unveiled in Ottawa.

Twenty-two
Déjà vu

In the Spring of this same year, 1939, I experienced a case of *déjà vu* which gave me a wider perspective on Canadian politics. In the early thirties, Lord Rothermere had used his political influence in Great Britain and the columns of his newspaper, the *Daily Mail*, to try to organize middle-class youth into a militant national movement against what he portrayed as the weak-kneed government and lily-livered liberals.

His demagogic rhetoric, for which he had a gift, would provide the oxygen to fan their latent fires of self-sacrificing patriotism and convince them to enlist in organized, disciplined national service – largely unpaid, one suspected, to judge by his rhetorical question: "Can a democracy which prohibits those in command from directing the individual citizen to the work it is needful for him to do ever hope for anything other than a bad organization for national defence?"

If you didn't agree with him, you were a "hysterical screamer" or "a pinhead pacifist." His bellicose prose appealed to many white-collar young people who found themselves squeezed between the established well-to-do classes above and the grasping workers below. That the movement never really got off the ground was – after my brief encounter with it – no surprise to me. My older brother who at that time was articled to a firm of chartered accountants and spent most evenings until bedtime cramming for exams, suddenly became interested in what sounded like a disciplined, accountable movement in which the books would always be in balance. He persuaded me to attend a local meeting with him. There was no more than a handful of young people present in the hall to listen to an uninspired young man spouting right-wing platitudes. The meeting broke up in a fistfight between the speaker and the sole reporter present who claimed someone had stolen his shorthand notes.

Years later, I was not surprised to find a Canadian publisher beating the same drum. At the beginning of 1939 I had been sent on temporary assignment to the McKim's agency's Toronto office where I started to read the *Globe*. While I was there, George McCullagh, the publisher, launched his Leadership League "to make the voice of the people supreme in public affairs." The League vowed that it would "if ever the urgency arises, smash the present political set-up with the launching of a potential new party of power and propriety…and independent thought and action." It is interesting to speculate on what action Commissioner Wood would have taken if the Communist Party had signed its name to a similar proposal to smash the existing set-up. McCullagh's real motive was better revealed in a *Globe* editorial which advocated "...registering all young men out of work…setting up camps in suitable locations tie up with industry supplemented by…military service." McCullagh's prose ran to alliteration: "…professional politics' pests have plagued the country beyond endurance…" and "…the greasy grinding of partisan politics must cease." McCullagh's movement fared no better than Rothermere's, probably because they were both better publishers than politicians and in the end had nothing to offer but words. There seems to be an international political virus which flourishes when times are bad and governments still worse, the symptoms of which are a fever of rhetoric and a rash of reform parties.

Twenty-three

The Movement

I returned to Montreal with the feeling that at last I was going home, to be among trusted and trusting friends who shared my view of life. These were people who accepted me, people with whom I could be myself and with whom I could let my guard down. They were also people who bluntly but without malice took a mallet to my sharp corners. I learned this early in my friendship with Ron and Dick over a couple of beers in the Peel Tavern. I was about to hold forth in my as yet unmodified BBC accent when Ron said: "Hold on to your hats boys, here comes the bullshit!"

I joined the artists' group and became a communist, if indeed I ever was one, by osmosis. I never formally joined the Communist Party, never held a membership card, never submitted to any kind of initiation procedure, never read more than a fraction of the gospel according to St. Marx, and only sporadically paid membership dues. Contrary to the elaborate 1907 scenario of secret oaths, cells and Machiavellian brain-washing that the RCMP's token Jew and police spy, John Leopold, scripted and foisted on Mackenzie King and the Taschereau-Kellock Royal Commission, life in the "movement," or at least in that part of it with which I became familiar, was informal, at times carelessly casual and even disorganized. We belonged to "clubs" or "groups" – never "cells." The Party line would be passed from the leadership down from echelon to echelon, following the principle of democratic centralism, until it reached the club secretary whose job was to pass it on to the members. Not surprisingly, it could become quite garbled by the time it reached its destination. As a means of brainwashing, if that was the intention, it was not very effective.

We in the artists' group may have been untypical of party groups in general, particularly genuinely working-class and union groups who were on the front lines in the class war and with whom we had very little direct contact. I do not remember any penetrating discussions of Marxism, or that there was anyone in our small group well enough read on the subject to conduct them – including myself who at one point became the club secretary whose job it would have been. Our main tasks were to supply copy and artwork for posters and leaflets on request, to help raise money for a variety of causes (from a strike fund to the League for Peace and Democracy or the Civil Liberties Union) and to keep abreast of current affairs, an area in which the received word was more instructive than anything gleaned from the newspapers. Our success was measured in new unions where none existed before, in successful or even unsuccessful strikes, in signatures on petitions, in minuscule increases in the number of votes cast for "our" candidates in local and national elections and in the rare recruit. This hardly rated as revolutionary activity. In fact the idea of revolution simply was not on the agenda. We might say "Come the revolution," but ironically, tongue in cheek, as for example: "Come the revolution my pipes will never freeze" or: "Come the revolution my husband will put the toilet seat down." If we appeared to act as revolutionaries it was because we were living in an authoritarian society which made the simplest of dissident acts revolutionary. We were forced to be secretive so as not to attract the attention of police Red Squads – municipal, provincial and federal – operating under the Padlock Law.

At first, coming from the London of Hyde Park soapbox orators, Communist members of parliament and the exuberant May Day celebrations of British labour and left-wing organizations, I thought my new friends were unnecessarily paranoid about this law. I soon realized that all of us lived daily under the threat of being locked out of our homes. The Padlock Law was an expression of the conservative ruling coalition of Church, politicians (like Duplessis) and right-wing societies such as the Knights of Columbus and Knights of Jacques Cartier. This extraordinary piece of legislation was devised by a committee of five presided over by none other than His Eminence Cardinal Villeneuve, although it has gone into history as largely the work of Maurice Duplessis and his Union Nationale party. It was passed without dissent in the Quebec provincial legislature, which is an indication of the pervasive hostility to left-wing sentiment of any kind in the province at the time. Even the federal government turned a blind eye to it. The law gave Duplessis, in his dual capacity as premier and Attorney-General, the authority to padlock the premises of anyone suspected of being connected in any way with propagating communistic ideas. What constituted "communism" was never defined. The law was left so vague that it could be invoked against almost anyone. The victim would then be faced with the onus of proving his innocence. Duplessis defined communism as a "virus." A person might be infected with it, like HIV today, without even knowing it. Duplessis put such a broad interpretation on the law that, just by declaring the Jehovah's Witnesses a subversive organization, he was able to jail them and hound them through the courts for years before the Supreme Court of Canada finally ruled the law to be unconstitutional. (That ruling was related to a case involving Montreal restaurant owner Frank Roncarelli. Much to the annoyance of Duplessis, Roncarelli insisted on posting bail for Jehovah's Witnesses arrested for distributing religious pamphlets. In 1946, the premier struck back. He had Roncarelli's liquor license pulled. Unable to serve alcohol, the restaurant quickly went bankrupt. Roncarelli challenged the action. And thirteen years later, the Supreme Court ruled that Duplessis had committed a civil wrong. It ordered him to personally pay damages to Roncarelli.)

I learned a lesson from another incident. Crossing the street with the pedestrian right-of-way at the busy Peel/Ste. Catherine intersection I was almost knocked down by a car sweeping round the corner. I let go a "Jesus Christ!" A policeman standing nearby angrily threatened me with arrest for blasphemy.

The Quebec Provincial Police reported a busy year in 1939, my first full year in Canada. Their Red Squad made 139 raids under the Padlock Law; arrested 15 communists and 11 Jehovah's Witnesses; seized 51,392 pieces of literature, 22 phonographs and 110 records. I happened to have witnessed, quite by accident, an arrest made by their colleagues in the Montreal Red Squad. Coming out of Morgan's department store, I saw a group of police moving in on a knot of people on Philip's Square. A man was being held with a cop on each arm while a plain-clothes man smashed a fist in his face. I later learned that I had seen Capt. Jack Ennis of the Montreal Red Squad in action.

Brutality like pregnancy is indivisible. To use the jargon of dialectical materialism, a punch in the face is qualitatively the same as being strung up on the parrot perch or some other instrument of torture – only quantitatively different. There had been a few examples of extreme police brutality, such as the 1934 shooting in the back at point-blank range of Nick Zynchuk for trying to retrieve his belongings from a building from which he had been evicted. Nobody was being thrown live out of helicopters or tortured with electric shocks to the genitals. Creative police who have a sense of humour have other ways to have their fun. The Nazis did not kill Chancellor Schuschnigg of Austria when they took over his country; they put him under house arrest in a tiny room and issued him with a hand towel for his personal use with which he also had to clean the SS latrines.

Closer to home, the single, unemployed men herded into remote camps by General McNaughton during the Depression, I learned, weren't issued with towels at all.

Later, in the early days of the war, Canadian anti-fascists were interned under the War Measures Act. The Commandant of Camp Kananaskis in Alberta put each internee into a hut with eleven German POWs who were encouraged to wipe the floor with the lone anti-fascist. (One internee, John Weir, refused the commandant's offer of compassionate leave to attend his father's funeral. The terms – he would be brought to the coffin in handcuffs and allowed precisely two minutes to mourn.)

Always present was the feeling that we were the prey of a special dehumanized police who took pleasure in hurting and degrading.

Lieutenant John Boychum, one of the Montreal Red Squad and widely known as Scarface, was a cop who brought personal venom to the job. He and his men broke into the Old Rose print shop in Montreal early one winter morning. While waiting for the owner to walk into the trap, they urinated on the floor, started a fire in the stove and burned up a case of antique, irreplaceable boxwood type used for handbill headings. On the other hand, Jack Ennis, whom I had seen in action on Philips Square, represented the "it's just a job" attitude we hear voiced today by off-duty torturers. He later took a job with Canadair as a security officer. A former party member working in the plant asked him how he felt about beating up workers, to which he replied: "There's nothing personal. I'd do it for you guys, too, if I had to."

The police, of course, have a duty to obey the orders of the government in power, even when that happens to be fascist-minded and anti-Semitic. But it does raise the question of personal responsibility; how to solve moral dilemmas in extreme situations – whether to turn people in dutifully, like Klaus Barbie, or shelter them at personal risk like Anne Frank's protector; whether to head for the hills with the French underground Maquis or stick around with a dishonoured Pétain; whether to kiss ass like Quisling in Norway or thumb nose like the King of Denmark.

Naturally, there were many levels of radicalism represented in the movement and also many private reserves of skepticism about the Party line. The obvious question is: How could you swallow the line so uncomplainingly? How could you go along with policies and pronouncements about which you obviously had secret reservations? You hadn't been brainwashed by Bolsheviks as Harvison would claim. You had come to your political stance in your own way, through your own observations, your own emotional and intellectual responses, the exercise of your own free will. So how could you voluntarily surrender your independence?

There must be as many answers to these questions as there were Party members. Militant trade union leaders like Bob Haddow, C.S. Jackson and Ross Russell, to name a few, presumably drew strength from the solidarity and political guidance of Party membership. But it wasn't necessary to be a Party member to earn vicious retribution from the Law. Madeleine Parent, while still in convent school, was so moved by the deplorable conditions of the young lay servant women that she decided to dedicate her life to "les ouvrières québécoises." Abused in the press, hounded by Duplessis' police, in and out of jail for union activity, she faced her tormenters with the serenity of a Jeanne d'Arc. Few artists or intellectuals had to face such persecution. (Some did lose their jobs, it's true. Agatha Chapman, Norman Lee and M.J. Brierley were amongst those fired from the Sun Life Company for belonging to the Civil Liberties Union.)

As for myself, the Party with all its faults – its sectarianism, its preoccupation with fighting social democrats when it should have been making common cause, its tone-deafness and colour-blindness when confronted with creative individuality in literature and the arts, the ghastly language of its polemics – was still the one that best worked for social justice, the one with the best track record in fighting fascism, the only one capable of inspiring a sense of international brotherhood as exemplified by the International Brigades in Spain, the one that put its feet and its fists where its mouth was. The Party touched a nerve in me with its disapproval of "bourgeois" thinking and attitudes – the nerve of my misgivings, perhaps even guilt, about my lack of commitment (guts?) when compared with so many others in the movement world-wide.

I admired the Soviet Union for what I believed then to be its enlightened worldview. I wished it well, but like most of my comrades, I suspect, I would not have wanted to live there or to make Canada over in its likeness. RCMP claims to the contrary notwithstanding, the real glue that bound me to my comrades and them to me was the shared desire for a more humane society, a fairer distribution of wealth – enough in itself, of course, to be considered deeply subversive of existing Canadian society.

This comfortable popular-front, anti-fascist, international-solidarity ambience, the emotional and intellectual magnet that had drawn us together, was badly disrupted in August 1939 when Stalin did the unthinkable and signed a non-aggression pact with Hitler. Not just the rank and file but also the leadership were caught with their dogmas down. Stalin maintained that, since France and Great Britain had rebuffed his efforts to join forces against Hitler, he was no longer willing to "pull their chestnuts out of the fire." The war was nothing more than an imperialist war that should be condemned and opposed.

Under pressure from the Comintern, the Canadian party leadership eventually fell into line. And I must admit I did too. Great Britain and France – and Canada, certainly – had shown very little enthusiasm for anti-fascist causes. They had been persistently hostile to the Soviet Union and unwilling to enter treaties or agreements designed to hobble Hitler. Just a few months earlier Great Britain had made it plain where she stood on anti-fascism by officially blessing the Franco regime. One could hardly blame Stalin for trying to forestall a German invasion. I bought the line (but not necessarily the rhetoric) of which this is an example from the Party Manifesto for the 1940 federal elections:

> "In this war the Canadian capitalists plan to revel in luxury at home, raking in the mounting piles of profits while sending sons to rot and die in the trenches [sic] of someone else's war on a far-off continent. Greedily they count the millions that they will make from the life of every Canadian boy sacrificed on their barbarous altar of profits. A degenerate, besotten, parasitical class, they are carrying on a traffic in death. What despicable pay-triots."

The program adopted by the Party also contained elements I had no difficulty in accepting, elements such as better union and wage conditions, taxes for the rich, slum clearance, the prosecution of war profiteers and, believe it or not, promises to enact unemployment and health insurance.

Twenty-four
Three Solitudes

I found Montreal to consist of not two but three solitudes – English, French and Jewish – which came together only at the edges where the exigencies of daily life made contact imperative. It was my first experience of a profoundly Catholic society with its ubiquitous reminders of the faith – the nuns and priests on the streets, the roadside shrines, the statues of Mary with her neon halo, the crucifixes in public buildings, the prison-like orphanages, the "*Ne me blasphémez pas*" signs, the terrible slums below the tracks, the general air of pious poverty. Less obvious but no less there, ignored but tolerated, were the sinful components of society – the blind pigs and the whorehouses plying their protected trade undisturbed. Who had not heard of de Bullion Street or the classier ménage at 312 Ontario Street East?

As far as life at McKim's was concerned, the French might as well not have existed. All contact with them was funnelled through a single translator. French creative services were yet to break free of the clerical mould. After-work hours were a different story. In "progressive" circles the three solitudes came together freely although in disproportionate numbers. I respected the social and political views of my new-found "comrades" certainly more than the bigotry of some of my professional colleagues. Bob Campbell, for example, thought it great fun to bait French-Canadians. One of his coups was to snatch the hat from an uncooperative streetcar conductor and fling it up on a balcony overlooking the tracks on Ste. Catherine Street. He also took pleasure from the humiliation of a young Jewish woman who had been hired by McKim as a librarian. She had been installed at a desk in a busy passageway just inside the entrance, buffeted by steady traffic. This was an era in which there were perhaps only a couple of token Jews in the entire Montreal advertising agency field.

I soon came to know that there was a Canadian left-wing artistic and intellectual tradition, crossing all ethnic and language barriers, with an honourable history of dissidence in spite of all the Red Squads and Padlock Laws, embracing people like poets Leo Kennedy and Dorothy Livesay, play director Jim (Jean) Watts, newspapermen Campbell Ballantyne, Fred Poland and Paul Gardner, advertising woman Irene Kon and her father – the incorruptible Louis whose admonitory letters to Mackenzie King always drew thoughtful replies – and architect and photographer Hazen Sise, back from Spain and now a regular dropper-in at 3610. There were many, many more. Let me not call them all communists. Whether they were or not remains their secret. Except amongst our closest associates we never asked.

As I came to know some of them, I became aware of the depth and breadth of the middle-class, professional, non-working-class elements of the movement. Norman Bethune had returned from Spain and gone to China before I arrived in Canada, so I never met him. But his aura still floated over us. Most of my new friends and acquaintances, it seemed, had known him or worked with him, some even claiming to have slept with him.

One woman in particular impressed me – Miriam Carpin Kennedy. Miriam K – so called to distinguish her from two other Miriams who moved in the same circles – was one of the many gifted people attracted to the movement who chose not to "take advantage" of society, to use Inspector Harvison's phrase, but rather to try to serve it and perhaps make it better. She had been married to Leo Kennedy, the poet, contemporary of F.R. Scott, A.M. Klein and Dorothy Livesay. The marriage had broken up by the time I met her. Her brilliant, well-stocked mind enabled her, even without a string of degrees, to pursue a career that later took her from social worker to internationally-respected expert in criminal psychology, working with Dr. Bruno Cormier at McGill University on a government-funded research project. She had read more widely, knew more about music and painting than anyone I had yet met, and she could talk about it without a trace of pedantry. I am indebted to her for, among many other things, unplugging my ears to chamber music, especially to the treasury of the late Beethoven quartets and piano sonatas.

People like Miriam K were in the movement only partly out of political conviction, although that was undoubtedly sincere. A sizeable section of the movement, including many of the uncommitted fellow travellers around the edges, was essentially a middle-class Jewish association of well-informed, culture-oriented, free-thinking people who did not or would not fit into conventional Montreal society and who would not accept the religious shibboleths, the bigotry and the philistinism of so much of contemporary Canadian society. For many, the odour of persecution and pogroms was still in their nostrils.

When I first met Miriam K she must have sized me up as a likely recruit as well as a potential ally in her mission to improve the quality and style of the Party propaganda. She showed me the draft of a pamphlet someone had written protesting the shipment of scrap steel from Montreal to Japan, where it would presumably be converted into weapons for use against the Chinese. She asked me for my opinion. The clenched fist heading was several lines long; the text was impenetrable jargon.

"It's garbage," I said.

"I'm glad you think so. How about rewriting it?"

"Okay, but it'll have to be in plain English. And it needs a short, snappy heading." I thought for a moment. "How about 'Death Sails from Montreal Harbour'?"

She was enchanted.

On this occasion, professional writing prevailed. In general, however, this kind of approach was thought to be too glib, too "bourgeois." The higher up the leadership pyramid one went, the greater the resistance to anything written by an advertising man in the contemporary idiom. All the clichés of Marxist expression had been worked out over the years and why tinker with them?

Part of the problem was the acceptance by Party pundits of the hammer-blow Comintern and later Cominform style of writing and the rejection as "bourgeois" of elegance and simplicity of expression. Questions of style aside, however, much of what leading Canadian communists wrote is astonishingly prescient when reread half a century later. It made good sense to skeptics like me whose appetite for information could not be satisfied by the fast food of mainstream media.

For example, soon after the war in an appeal to *Keep Canada Independent*, Communist Party leader Tim Buck wrote:

> We are threatened with complete national enslavement to a foreign power, but that power is not, at least not yet, imposing its control by the force of arms. Canada is being sold into United States control by "her own" ruling class; the parasitic, speculative, Canadian manipulators of stock market deals, politics and governmental concessions, who are enriching themselves by trading the national future of Canada for junior partnership in the United States monopolies.

And this long before Brian Mulroney – whose government would bring in the North American Free Trade Agreement – had begun to shave! The tragedy of Tim Buck, unrevealed to us at the time, is not that he was mistaken about the Canadian scene and the hidden capitalist agenda – he was often brilliantly clairvoyant – but that he failed to see the crimes of Stalinism; or, worse, that knowing about them, he failed to come clean with the Canadian rank and file.

Like the Catholic Church and other authoritarian organizations, the Party dictated what you could and couldn't read. There was no formal Index of proscribed books, but books by Trotskyites, by deviationists, by expelled comrades were on the no-no list. This included *Darkness at Noon* by Arthur Koestler. It is an indication of how binding, even venomous, this prohibition was that it took me ten years to get around to reading this great book.

Soviet literature, on the other hand, was held up as an example of socialist realism to be admired and emulated. New novels by Soviet writers appeared from time to time amongst the Marxist classics and Comintern pamphlets trotted out by the group's literature representative at the end of the weekly club meetings. We bought them, somewhat reluctantly, and partly because they were so inexpensive (another one-up for the Soviets, where books for the mind like bread for the body were a subsidized necessity).

The cultural buffs – amongst them Miriam K – explained why the didacticism of Soviet writing and the stereotyped characters of socialist realism were necessary cultural steps in the development of Soviet man (the "person" substitute was still far in the future), although I suspect that those who read the books did so more as a duty than a pleasure. Miriam K, who had been brought up on Wordsworth, Jane Austen, Tolstoy and Fielding, and who could unerringly sieve out literary dross (or "drek" as she might have said) summed up the situation with characteristic irony: "Workers and peasants of the Bronx, unite."

Twenty-five
Fetid Brew

I was one of the few members of our artists group to have a steady job, and a very good one by the standards of the day. Most of the others were Jewish and living precariously by free-lancing or working at subsistence wages at unrelated jobs. One of them was a multi-talented fellow who brimmed with ideas. He could write. He was at home in the graphic arts. He was a natural advertising man, which was how he saw himself. When he approached me to get him a job at the agency my heart sank. His heavy accent, his frankly disgusting eating habits would be enough to disqualify him from the WASP enclave of agency and clients, but the deciding black ball would be the mere fact of his being Jewish. He had a better chance of becoming a teller at the Royal Bank of Canada on St. James Street. He accepted with good grace the fact that I had no magic wand to wave and went on to eventual success as an independent entrepreneur. But the encounter made me still more sensitive about anti-Semitism.

Someone in the group, perhaps thinking it was about time I clued in to the systematic promotion of anti-Semitism, gave me a pamphlet to read, *Fascism over Canada* by a certain Fred Rose. This documented the pro-fascist, anti-Semitic philosophy shared by Church and State which, in the words of feisty civil rights lawyer R.L. Calder, was "encouraged by bench, pulpit and council chamber."

Unbelievably, the discredited *Protocols of the Elders of Zion* had been trotted out in a campaign of anti-Semitic slander master-minded by Adrien Arcand, an avowed fascist and admirer of Hitler and Mussolini. The same Arcand had close ties with Premier Duplessis and R.B. Bennett, the Tory "Iron Heel" prime minister of Depression days. Arcand was the editor of the semi-official Union Nationale party newspaper, *L'Illustration Nouvelle.* Arcand and his disciples favoured banishing the Jews to a colony on Hudson's Bay. His verbal violence rivalled that of the worst Nazi Jew-baiters. Castigating a Jewish member of the Quebec Legislature for having the temerity to speak up in defence of Jewish citizens of Quebec he called him "this left-over from the justifiable furnaces of Nebuchadnezzar…this illustrious descendant of the assassins of Christ." This was the man whose fascist organization RCMP Commissioner Wood, would later call "purely Canadian" in spite of it having ties with Germany and Italy. Arcand's ideas had support also from the Anglo establishment, although shipping tycoon Ross McMaster was more outspoken than most when he said: "Democracy is not the best form of government to deal successfully with the problems facing us." The Quebec government was well aware of the attraction to corporations of a submissive, underpaid work force and seduced them with ads in publications like the *Gazette Annual Report on Business* with promises of guaranteed labour peace.

There have been such profound changes in Quebec society since the war that many citizens feel that the fascist and anti-Semitic tendencies of those days have been much exaggerated. But in 1939, Montreal Mayor Camillien Houde created a furore when he said that Quebecers were fascist by blood if not by name, and that their sympathies would be with Italy should England go to war. Italy meant Mussolini, darling of the Pope, so surely acceptable to the faithful of Quebec. In spite of the angry denials, Houde stuck to his guns, insisting that "Quebecers are accepted as fascist." Eugene Forsey, feisty, outspoken, openly left-wing, and no doubt on the RCMP hit list in those days before he became a senator and an almost sacred symbol of democratic wisdom, wrote to Minister of Justice Ernest Lapointe: "There is in fact a formidable Fascist movement in the province."

This persistent aura of corporatism and Church-inspired authoritarianism – if not downright fascism – hung over the province for a long time. *LIFE*, the American picture magazine at the height of its popularity in 1942, commented in patronizing style:

> The French-Canadians are among the nicest people in the world...sweet-tempered...frugal...industrious... honest...The church and farm dominate most of their lives. The people are not radical...they feel it their sacred duty to combat "Communism and Bolshevism" which may include almost anything from state allowances for mothers to American atheism. This makes them more than a little troubled by a world war being fought by Russian Bolsheviks, Chinese Buddhists and English-speaking Protestants against, among other places, Rome, the home of the Church.

Cardinal Villeneuve strongly objected to the article as slanderous, in spite of the fact that he had consistently opposed giving women the vote because it would destroy the unity and hierarchy of the family (in any case, he argued, women did not want it) and that he fully supported Duplessis in opposing compulsory education and reform of the education system – something that would only result in substituting schools for the authority of priests and parents.

Twenty-six
3610 Oxenden

One of the least popular tasks we had to face was peddling the Party newspaper *The Clarion*. To be caught with even one copy would put you out on the street under the provisions of the Padlock Law. At 3610 Oxenden there was enough concealed evidence to padlock the whole street. We had allowed the local *Clarion* agent to use 3610 as distribution depot. The papers were stored not in the apartment itself but on an enclosed staircase at the rear of the building. One afternoon, I came home to find a very nervous young *Clarion* agent sitting in our living room amid a pile of prune stones. The RCMP must have tailed him to our house where they conducted – or so they thought – a very thorough search. But they hadn't gone down the back stairs. While the search was going on, our young friend had nervously eaten his way through a week's supply of dry prunes.

Ron, Dick and I would also be called on for help in making sure our candidates for union office were democratically assured of victory by means of the time-honoured Quebec tradition of "telegraphing" votes. Pat Sullivan was President of the Canadian Seamen's Union. He normally had the membership cupped in his hand. But with a leadership election coming up, he feared there were the makings of a revolt within the ranks. Not one to take any chances, Sullivan called on us – among others – to go to a membership meeting and cast votes for his slate. On the appointed evening I dressed in what I hoped would pass for suitably off-duty maritime gear and went with Ron and Dick to the union hall. We'd been advised to sit anywhere but at the back which was where the cops and stool pigeons would usually sit. It was a rough-looking and noisy crowd. We had no credentials except our fists. I knew nothing whatsoever about lake-shipping should anyone question me, so I was much relieved when Sullivan began to speak. The hall fell silent as he mesmerized the union brothers with his speech – an Irish fugue of poetic blarney, union evangelism and veiled violence. It was almost enough to make me sign on as a deck hand on the spot.

During these times, our thoughts were not exclusively on political matters. The Depression still hovered in people's thoughts like a nightmare carried over from sleep. Thousands of unemployed single men, it is true, were finding better board and lodgings in the armed forces than they had ever known. But for many others, life was still pinched and uncertain. The country – Quebec in particular – took a long time to shake off the depression conditions. The war brought something close to full employment, but wages still had to be fought for tooth and nail – and often scalp, too. Dick Hersey's girlfriend, a young, educated, able-bodied, intelligent woman, worked as a saleswoman in a department store where her abilities won her top slot in the women's wear department. By working fifty or more hours a week, she was able to take home from sixteen to eighteen dollars. The average weekly wage for women ran from seven-and-a-quarter to eleven-fifty. Men might make up to twenty-one dollars. Any attempt to organized white-collar workers was met with particular savagery.

Unemployment insurance had just been introduced in 1940 with minimum payments of about four dollars a week. But service workers and those in the public sector were not eligible for benefits. Almost daily, somebody's tragedy would turn up as a single paragraph in the newspapers.

Ron, Dick and I were rich by comparison. We could indulge in ten-cent steins of beer at the Peel Tavern where an extra fifteen cents would buy a sandwich stuffed with Oka cheese, or a "frog" – a glass of beer poured over a few raw oysters. Smoked meat sandwiches at Ben's were two-for-a-quarter. On a lean day before payday we would spend twenty-five cents each on an evening pub crawl – a nickel beer at each of five pubs. At the end of one such evening, we headed for Ben's. On the way, Ron snatched a red flag from a road works barricade and led us into Ben's singing the *Internationale*. A horrified Smokie – the carver – flashed his formidable carving knife at Ron and threatened to circumcise him on the spot, whereupon Ron unzipped and demonstrated that the operation would be redundant.

We walked everywhere under Ron's urging, covering the city in every direction by following a "first left, first right" route and seeing where it would take us. Panhandlers – "Gotta nickel, mister, for a cuppa coffee?" – were common. Dick, who had done his share of panhandling, never turned them down. "The hell with coffee," he would say digging his hand into his pocket, "have a beer on me."

Money-raising, which was an important activity of the group, merged with our social life. The flat at 3610 Oxenden, because of size and location (but even more so because of the carefree nature of its three bachelor tenants), became a Saturday night social center combining good parties with money-making through raffles, draws and the sale of beer. A quart bottle sold for less than a dollar and still paid a worthwhile profit into the kitty.

During the fifteen months or so that we occupied the flat, scores of trade union organizers, fellow travellers, academics, architects, doctors, lawyers, artists, newspapermen, along with career communists passed through – some passing out. (Judging from RCMP Inspector Harvison's well-filled ledger sheets, there must have been a fair sprinkling of finks, informers and stool pigeons, as well. One not-so-smart borer-from-within – ostensibly a night clerk at the Berkeley Hotel – rented a room in the house of one of the members of the artists' group. The artist became suspicious and searched the man's room in his absence. He found an RCMP uniform hanging in a garment bag in the closet.)

It was at one of these parties that I met Phyllis who would become my first wife.

Twenty-seven
Phyllis

Phyllis had come to Canada from Lodz, Poland, at the age of twelve not speaking a word of English. A decade later, when I met her, she spoke a beautiful, educated English without a trace of accent, an indication of her confident determination to beat all the odds on her way to excellence. Her father, Barnett – *Tatele* to the family – had come to Canada a year or so earlier with the oldest son to establish a suitably prosperous living for the family, to which they felt entitled. They were not exactly poor in Lodz; Barnett's father was a baker to the Jewish community. Unfortunately Barnett had socialist leanings. He made the mistake of trying to organize his father's workers into a union and was persuaded to leave not just town but preferably the country and the continent, too.

He settled in Sudbury and opened a general store hoping to cash in on the mining trade. One of his first disbursements was for an imposing letterhead with the title NEWMAN GENERAL STORE which he used to write encouraging letters back home. Unfortunately, the store went belly up within the year, partly because *Tatele's* son-and-heir took his inheritance in advance from the till and beat it to New York where, during New Deal years, he set himself up as an artist, supported by the Work Projects Administration (WPA) under the New Deal.

When the mother and remaining four children eventually arrived in style by ocean liner, draped in fox furs and anxious to join *Tatele* who, to tell by his letterhead, was already a general after only a year in Canada, they were not prepared for the state of near poverty that awaited them. Fierce family loyalty held them together – the children, as they grew old enough to work and contribute, helping to eke out *Tatele's* meagre earnings as an insurance agent.

Under these circumstances, Phyllis had to go to work as soon as she had graduated from Montreal High School. These were Depression days but also, in Montreal, nightclub days. She got a job as flower girl at the El Morocco nightclub where her natural sales ability and aura of unfeigned innocence made her a success. And, oh, what a tangled web she wove. Threaded in and out of her life were people like McGill guru and future biographer Leon Edel, Dominion Textiles president Blair Gordon, comedienne Fanny Bryce, mobster Lucky Luciano and most of the working and unemployed newspapermen of the day who at one time or another turned up at the club.

Amongst the unemployed was Campbell Ballantyne. He'd been working as a reporter on the Montreal *Gazette* but had had the gall to try to organize journalists into the Newspaper Guild and was not only fired but also black-balled as a newspaperman from coast to coast. Cam's girlfriend was Lizzie, a chorus girl at the club who took Phyllis under her mother hen's wing and saw that she came to no harm. Lizzie later worked at Billy Rose's Diamond Horseshoe nightclub in New York, married a CIO organizer and at great danger from the mob organized the chorus girls into a union.

At a point when Phyllis' father's affairs had more or less stabilized, she decided it was time to think of training for a better career. She went to Boston where, because of her photogenic hands and nails and her way with hats, she was able to support herself working as a photographer's model while learning to become a dental technician. One evening, sitting at a table in the renowned Coconut Grove night club with a friend (Mayor Curley's son, no less), she saw two men come into the room, produce tommy guns and start firing at one of the patrons. A moment later the room seemed to be empty, except for a bleeding corpse slumped over a table. All the customers except Phyllis were out of sight on the floor or under the tables. When the police came, it was clear to them that she was the only acknowledged eyewitness to the shooting. She went home to her apartment to spend an uneasy couple of days until, early in the morning she was awakened by a knock at the door. The caller had slipped an envelope under the door and left. The message was short and sweet: Get out of town. Also in the envelope were five fifty-dollar bills. She left for New York to join her married sister without even packing a bag and stayed there until she returned to Montreal a couple of years later to stand by her mother who had been badly injured in a fall. It was then, in the spring of 1939, that I met her.

It was hardly love at first sight. We were drawn to each other as much by the contrast of our backgrounds as by our similarities. If Phyllis had marriage in mind, whether on her own account or because of family pressures, she gave no sign that she expected it of me. The closest she came to an oblique hint was to rebuff the boyfriend she had left in New York, who made a special trip to Montreal in a vain attempt to claim her. We behaved as comrades rather than people in love. One thing we did have very much in common was our willingness to put our time and talents at the service of the "movement." Phyllis' talents were considerable. She was a persuasive speaker, poised and confident, and a single-minded manager and chairman who usually got her way. I was no virgin; but neither was I a confident, experienced Lothario (although I tried to present the appearance of one). It took us a while to become lovers, but when we did she moved in to 3610 which now became a ménage of six, Ron's and Dick's girlfriends having already moved in.

Twenty-eight
Norval

During this summer I invited my youngest brother, Norval, for an extended visit from England. He had finished school and would be going on to Oxford on a scholarship in the fall. He was the youngest by a few years with the advantage of having had three brothers ahead of him to trample a path through the thorny parental thickets that had left them bleeding and scarred. He had been free to develop his considerable talents, admired, praised and encouraged along the way. At the age of fifteen he astonished the family by admitting that he had been quietly contributing poetry to leading British poetry reviews without revealing his age. We found this out only by seeing the complimentary copies of the publications sent to him as a contributor.

His Canadian holiday ended with unexpected suddenness. Phyllis and I planned to go to New York to visit her sister and we invited Norval to go along. Leon Edel was at that time night editor for Canadian Press in New York. Phyllis knew him well from her Montreal nightclub days. During the afternoon of September 3rd she suggested we go up to the Canadian Press office to say hello to Leon. We arrived as the ticker was clattering away. Leon motioned us to be quiet. As we watched, the ticker delivered the news that England had declared war against Germany.

"I have to go back right away," Norval said.

He did, in fact, wangle passage on a liner leaving a day or two later from New York. He returned to a long involvement in the war, winding up a British paratroop captain. He had learned to speak and read fluent Russian at a six-month army cram school at Cambridge University. And he was seconded to the Red Army of Occupation in Berlin immediately following VE Day – an experience, he claimed, which put him off Soviet-style socialism for life.

(In 1946, I wrote to him from the RCMP barracks in Rockcliffe telling him, amongst other things, that I had left London in such a hurry that I had forgotten to take my typewriter. He could dispose of it, I wrote, in any way he thought fit. He got the message all right. He took a hammer and smashed the machine to pieces. Unfortunately, he stashed the pieces in a box under his bed where the police soon found it, probably as a result of my letter, and returned it to Canada. Inspector Whitehead of Scotland Yard had a great time in court in Montreal playing his bit part in the well scripted Fred Rose trial as he opened the box and poured out the scrap metal which, he had to admit, was of meagre value as evidence.)

Twenty-nine
Tying the Knot

As it did for many other young couples, the advent of war dramatically telescoped life's expectations for us. We decided to get married as soon as we got back from New York. *Tatele* drummed up enough money to buy Phyllis a trousseau of three dresses at the Henry Morgan Department Store and Rev. McCutcheon consented to unite us in holy matrimony in his front parlour – a gracious gesture on his part because there were no civil marriages in Quebec at that time, and rabbis recoiled from mixed marriages.

We soon decided we had had enough of life in a combination commune and part-time nightclub and moved to our own one-bedroom apartment on Union Avenue. The forty-dollar-a-month rent seemed to be well within our joint means of $54.50 a week, especially as we would still be able to walk to work and save car fare (four tickets for a quarter). At the lease signing, the owner, Mrs. Heriot, who lived in the apartment above us, served us tea and told us how pleased she was to have a nice young couple like us as tenants instead of Jews. She was not the first to have been misled by Phyllis' china-blue eyes, high Galician cheekbones and upper-crust accent. She was won over, however, when I proposed to renovate the kitchen at no cost to her for labour if she would supply the materials, which she agreed to do. Meanwhile, we had been busy with all the nest-building tricks of the times – the bricks and planks for bookshelves, the Chianti-bottle lamps, the burlap curtains and the cretonne-covered packing cases. Jean Palardy's wife, the painter Jori Smith, had some old catalogne rugs for sale – not the stiff, garish commercial product, but the genuine habitant article in beautiful, washed-out pastel colours. We bought one for ten dollars to act as a cover on the inevitable studio couch.

This ability to improvise and make things must have impressed Gordon McCutcheon, a friend who often called at the apartment. One day he asked me if I could make a stencil duplicator for the Party. The Padlock Law made it almost impossible to get anything printed through regular commercial sources. The Party put out an endless flow of leaflets which had to be run off surreptitiously, usually on legitimate duplicating machines to which members had access. The standard duplicating machine of the day was the Gestetner. These machines were expensive, bulky, noisy and difficult to conceal or to move at a moment's notice should a neighbour become suspicious or if the Red Squad were to trace the sale through the dealer. It occurred to me that a very efficient duplicator could be made on the principle of silk screen printing. The only elements needed would be a piece of silk-screen fabric stretched on a hinged wooden frame, a piece of ground glass and a standard photographer's roller – all easily obtainable items. The operator would roll out the duplicating ink on the glass, put the typed wax stencil on one side of the silk, close the frame on a sheet of paper and pass the roller on the other side of the silk. After the first impression, the ink would hold the stencil in place on the frame. Slow, maybe, but simple, portable and cheap – less than ten dollars for materials.

In June 1940, a few months after we moved in to the apartment, the Party was made illegal, which meant that most of the leaders and functionaries went underground to avoid arrest. In fact, most of them managed to operate fairly freely, although at the expense of moving often or finding haven in the households of middle-class professional fellow travellers who were politically virgin. Soon after this, McCutcheon asked me to go with him to a meeting in Toronto. It would cost me nothing; we would drive and friends in Toronto would put us up. I agreed to go although he was tight-lipped about what the meeting was all about. The meeting was in an elegantly furnished living room in a suburban house with a friendly, informal group of perhaps twenty people present. The speaker was an immaculately-dressed, grey-haired man. I remember especially his well-polished penny loafers which were beyond my financial reach at the time. He spoke for over an hour on Canadian and international events, seemingly never at a loss to unravel the tangled skein of events. After the talk, McCutcheon took me to meet him but without introducing him by name.

After a short talk he said to me with amused surprise, "You don't know who I am, do you?"

It was, of course, Tim Buck himself – a name security-conscious McCutcheon could not bring himself to say, even in the safe-house of the meeting itself. Clearly I was being passed around for appraisal.

Occasionally Phyllis and I would be asked to lend the apartment for two or three hours for the *ad hoc* meetings of Party functionaries on the move, which we agreed to do. We were almost never present at these meetings, but I happened to be there on one occasion that stuck in my mind not for the gems of political insight but for the behaviour of Charles Simms, one of the Toronto leaders in for the occasion. Simms had a reputation for verbosity that I found to be fully justified. It was not the words, though, that I remember; they rolled out of him non-stop, as exciting as elevator music. As he spoke he was reaming out his nose with a forefinger. From time to time he would examine his find then wipe it off on the catalogne. Luckily, Phyllis was not present to express her bourgeois outrage.

Thirty
Mamele and Tatele

I have no idea what Phyllis' family's thoughts were on acquiring a Gentile for an in-law but they certainly could not have made me more welcome. They were not at all religious or even much concerned with traditional observances; their style was more that of European socialist secularism.

Mamele felt it her motherly duty to fatten me up, so we had to submit to the weekly dinners at which two and sometimes three meat dishes were offered. She believed that the longer meat was cooked the healthier it became. This made it difficult for me to chew my way through enough of the less tender kosher cuts to satisfy her that she had done her maternal duty. My repeated refusals of third or fourth helpings did not deter her. She would arrange the serving spoons on the dish with handles facing towards me then inch by inch nudge them right up to my plate.

Tatele spoke German as well as English, and fluent Yiddish and Polish. My imperfect German gave me a handle on Yiddish which was the language of the Saturday night poker games to which I was invited along with a half dozen of *Tatele's* contemporaries. The stakes were nominal, just enough to make the game interesting, so these wily bluffers had no compunction in taking me to the cleaners as part of my higher education in survival tactics.

(I would occasionally speak German with my father-in-law in an effort to improve it. Later during the war, bored with my army job, I responded to an appeal for German-speaking volunteers and was called up for an interview by a professor of German at the University of Toronto. He concluded that my German was good enough to qualify after a brush-up course. "But where did you learn to speak German with a Jewish accent?" he asked.)

My relations with the family were always good, even when I refused to connive at encouraging *Tatele* to sponge on his children. For example, I could not condone subsidizing his four-dollar broadcloth shirts while the rest of us working stiffs had to be content with the regular two-dollar item. He was always impeccably dressed and squeaky clean, partly because he bathed twice – first to wash and then to rinse in clean water. He would have been a handsome man had it not been for his teeth. Only two were visible, long yellow tusks, one in his upper jaw and one in the lower, at different sides of his mouth. His other teeth had been pulled out in a move to avoid being conscripted by the Czarist army. (He felt this course of action was preferable to injecting one's legs with gasoline which was another popular ploy.) In spite of his dental disability he could reduce a chicken leg to bare bone and gristle in quick order.

I refused from the start to co-sign the stream of small loans which financed the little luxuries *Tatele* couldn't be denied. But he seemed to think none the worse of me, although the emotional chasm between the uptight Scot and the demonstrative Jew must have puzzled him at times.

Later, while I was in Kingston Penitentiary, *Tatele* suffered a massive heart attack from which he was not expected to survive. But survive he did to live for many more years. Long after I had ceased to be a member of the family I learned that he had developed a cancer which eventually blocked the esophagus so that he had to be fed through a hole in the chest below the tumour. He had been sent home, presumably to die. Brutus Rubenstein, a long-time family friend, called me to say that the old man would like to see me. I found him in bed, wasted to a near skeleton, the huge prow of a nose looking more defiant than ever. Presently *Mamele* came in with a tray bearing a pitcher of what looked like eggnog, and a glass funnel. She motioned me to leave the room, but he insisted I stay. She pulled back the sheet, revealing the obscene orifice in his chest, inserted the funnel and began to pour in the mixture. The old man gave me a wink, smacked his lips and said "Mmm…deee-licious." A couple of weeks later I heard that he had become so frustrated at not being able to drink and swallow that he had taken a mouthful of orange juice and swallowed so hard that he forced open a passage. From then on, he took his food by mouth.

Months later I had another call from Brutus. The old man had finally died – from a stroke, not the cancer. If I wasn't too busy, said Brutus, would I mind coming to the funeral? They weren't sure of having the necessary *minyan*.

When I got to Paperman's funeral parlour I saw at once the reason for Brutus' concern. Only a scattering of people were present, not enough probably for the requisite quorum of ten adult Jewish males to be present at the burial. I was assigned to the rabbi's limousine with instructions to keep my *goyishe* mouth shut. At the gates of the cemetery I took my assigned handle of the coffin immediately behind my former brother-in-law at whose side the rabbi walked, praying in Hebrew. At intervals as we carried the box to the grave we lowered it to the ground to pray. No words came from my ex-brother-in-law. The rabbi looked at him in astonishment then gave him a vicious jab in the ribs with his elbow. This produced a pained grunt followed by a stream of Hebrew from God knows what atavistic recesses of the soul.

Mamele had been a vigorous woman in mid-life, active in the left-wing Jewish community. An accident had extinguished her spirit, reducing her to a tearful, worried state. Even so, she showered me with the full bounty of Jewish mothering.

Many years later, after my marriage to Phyllis had broken up and I was preparing to remarry, again it was Brutus who called me to tell me that *Mamele* would like to meet my intended. Miriam agreed to go with me. We were received with warmth and tears and blessed with every good wish. As we were about to leave, *Mamele* grabbed me by the arm, pulled me back and said "Remember, you'll always be *mein Sohn*."

Thirty-one
Not Quite Madison Avenue

Soon after I started at the agency, the creative atmosphere brightened with the arrival of Geoff Grier as art director. Geoff had been working for a big periodical publishing house in Philadelphia before being seduced back to Canada by McKim's. A son of Sir Wyly Grier, the establishment portrait painter, Geoff was no stranger to Canadian high society, having amongst other things passed around cups of tea at Governor Generals' levees at Rideau Hall. But he was aghast at the reaction to his buying a house on Victoria Avenue in Westmount. Nobody – it seemed – who was anybody lived on Victoria Avenue. To make matters worse, Geoff and his wife installed a prized antique Pennsylvania Dutch dresser in the living room. The piece had spent some years in a barn and bore the tooth-prints of a horse. Would-be friends and arbiters of taste were scandalized. As everybody knew, the proper furniture was Duncan Phyfe reproductions from Eaton's or Morgan's department stores. Over his peers' protests, Geoff later enrolled his young daughter in the art school being run by Ghitta Caiserman and Alfie Pinsky who were considered to be dangerously left-wing.

Another copywriter, Hugh Trill, was hired to team with Geoff Grier. He had published a novel and made it plain he was not going to sit in any bullpen, so they gave him his own cubby-hole next to Geoff. Hugh was responsible for introducing the public to the word "allergic" in a campaign for Sweet Cap cigarettes, the theme being: you may be allergic to all kinds of things, but nobody is allergic to Sweet Cap cigarettes. The campaign almost didn't get off the ground, being a bit too *avant garde* for the account man. He didn't know what the word meant and was convinced that nobody else would.

Trill's addition to the copy team pushed me, already low man on the totem pole, still further into the cellar. When another agency – McConnell, Eastman – advertised for a copywriter, I applied for and got the job. The agency was a branch office with a staff of only eight or nine headed by Keith Crombie, a congenial boss with a reputation as *bon vivant* and writer of wit. The accounts here were also incestuously tied to the agency and to each other by interlocking directorates, corporate back-scratching and political promissory notes. Canadian Oil Companies (White Rose) was the flagship and John Irwin the admiral of the fleet. Crombie would bash out full-page newspaper ads in a couple of hours, writing the copy ten or twelve words to a sheet, bearing down with his 6B pencil so hard that the sheets would dish like saucers, while free-lance artist Roy Still would sit at his side doing the finished art on Ross board with a wax crayon. The resulting ad would run in every daily newspaper coast to coast plus a string of weeklies. With this kind of man-hour to profit ratio it is not surprising that the agency prospered.

My first Christmas at the agency we all received bonuses. Crombie's was in the princely amount of three thousand dollars. That year, the agency Christmas party was held at the home of his secretary. When I got there, Crombie was already well in his cups. The secretary, who obviously knew his habits, asked me and another young employee to get him into a taxi and stay with him until he was delivered safely home. Despite his protests and threats about our job security, we managed to get him into a taxi. But before we could get in ourselves he exited by the other door and disappeared. This was the last we saw of him for the ten days it took him to drink his way through the three thousand dollars.

Part of my job at McConnell, Eastman was to compile and edit the Canadian Oil Companies house organ, *White Rose News*, for its nominal editor, Ira Peacock, the company's divisional manager. Peacock was a talented executive with a flair for what was called "man management." He took pride bordering on love for the family "teams" of nine, eleven, even fifteen children of company employees across the province whose photos we solicited for publication in the *News*. "Just put a little more water in the soup" was the universal reaction to the annual increment in offspring. I was surprised later to find that Peacock – this kindly, thoughtful person – had been one of the more damning witnesses against the alleged Regina rioters before the judges at the subsequent board of enquiry.

Another, less agreeable client was Bill Moffat of Alexander Murray, the building materials company. He was a military man with a military sense of rank and discipline. Worse, he was also a director of the agency, so he would switch hats disconcertingly from client to agency boss. In both roles he would pull rank and disparage my best efforts to the point that I became so frustrated that tears of rage pricked my eyeballs – a weakness he was quick to exploit.

Looking back at those days, I marvel at the dichotomy of my working and after-hours lives. Each occupied a separate compartment, neither impinging on the other nor presenting insoluble contradictions. I was sufficiently security conscious not to mention my political association, but otherwise I made no secret of my outspoken "liberal" views. The agency was a satellite of the Conservative Party, so naturally the staff tended to be Conservative. I got away with my maverick views probably because they made allowances for my immigrant British background.

During this agency period, the Communist Party was declared illegal. This made very little difference to me or my friends since the Padlock

Law had long had the same effect. The friendly Rapid Grip and Batten engraving house rep who called on us daily was proud to tell me he had joined an RCMP anti-subversive auxiliary. One day in June, Sgt. René Noël of the RCMP (of whom I would later see much more) commandeered the agency switchboard to intercept anticipated phone calls from some Italians on our client list in an effort to catch them saying something for which they could be interned.

It was a time of all-round contradictions and paradoxes. The so-called phoney war was underway. The evacuation of Dunkirk had been completed. All was quiet on the Western front, leaving many of us to question the motives of some of the high-ranking Britons who were still leaning towards their fascist friends of appeasement days, in spite of Churchill having taken over from Chamberlain. For example, Sir Samuel Hoare, who was now ambassador to Spain, gave a cocktail party in Madrid for the élite of Franco society to meet the Duke and Duchess of Windsor.

Here at home, Free French leader General Charles de Gaulle had his base in Trois-Rivières, not being welcome in Montreal. Judge Sturveyer made a speech in August calling de Gaulle "a soldier of fortune." He told the members of the St. Lawrence-St. George club in Montreal that "Marshall Pétain is rebuilding France and leading her back to her old glory." A couple of months later, Pétain made what William Shirer was to call "his odious deal" to collaborate with Hitler against Great Britain. I have to admit that in some respects Inspector Harvison had it right: We did think we were better informed, more democratic, morally superior to this brand of established authority.

Thirty-two
Quebec Committee for Allied Victory

For the Russians, June 22nd, 1941 – the day the German armies swarmed into their homeland – was a day of disaster. But to communists and sympathizers it brought a huge sense of relief.

Here at last was where we truly belonged – in the thick of the anti-fascist fight which we had been the first to join and which we had never abandoned. In spite of being hobbled by its illegality and the absence of many of its most effective members who were either in jail, internment camps or in hiding, the "movement" swung into action. The "movement" was more than a euphemism for the Party; it embraced thousands of sympathizers who never walked the plank to openly avowed membership. Thanks to "democratic centralism" –accepted Party jargon for the sanctity of the word from on high – but also because of the pent-up enthusiasm of most of the members for the anti-fascist fight, the "movement" swung overnight from underground anti-war to aggressively public one-hundred per cent pro-war activity. The artists' group was co-opted to supply the graphics for the posters, programs, publicity and stage settings for the public meetings and concerts which had suddenly become kosher. Within weeks a committee to supply medical aid to the Russians was organized to raise huge sums of money through concerts, rallies and mass meetings. At the first of these, former US ambassador to the USSR Joseph E. Davies spoke, Hollywood star Luise Rainer emoted, and famous baritone Thomas L. Thomas sang to a crowd of thousands in the Montreal Forum from a platform studded with a score of dignitaries from industry, finance, medicine and the arts.

The RCMP proved to be less flexible in accepting the Russians as allies. They were also reluctant to accept us as loyal citizens since we were the very reds whom only a few months earlier they had declared to "have joined hands with the Nazis and fascists to undermine public confidence in democracy." Yet here we were, working so effectively, and so democratically, sucking in so-called well-meaning but misguided dupes like Sam Bronfman of Seagram's, Dr. Francis McNaughton of the Montreal Neurological Institute and John McConnell, owner and publisher of the *Montreal Star.*

On a humbler scale, Marion Roberts, Secretary of the newly-formed Quebec Committee for Allied Victory, announced the formation of neighbourhood Victory Clubs organized under its auspices. These were based on existing Party clubs which were able to greatly expand their membership with their now virtually legal status and a program of supporting the war effort in every possible way at the community level, through blood donor campaigns, salvage drives, War Bond campaigns and pro-conscription rallies. I became an executive member of the QCAV largely because of my writing and publicity experience and the ability to work with the many artists in our orbit, both fine and commercial, to produce the posters, programs and graphics for the projects on our agenda.

We had acquired John Kerry as our Honorary Chairman. Kerry was a Montreal city alderman who had crossed swords with the Establishment a number of times over what he considered to be their lack of enthusiasm for the "crusade against Hitlerism" and their tolerance of "high placed native fascists who would like to see Nazi methods used in Canada." White-haired, pink and plumpish, he looked the very model of respectability in his blue serge suit and polished Oxfords. Unfortunately, his powers of eloquence were no match for his explosive themes. He had the dullest, plaintive, monotone delivery combined with a free-wheeling style which seemed always to be groping without success for a convenient exit. We tried (not always successfully) to confine him to brief introductory speaking roles.

There were a number of issues jostling for attention during this critical year – the stiffening of anti-conscription sentiment in French Canada; the growing demand for a war on two fronts; and, for us, the continued internment of hundreds of our people considered by the authorities to be a threat to national security. Justice Minister Louis St. Laurent was unbending in his opinion that "their prime objective involves a threat to Canadian institutions." In the early days of the war, the Montreal *Gazette*, furiously anti-left and anti-labour at that time, saw nothing illogical in reporting indignantly on Pastor Niemoeller being thrown into a concentration camp by the Nazis, and the torture and murder of his fellow prisoners, while editorially campaigning for R. B. Bennett Depression-style iron heel laws against the reds. These laws, in the newspaper's opinion, should never have been repealed. The *Gazette* railed against "unlawful assemblies and unlawful doctrines." And it denounced what it described as "innocent and earnest people" who co-operate in activities with the communists: Though they may be "loyal and sincere, they do incalculable harm." Upstanding citizens from business, the professions and the arts, such as William Birks, Jean Louis Gagnon, Rev. R. G. Katsunoff, Goodridge Roberts, Hans Selye, B. K. Sandwell and A. Y. Jackson were just a few of the three hundred "dupes" who signed an open letter to the government in July 1942, urging it to rescind its internment order.

St. Laurent eventually bowed to this kind of pressure, but even after most of the internees had been set free (on conditions that treated them like enemy aliens), he still maintained the ban on the Party itself, insisting that it worked for the revolutionary overthrow of the government. He agreed that people were technically free to entertain certain political opinions but saw nothing contradictory in maintaining the ban on the communists.

Duplessis, in a speech to the Canadian Club in 1939, had been more graphic in his condemnation of the reds.

"Communism merits the same treatment as small pox," he had declared while arguing that there was nothing in the Padlock Law inimical to freedom of speech. The RCMP in its annual report now came up with a suggestion for an anti-red vaccine. Their hands were full dealing with the problem, they said. It was about time the government undertook its own propaganda campaign to counter communist literature that advocated – amongst other unacceptable notions – the conscription of wealth, the restoration of free speech and civil liberties and repeal of the Defence of Canada Regulations.

Our best and considerable contributions to the war effort were about as welcome to the authorities, especially the Quebec hierarchy, as a bevy of bag ladies at a Governor General's levee. The Establishment had not yet resolved the dilemma of hating Russia while at the same time taking her to its bosom as a powerful and possibly decisive ally.

Thirty-three
Conscription if Necessary

The government seemed to us to need all the help it could get on the conscription issue, especially in view of its appeasement of pro-Vichy sentiment in Quebec and the anti-war and anti-communist sentiment of a vociferous group in the province. In a period when the Red Army had turned the tide against the Germans and was winning back lost territory while inflicting huge losses on the enemy, Canada was in the middle of a conscription crisis which would be resolved in typical Mackenzie King style by means of a plebiscite thus releasing the government from its "no conscription for overseas service" pledge. That pledge would now become "conscription if necessary but not necessarily conscription."

The Montreal *Gazette* published a letter in March 1942 quoting the percentages of enlistments per thousand of population. This put Quebec at only 19 per cent as compared with 46 per cent for the Maritimes, 39 per cent for Ontario and 45 per cent for BC. Efforts were made to play down the importance of military action in support of the Russians as being of less importance than sending them arms and materiel. Apologists, including Louis St-Laurent, chief federal spokesman for Quebec, took to the rostrum. In a speech at the Ritz-Carlton Hotel in Montreal, he explained that not everyone could possibly be granted the great privilege of joining the armed services since there was only one manpower pool out of which our brave fighters had also to be supplied with services and food!

This argument was diminished somewhat by the complaint of Colonel J. E. McKenna, an army recruiting liaison officer, that recruiting was not good. The famous phrase "give us the tools and we shall finish the job" was disastrous, he said. "It is only an alibi for not joining the army."

Also, some doubt was beginning to be expressed whether greed or inefficiency were not greater factors in the flow of war materiel to Russia than a sense of allied solidarity. James Reston of *The New York Times* reported in February that US deliveries of war equipment to Russia were only half of what had been promised in the first three months. Later in the year the Annaconda Wire and Cable Company would be charged with what the U.S. government called "reprehensible" fraud in supplying the Red Army with defective wire, 50 per cent of which failed under combat conditions. War industries were not exactly suffering from hard times. For example, a U.S. court had upheld the 22 per cent profit of Bethlehem shipbuilding as not excessive and "conforming to the standard established by common practice" at that time. In Canada, company profits had hit an all-time high in May of 1941, CPR reporting a 60 per cent increase in net profits for March of that year compared with the previous year. In 1942, receipts were again higher, by 24.4 per cent.

Meanwhile, the conscription issue was heating up in the House of Commons, Mackenzie King trying desperately to form a workable emulsion of the oil of the English conscriptionists and the water of the French opponents, the latter threatening to form an anti-conscription party. The Canada Defence League was formed. Under its banner young activists such as Jean Drapeau, André Laurendeau and Gérald Filion began to organize against the war effort in much the way we were organizing in support of it. The only difference was that their rallies sometimes ended up with riots, broken glass and mass arrests.

There were also what looked like spontaneous street corner anti-conscription speeches. These so annoyed a young woman of American upbringing, Marguerite Jean Preston, that she took to the soapbox herself to roast the anti-war activists, was arrested for her trouble and hauled into court for making speeches without having a permit.

In March, Mackenzie King was given virtually unanimous parliamentary support for a so-called conscription plebiscite bill aimed at releasing the government from its previous undertaking not to have conscription for overseas service. Plebiscite day would be April 27th. The "anti" forces responded with a third mass rally in Montreal, but the "pro" forces were strangely silent. Montreal Member of Parliament and cabinet minister Brooke Claxton thought that if the government just dropped the word conscription, the whole problem would disappear. One group of General McNaughton supporters organized a mass meeting that drew two thousand people but turned out to be more of a "Hate Mackenzie King" demonstration. Their support of a Yes vote in the plebiscite was contingent upon the formation of a new, non-party, national government under the leadership of McNaughton. They would not say who financed the meeting.

The QCAV Victory Clubs, of course, along with trade unions, youth and study groups – wherever the movement had influence – went out to beat the bushes for Yes votes. When the results were tallied Ontario led the pack with 84 per cent in favour. In Quebec, the results were very different with 72.9 per cent voting No. But the overwhelming support for Bill 80 in Ontario and the other provinces was enough to allow Mackenzie King to claim success – the bill was passed. For us in the movement, the sign of success was a Montreal *Gazette* editorial that credited the communists with being the first political party to get out and organize for an affirmative vote.

Thirty-four
King Might Need You

The Quebec Committee for Allied Victory decided to kick off the post-conscription era with a recruiting rally in the city-owned Atwater Market Hall. Ironically, this was easier to rent than comparable privately-owned halls – no nit-picking scrutiny of our pedigree and motives nor the possibility of being locked out at the eleventh hour by the owners for fear of the Padlock Law, because one of the Red Squads had tipped them off. The rally was co-sponsored by aircraft and textile workers unions and by the Montreal Youth Council, and was chaired by Paul Fournier, president of the Montreal Trades and Labour Council. Lt-Col. Mackay Papineau, district recruiting officer, was only too happy to attend in the expectation of improving his woeful figures. One of our artists had access to his family's textile silk-screening facilities where he designed and printed four huge portraits of the Big Four of the day – Roosevelt, Churchill, Chiang Kai-Chek and Stalin. These we rolled up like blinds, tied with strings, and fastened to the iron railing fronting the gallery which would seat the speakers and honoured guests. At the appropriate moment, I pulled at the strings, unfurling the portraits in sequence. A round of applause greeted each as the picture was revealed to the audience. As the fourth one unfurled, however, the hall broke into thunderous, prolonged cheers.

"Who was that?" a startled Mackay Papineau asked me.

"I think it must have been Stalin," I told him in my most innocent tones.

The meeting ended with an appeal for volunteers, to which seventy-seven men responded, coming forward in dribs and drabs to milk the scene of its maximum PR value. The Montreal *Gazette* reported the meeting, albeit briefly and on page 14, but damned the volunteers with faint praise as being "principally of foreign extraction" since many had foreign-sounding. This mass recruitment started a trend which much disturbed Lt.Col. Mess, Director of Army Recruiting for Canada. He warned that the country faced "a communist menace." Why? Because communists were flooding into the army. He particularly disliked those who called themselves anti-fascists. Some of these volunteers were turned down by the armed services because they'd fought in Spain. (One "dangerous patriot" who slipped through their sieve was Bill Walsh. He would take part in the Normandy invasion and, although only a private, would be appointed by the colonel to replace the unit's wounded intelligence officer. An intrepid Mountie would ferret him out under fire in the front lines and insist the colonel tell him who Walsh associated with and whether he was likely to lead the men over to the Russians.)

We followed up with other "Victory Rallies," conferences and mass meetings. One of the most successful of these came out of a casual brainstorming session. I was sitting with Sol Pomerance, publicity consultant to several war plant unions, in his office one day, looking for ideas. "How about Paul Robeson?" Sol said. It sounded fine to me. But the great American singer was then at the top of his career – How would we ever get him? Sol had already picked up the phone and was grappling with the long distance information operator. A few minutes later he had not only tracked Robeson down to his home in New England but had obtained his promise to appear, waiving his customary fee. An audience of twelve thousand, including a thousand servicemen who were admitted free, were at the Montreal Forum to hear Robeson singing in French, Hebrew, Russian and a few other languages. And they gave him one of the biggest ovations of his career. Robeson – who was black – was better received in Montreal than in Winnipeg. In Montreal, he was put up in style at the Windsor Hotel while in Winnipeg they grudgingly gave him a hotel room but insisted he use the freight elevator.

Thomas Archer of the Montreal *Gazette* wrote: "There is the fact that Mr. Robeson has a mission and that he has faith in that mission. He is a champion of the underdog and the choice of songs and the way he sings them tells of it. Those who heard him previously in Montreal heard the artist…this time they heard the artist and the man, perfectly blended."

By this time even the CBC was showing interest. They were on hand a month later to broadcast part of our next production, *Salute Fighting Russia*, which drew a crowd of five thousand to the Atwater Market Hall. I remember this one because of the efforts of one of the plain-clothes police to sabotage the CBC equipment by tampering with their microphone leads, and by the spontaneous community singing which developed. Inspired by offerings from the Montreal Russian Choir who were on hand to entertain, the crowd began to sing popular war songs, winding up with La Marseillaise, O Canada, the Star Spangled Banner and – what else? – the Internationale.

Thirty-five
A Distant Second

The year 1942 had opened with headlines on the Red Army's resurrection from its staggering early defeats:

"REDS OPEN NEW YEAR WITH SMASHING SUCCESS"
"SIX NAZI CORPS CLAIMED ROUTED"
"RUSSIAN GAINS IN CRIMEA"
"GERMAN CASUALTIES 10,000 IN 5 DAYS"

And by the end of January:

"EXULTANT REDS ROLL BACK FOE,
POISED TO OPEN MAJOR FRONT."

General A. G. L. McNaughton, commander of the Canadian troops overseas, on a visit to Canada in February, said European invasion plans were ready; he believed that an invasion had to come. Later the same month,

Soviet Ambassador to the U.S. Maxim Litvinoff made the first public request for a second front. In March, McNaughton was in Washington with Vice-President Truman, General George C. Marshall and General Sir John Dill, head of the British military mission in the U.S., leading the press to conclude that a European invasion was near. Litvinoff repeated his request in a speech in New York. And a week later his colleague at the Court of St. James, Ivan Maisky, bluntly called for second front…now – not in 1943 –because Hitler could very well win the war in 1942.

U.S. newspaper correspondent Drew Middleton noted the "public agitation" for a second front in an article from London. But it was not until a month later that the big non-Russian media artillery opened up. Lord Beaverbrook in a speech to the American Newspaper Publishers Association in New York came out with guns blazing in support of a second front. He said he could not understand the complaints of short-sighted people who said that Britain did wrong to put weapons in the hands of communists. Russian communists had provided us with examples of patriotism "equal to the finest annals of our history . . . and has produced the best generals of the war." He claimed Britain was now well equipped to launch such an offensive.

Whatever the historical analysts may conclude about the politics and logistics of the opening of a second front in Europe, the idea caught the public's interest not only in Canada but also in Britain and the United States.

It was a recurring theme in the press throughout 1942 and 1943. More and more high-placed persons came out publicly in support, and the movement and declarations – as well as the evasions – of politicians and generals were scrutinized and interpreted by the press in relation to second-front intentions.

By June of 1942, newspaper headlines had U.S., Britain and Russia reaching complete agreement on a second front in 1942. When Mackenzie King went to Washington in June, speculation was that he went to talk about the second front. The American press was becoming the most outspoken over the delay. U.S. Maj. Gen. M. W. Clark went public to say the sooner the better. Wendell Willkie, returning from a visit to Stalin as President Franklin Roosevelt's special emissary, claimed to be "haunted" by Russian resentment over the Allied failure to make good on its pledge and added his voice to the campaign. Lord Strabolgi upset his fellow peers in the House of Lords by suggesting that some allied generals might need prodding, a not unpopular thought. Even *The Times* of London, that bastion of ultra-conservatism, in what was seen as a calm, logical editorial, advocated the speedy opening of a second front as the only means of complete victory.

Finally, Stalin in his didactic, question-and-answer style put the matter in a nutshell: "Why were [the Germans] able to muster all their reserves and hurl them into the Eastern front? Because the absence of a second front in Europe enabled them to carry on this operation without any risk to themselves. Contrast this with the situation in World War I when there were two fronts and divided German forces."

The Montreal *Gazette* agreed that Stalin had "put clear and just emphasis upon the burden which lack of a second front has laid on Russia."

Another year and a half of speculation and unfounded predictions would pass, however, before the burden was lifted and the invasion actually took place. The second front continued to be headline material all through 1943. Strabolgi and Beaverbrook were mauled by their fellow peers for charging that the government had missed an opportunity to invade Europe in the winter of 1942 when it was known that the German army was on the verge of collapse. Such talk, it was said, did nothing to help our boys in Tunisia.

In August of 1943, Churchill made a speech widely hailed as the long awaited decision. He forecast British and American liberating armies crossing the channel in full force "to come to close quarters with the German invaders of France." But what happened was the allied invasion of Italy.

By the time the real invasion had taken place and the war was finally won, the total "burden" as later estimated by war historians is as follows:

	Military Casualties	Civilian Casualties
USSR	13,600,000	7,700,000
UK	326,000	62,000
USA	295,000	–
Canada	39,000	–

C. A. Cummings of the *Ottawa Citizen*, writing from the paper's London Bureau in the spring of 1945 under the headline "Without German Invasion of Russia, London Might Have Fought 12 Years," told his readers "…only now, as newspapers here admit, is it realized that if Hitler had not invaded Russia, the British Commonwealth might have fought a ten or twelve year war against a Germany constantly growing stronger because of her continental conquests which gave her millions of foreign slaves for war factories."

We at the Quebec Committee for Allied Victory were not so naive as to think that the second-front equation contained only military and no political factors. North Africa, the Middle East – the soft under-belly of Europe – we knew to be British imperial preoccupations. But we failed to see why the same establishment which had for so long appeased fascism should now be trusted to deal fairly with the Russians, even with Churchill at the helm. We suspected that the same people who had nudged Hitler eastwards would be only too happy to see much more Russian life-blood spilled before supplying a desperately needed transfusion. We did not need any prompting from the Soviet Union to reach this conclusion, but clearly the Russians thought likewise. A Russian movie released in 1947 featured Stalin charging that Britain and the United States had broken a solemn promise to open a second front in 1942 in order to bleed Russia white, reach the Balkans ahead of the Red Army and dictate the peace.

In spite of the support for a second front by eminent Americans and Britons, and by Canadian General McNaughton, there was a feeling in Canada that this was strictly the domain of "established authority," and anyone who meddled in such matters must have subversive motives, especially since the Russians would appear to be the principal beneficiaries.

Nevertheless, we decided to use our advertising skills to produce large space newspaper advertisements presenting the case for the second front. The first ad appeared on July 20th, 1942, in the *Montreal Star* which accepted it with some hesitation from such non-kosher sources, and then only with cash on the line. I wrote the ads in plain English, staying clear of political jargon, and had them illustrated in the best contemporary style. They cited Beaverbrook, McNaughton and Gen. Somervell, Chief of U.S. Army Supply, in support of opening a second front. As far as the RCMP was concerned, it proved to be the final straw. A few days after the first ad appeared, I was called in to Keith Crombie's office. His manner was friendly but he was still recovering from a drinking bout, reeking of paraldehyde and trembling so badly that he could not hold on to his customary 6-B pencil. He told me I was fired – not by his choice, of course, he would never have done such a thing. The RCMP had come to him direct, but when he had taken no action to get rid of me, they had gone to a few of the agency's clients who made sure Crombie toed the line, or else.

The following day I accepted the Quebec Committee for Allied Victory's offer to work for it full time, and a few days after that I answered the phone to find Bill Moffatt on the line, scandalized at the news of my firing, scathing about Crombie's spinelessness and promising to help me in any way possible to obtain redress. Sometimes a principled reactionary is a better friend than a spineless liberal.

Thirty-six
General's Election

In November 1942, it was announced that a by-election to fill the vacant Outremont seat would be held in December. Mackenzie King, having skilfully threaded his way through the conscription minefield, had come up with what looked like the perfect candidate, Major-General the Hon. L. R. LaFlèche, DSO, impeccably French, Catholic and pro-war. The general was unquestionably a man of great courage and moral strength. He bore the scars of wounds which had almost cost him his life in World War I. The story goes that he was being carted off the battlefield near death when the two stretcher-bearers decided he would never make it and twice dumped him but were each time firmly ordered by him to reload him on the stretcher.

LaFlèche's addition to the wartime cabinet was politically important to King because he was still fencing with the Quebec Vichyites whom he was unwilling to offend. Quebec nationalist Henri Bourassa was claiming that the only Catholic countries left in the world were the France of Pétain, the Spain of Franco, the Portugal of Salazar and the Italy of Mussolini – and presumably the Quebec of Duplessis.

This same week, the Vichy government broke off relations with the United States. King was hard-pressed to explain once more to an angry Parliament why Canada still kept up relations with what looked more and more like an independently hostile state rather than a victim of Hitlerism. King's reply to his critics, in the words of the Montreal *Gazette*, was "a masterpiece of ambiguity." He rationalized that even if Allied troops met opposition from French forces it wouldn't really be French resistance but German resistance. A few days later Pierre Laval, who had done so much to appease Mussolini and who would later be executed for his collusion with the Nazis, became dictator of Vichy France. King must have been relieved when the pro-Vichy, anti-conscription Bloc Populaire Canadien joined other parties in announcing that it would not oppose LaFlèche.

The very next day, however, twenty-six-year-old Jean Drapeau, an articled law student, prominent anti-conscription organizer and future long-time mayor of Montreal, launched his official political career by declaring his candidacy in the by-election. The election had now clearly become a pro-war/anti-war contest. The Quebec Committee for Allied Victory decided to join the fray behind the general.

It was not easy to persuade the LaFlèche camp to accept our help. The French-Canadian pro-war establishment rallied around the candidate, first at a eulogizing dinner at the Cercle Universitaire given by regimental comrades from the Royal 22nd Regiment – the Van Doos – and then at an opening meeting of dignitaries resonant with mutual admiration and high-minded platitudes. And, of course, the usual gang of hoodlums, vote telegraphers, ward-heelers and back-room boys were on hand to lubricate the traditional Quebec democratic process. But a few days earlier, Drapeau had kicked off his campaign with a scandalous meeting which mocked Major Reverend Father Sabourin, revered hero of the Dieppe debacle, and LaFlèche himself. Drapeau's eighteen-year old lead speaker boasted of ignoring his military call-up notice and claimed he and others like him would never spill their blood on foreign soil and come back crippled, or with some loathsome disease, or as drunkards. The RCMP promptly picked him up and interned him. The campaign had now heated up to the point where the LaFlèche people were willing to talk to us.

Noah Torno – scion of a prominent Ontario winemaking family, and LaFlèche's aide-de-camp and campaign manager – came to 2048 Union Avenue in a skeptical frame of mind to sound Phyllis and me out. He wore the navy blue uniform of the Canadian Firefighters, a non-combatant unit which had been inaugurated by Mackenzie King on a visit to England and was one of LaFlèche's special interests. Something about the custom cut of Torno's uniform and his patronizing, rich boy's manner got under Phyllis' skin so that she evidently decided to deflate him. By the time she had finished with an analysis of his limited and faulty grasp of the political realities of Montreal life and the huge bonus of support from the Victory Clubs that was within his grasp if he were not too vain or stupid to reach for it, he realized that we were not bluffing.

Now officially – albeit reluctantly – accepted as part of the campaign team, the Victory Clubs went into high gear, canvassing door-to-door, organizing block meetings and carrying out all the other activities which so irritated the authorities because they were done so well and independently of official auspices.

It soon was clear that the club members felt that their efforts were not being appreciated by the general who had so far failed to acknowledge their work by the slightest message or gesture of appreciation. They began to balk. We told Torno he had better do something quickly and we proposed a meeting – a mass meeting, naturally – at which the general would be the featured speaker. We engaged the biggest hall available in the riding and put the word out to the faithful to get busy.

At eight-thirty on the evening of the meeting the hall was packed to the rafters with a standing-room-only crowd. Like a prizefight, we had arranged for a handful of preliminary speakers to warm things up for the main event. By nine-thirty LaFlèche had not yet arrived; we were running out of speakers, who were beginning to repeat themselves. The crowd was moving from restlessness to noisy protest. By ten o'clock we were becoming desperate. By good luck we had a small group of amateur entertainers with us whom we pressed into service to perform a couple of skits and lead a sing-song. Meanwhile we had sent out a search party for the missing candidate. It was close to eleven o'clock when Laflèche finally arrived accompanied by Torno who had winkled him out of some safe bourgeois haven. He was received by a deafening prolonged ovation which, to my ear at least, had overtones of sarcastic overkill. The good general appeared stunned. Not even his beloved Van Doos had given him this kind of reception. He appeared to be at a loss for words and in fact seemed to find the conventional platitudes inappropriate for this astonishing polyglot "communist" crowd. So, out of consideration for the hour, he contented himself with a few sincere-sounding "thank-you"s and "God-bless-you"s.

On the following Friday, the last one before the election, LaFlèche was back on more familiar ground at a love-in with friends to celebrate the glories of race, blood, Catholic honour, sacred historic duty and so on. As reported in the Montreal *Gazette*, J.J. Penverne KC (King's counsel), who had once run in the same constituency as a Tory, but who had deferred this time to his dear Liberal friend Leo, said "We bow upon our knees before our old mother [France]" and became so moved that further words failed him. The *Gazette* reporter was also so moved that he coined a new word to describe it – "choken up."

Because of Drapeau's campaign and the hostility aroused over the internment of the young anti-conscriptionist, the *Gazette* began to show doubts about the outcome of an election that they had once considered in the bag. Computer predictions were a thing of the future. The paper's political pundits had done elaborate language and demographic analyses of the earlier conscription plebiscite results in the riding in an effort to predict victory. But nowhere did they give much weight to the "ethnic" vote and made no mention at all of labour or the working class as an element in the campaign, and certainly not of the QCAV contribution.

Election day was Monday, December 1st. On the preceding Saturday the *Gazette* ran an editorial which betrayed deep doubts about the chances of a LaFlèche victory. It warned that the nationalists would surely vote and it urged supporters to turn out and not let the case for total war fail by default. In the event, LaFlèche won with 12,288 votes to Drapeau's 6,920. In a post-election mass meeting, Drapeau claimed a moral victory, saying that if the war workers' long working day had not made it impossible for them to vote, he would have won and LaFlèche would have lost his deposit. Thousands at the meeting applauded mention of Pétain who, only a month earlier, had broken off relations with the U.S. and declared that he would resist any Anglo-US invasion.

I was in the Liberal campaign office late in the evening of Election Day when Torno came in, saw me and beckoned me to follow him. We went to a dirty little toilet at the back of the building with no lock on the door. Torno stood on one leg with the other leg braced against the door to hold it shut, then pulled a huge roll of bills from his pocket.

"How much?" he said, making peeling-off motions.

"We don't do this kind of thing for money," I replied.

He looked at me in disbelief. In retrospect, why I should have thought that Liberal slush funds were not to be shared in is beyond me, but Torno shrugged and pocketed the roll.

"But there's one thing I do want," I said.

"Ask away."

I want a meeting with the general. Not just to shake his hand but a long meeting, long enough to present our views on the war and what we think he should be doing now that we helped to elect him."

LaFlèche did in fact grant my request. He received a delegation consisting of myself, Mary Jennison who had joined the QCAV as Executive Secretary, and a former Liberal worker who had associated himself with the Victory Club movement and had parlayed his political savvy into membership in our delegation, but whose real motive, it turned out, was to try to get the general to pull strings on his behalf and get him a commission in the army. LaFlèche listened to us patiently, made no promises and wished us well. It was probably the easiest political debt he ever had to pay and one that had zero effect on his conduct of the war effort. The "zombies" – the name given to those conscripted for service in Canada only – continued to greet him with a chorus of boos whenever he appeared before them. He never learned how to edit his rhetoric in such a way as to bridge the gulf in patriotic thinking that put them mutually beyond reach.

Cases of Quebec doctors (both in and out of uniform) charged with selling falsified call-up exemptions or medical discharges began to show up in the courts. Crude jokes about "Quebec Highlanders" circulated, referring to draft-dodgers taking refuge in nuns' habits or hiding, sometimes two at a time, inside the sisters' capacious old-style skirts.

At the end of the interview with LaFlèche, he asked me pointedly what I now intended to do. Phyllis and I had already discussed what I should do and she had readily agreed that the proper course was to volunteer for active service.

"Join the army," I told him.

And that is exactly what I did.

Thirty-seven
You're In The Army Now

I joined the thirty-four other would-be officers who formed No. 2 platoon of Baker company, "A" army, at Brockville cadet training camp. It was a cold January morning but I was sweltering with vaccine-induced fever inside my greatcoat as the tetanus, typhoid and paratyphoid anti-bodies waged war in my arteries. My fellow cadets had all had months – even years – of military life and a few had been recalled from overseas to take the course. I was the only *bona fide* rookie. I turned out for the first parade without the slightest idea of what to do. But somehow I survived the numbering and forming threes, probably because the young gung-ho captain instructor expected us to behave like a bunch of recruits needing to be whipped into shape. He lectured us on our slender hope of measuring up to his high standards. He threatened us with all the traps waiting to snare us and deprive us of our precious officers' pips. Boots and belts, brass and buttons, and especially the white patch we wore on our caps under our corps or regimental badges were especially vulnerable to his perfectionist eye. Flu was prevalent that winter but he warned us against catching it. Anyone who reported sick would automatically be thrown out of the platoon and returned to where he came from.

This officer, we soon learned, was a Saturday-night soldier with little experience of active army life. The overseas men predicted a short life for him if he ever found himself in action. Unfortunately they were right. He went over in the draft of Canadian officers in 1944 and was killed within hours of going into action. His sergeant was of a similar macho cut but luckily these two were balanced out, like a good cop/bad cop routine, by a second in command (who had been wounded overseas and sent home for a rest) and by an elderly corporal, both of whom were more interested in avoiding problems than in promoting them. We tamed Capt. Gung-ho somewhat by outdoing him at his own game – for example, by following closely behind him on the gruelling cross-country runs, treading on his heels from time to time, to make him run faster and faster until he finally had to surrender the lead.

Probably the main reason I had been lofted into this company straight off the street and assigned to the Signal Corps, who considered themselves the intellectual élite, was that I had scored in the top few per cent in the Army "M" test. This was a quiz given to everyone entering the service. The test is not so much an intelligence test as a means of determining one's ability and aptitude in a wide cross section of fields. I got high marks simply because I was familiar with hammers and electric switches as well as with words like "homunculus." So the Army, in its wisdom, assigned me to Signals in spite of the fact that I had no knowledge of physics or electricity and certainly knew nothing about electronics. During my time in the Army, I never did get to use the word "homunculus" in context although I did encounter a few men who fit the description, figuratively at least.

Part of the platoon training was so-called "lecturettes." We were required to take turns giving a two-minute lecture to the platoon on a military subject of our choice. These were dreaded by most of the others. Gas training, being locked in a cement blockhouse and deliberately exposed to tear and nose gases, crawling through mud on their bellies with live machine gun fire a few inches over their rear ends, being wakened at three in the morning for a five mile forced march in full battle gear – all this they took without complaint. But lecturettes – the very prospect left them literally speechless with fright. I had got over my stage fright during my political work so I found no problem in holding forth for a mere two minutes, barely enough time to get my second wind. I would talk about subjects that were obliquely military – things I had learned about through the left-wing grapevine such as the underground activities of the French Maquis or how Russian kids frustrated the Germans by peeing in their gas tanks or placing dinner plates in the roads to simulate mines.

This willingness to make a public exhibition of myself, rather than my proficiency as a soldier, led to my being elected commander of the graduating class. (Most of the others were far better qualified than I was for the job. But they were also more experienced in never volunteering for anything and carefully avoiding eye contact with anyone in authority looking for a volunteer.) I have no doubt it also was responsible for my later being recalled to Brockville as an instructor. But first I had to submit to advanced training at Vimy Barracks, permanent headquarters of the Canadian Corps of Signals at Kingston, Ontario.

Thirty-eight
Signal Success

Vimy Barracks at Kingston was as different from Brockville as Cambozola is from Cheez Whiz. Solid, permanent buildings for learning, eating, sleeping and fraternal bonding replaced the flimsy shacks and Spartan facilities I had become used to. We slept two to a room in hotel-like comfort with washbasins in every room. The mess hall was a quarter of an acre of polished parquet; the food abundant and well prepared, with service provided by young ladies from the women's army. Our uniforms, haircuts and housekeeping habits were no longer under constant scrutiny. We were expected to adopt and maintain for ourselves the highest standards of deportment as befitted the élite of the army. This presented no problems to the older and senior officers, many of whom had moved over to Vimy from engineering practice or executive positions with Ma Bell and were trading civilian club life for mess life. It was a more difficult adjustment for some of the younger newcomers who were officers but proved to be no gentlemen. I still remember the outraged screams of one of the CWAC table girls as a young subaltern ran his hand up the inside of her thigh as she leaned over the table to remove a dish. He was gone by the next meal.

My roommate was Harold Acker. I knew him by reputation as a left-winger and physicist of some note. Harold was an individualist, even an eccentric, with a logical, skeptical scientific mind – qualities which were not held in the highest esteem by the army. He was completely at home with electronic circuits and "wireless" as we had to call radio in deference to the British. But he lacked the skill and assurance with vehicles that is taken for granted in the army. Soon after he arrived he managed to back a truck into one of the elegant cement light standards that graced the facade of the dormitory building, knocking it to the ground. There was something strangely symbolic about this act which Harold was never allowed to forget. After graduating in Signals, he was posted to an artillery unit with which he saw action in Italy. The next time I saw him was in Ottawa at the Wartime Information Board where he joined the inter-service group I was with as a writer. He had been sent back to Canada more or less in disgrace as far as the army was concerned, his sin being that from his advance observation post he had impetuously called for fire on an enemy position on his own authority without going through the chain of command.

What I remember most about Vimy was the quality of the instruction, especially the audio-visual aids which enabled me to grasp the rudiments of electricity, radio and electronics within the first two or three lectures and somehow stay in the same ball park with the Bell, CBC and Northern Electric types. Of course, the conditions for learning were ideal: highly motivated students, discipline which guaranteed good behaviour and concentration and tangible rewards for successful completion of the course. These seem to be sadly missing for many in today's classrooms, along with another important element, namely the latitude for teachers to plot their own course and wax inspirational in their individual way as long as they get results. My brief subsequent experience as an instructor taught me how difficult teaching can be and how dispiriting is even one pair of closed eyes in the class. (However, my one chronically-sleepy pupil turned out to be the son of a regular army colonel and was unfailable in his own estimation as well as that of my senior officer.)

About halfway through the course I was called before the second-in-command who told me that the RCMP kept bugging him for reports on me.

"Look, I don't know what the hell it's all about," he said. "But I keep telling them you're a good officer and are doing well, so I've told them to go peddle their fish some place else. I feel you should know about it, that's all."

Once again my classmates outsmarted me at the end of the course by electing me class commander for the graduation ceremonies, more a reflection of their polished sense of survival than a tribute to me. There would be a formal mess dinner on the Saturday evening with a Corps church parade the following morning on the huge drill square.

The mess dinner went off well. There was a gentlemanly gathering for cocktails at which, as the guest of honour for the evening, I was passed around for small chat among the senior officers. The atmosphere was similar to a corporate gathering at which the pecking order was being discreetly established and judgments stored away for subsequent retrieval without impinging on the cordiality and good fellowship of the occasion. At a signal which eluded me, we clustered around the wide double doors to the dining room which were opened by two corporals. A startled rat crossing the polished floor looked at us briefly before scurrying to safety as the colonel and I led the party to table.

One of my neighbours at the head table, a major, began to tell me about an amazing fellow who had turned up in one of the units under his command. He described a short, uncoordinated, hopelessly unsoldierly signalman – a foreigner, Jewish maybe – who had given them all kinds of trouble. The major had discovered that the man was brilliant, highly educated, a graduate of the University of Montreal, a linguist with fluency in several languages. I realized that he was talking about Boris Rubenstein – or Brutus to his friends, who included me. The major might have mentioned another of Brutus' characteristics, his fruity baritone voice and his repertoire of Yiddish and Slavic songs which I had heard and sung along with so many times at 3610 Oxenden and elsewhere. Brutus was born in Romania into a large family that included his aunt Helena of cosmetic fame. When I met him in the late thirties before the Depression clouds had yet lifted, he had funnelled his talents and irrepressible high spirits into peddling watches and having a good time. The major recognized his abilities and saved him from a useless army existence by having him moved to an area where at least his languages could be exploited.

I had my comeuppance the following morning at church parade. I had my gang fall in and marched them from our quarters to the corps parade grounds at the appointed hour. As we came in sight of the square I saw what looked like several thousand men already drawn up in faultless formation. I realized that we were the last to join the parade and that the whole operation would have to be done under the critical eyes of the entire establishment, including the little group facing the parade which included the colonel and the regimental sergeant major. What little I knew about drill procedures vanished from my mind. How to get the group converted from rank to file, or was it the other way round, and park them on that distant marker facing forwards was completely beyond my powers. Apparently I had also lost the ability to distinguish between right and left because at my command the group suddenly started to march in the opposite direction from the parade ground. I about-turned them and found the one command that would work: "Listen, you sons of bitches, march right on to that marker and halt...get it?"

Thirty-nine
Battle of Niagara Falls

I joined the Edmonton Fusiliers, 2nd Battalion, at Sussex, New Brunswick, as Signals Officer in the depth of one of the coldest winters on record. We occupied the usual flimsy, uninsulated army huts, three or four officers to a room. To keep the huts at least above the freezing point, stoves were kept going, burning soft coal. The air was dense with sulphurous fumes and we spat soot each bitter morning as we staggered out to the six o'clock parade. We had to turn out in full battle gear, although on especially cold mornings – zero degrees fahrenheit or colder – the commanding officer, Colonel Harcus Strachan, VC, sanctioned greatcoats.

Colonel Strachan was a bank executive from British Columbia who had jumped back into uniform in a patriotic reflex like so many other army reservists – accountants, hardware store proprietors, customs officers and funeral directors – all of whom were represented in the Edmonton Fusiliers 2nd Battalion mess. He dreamed of commanding a regiment composed entirely of officers. They'd soon put the Hun in his place. The war would be over in no time. He had some reason for feeling this way as his Victoria Cross escapade reveals. In November 1917, his regiment, the Fort Garry Horse, got the job of taking the town of Cambrai against fierce artillery defences. Strachan's squadron of cavalry got ahead of the rest of the regiment through an excess of zeal and wound up cut off, flanked by the enemy on three sides. By the time Strachan and the remnants of the squadron got back to the regiment they had destroyed an enemy artillery battery (seven members of which he had personally sabered to death), inflicted well over a hundred casualties, disrupted German communications over a wide area and taken more prisoners than the original strength of the squadron.

At the age of sixty-plus the colonel must have known that he'd never again lead anyone into battle, let alone an élite regiment of officers. His natural Scottish dourness was accentuated by the boredom and frustration of presiding over a battalion of reluctant conscripts. But he hadn't been able to seal every crack in his Calvinist carapace so that once in a while, unexpectedly, a little *bonhomie* and humour leaked out. He loved to recall how, after winning his VC, he and a fellow hero who had lost a leg in action were lionized in London society. After taking tea in some fashionable Mayfair drawing room, his friend would ask the ladies if he might smoke his pipe.

"Of course, please do."

Out would come a solid plug of cheap tobacco and a formidable jackknife. Slowly he would pare off flakes of tobacco until he had a pipeful in his palm. Then suddenly he would plunge the blade of the knife through his tartan trews into his cork thigh.

"He ruined a few pairs of trews but the ladies' screams made it all worth while," chuckled the colonel.

This was my first posting in the field. It was not easy, first to detect then to absorb all the nuances of army life with its tri-level social structure – officers, non-commissioned officers and other ranks. The others, with years of Saturday-night soldiering and months of regimental life together, followed the military shibboleths without giving them a thought. It took my sergeant no time at all to figure me out as an impostor, with no real love for or understanding of army life. I won him around in the end by teaching him all I knew about the mysteries of wireless, which wasn't very much. My batman, a pleasant young farm boy, grew increasingly distant although I was careful not to make too many demands on him out of a sense of socialist reluctance to "exploit" him by taking advantage of my rank. How wrong I was. He was annoyed that I was withholding all the demands for extra personal services for which he expected to be paid.

It was also my first experience of small-town life. The camp was some distance from the town of Sussex. But Sussex was the centre of everyone's thoughts. Sussex was where the girls were. Sundays were the best days to establish and pursue relationships. Church services and the family dinners that followed were the hunting grounds. Officers, of course, with more pay, nicer uniforms and greater prestige, were competed for not only by the daughters but also by the parents determined to do their patriotic best for the boys in uniform. The parents seemed to take the charade of church attendance, ever-so-polite conversation over roast beef, mashed potatoes and apple pie, and hymn-singing around the piano afterwards at its face value, unaware of the sexual undercurrent and the lascivious intentions on both sides.

A number of cosy arrangements were abruptly broken up when, soon after my arrival, the regiment was moved to Chippewa, above Niagara Falls. Training days were now behind us. This was real action – defending the Falls and associated canals and power houses from enemy sabotage!

We were housed in an abandoned factory within earshot of the Falls with small detachments of men dispersed in huts strategically placed throughout the sensitive area. It was a boring enough existence for the officers, most of whom wanted above all to get overseas. But for the men, cut off from society for weeks on end, it was especially soul-destroying. The company of Veterans whom the Fusiliers were relieving had left behind the evidence of their way of handling the situation in the form of cartons of empty lilac lotion bottles. The Chippewa power canal took water from above the Falls and fed it several miles to the powerhouse at Queenston. The canal was deceptively placid looking. It was far deeper than it was wide and the huge volume of water packed a fearsome punch as one lilac-lotioned veteran discovered when he tried to draw a pail of water. Not wishing to lose the pail, he attached it to his wrist by a rope. The water snatched the pail like a hungry shark and the poor vet with it. He was eventually found behind the grating at the bottom of the powerhouse penstocks.

Perhaps in anticipation of the men's travail, some pimp in their ranks procured a local girl for a so-called gang splash. I got the appalling story from my sergeant, an otherwise strait-laced young man. It took place in an abandoned church next to the barracks. After dark on the first Sunday evening after arrival, the intrepid Fusiliers were lining up outside the church awaiting their turn. A couple of hours later a score or more had passed through, leaving a semi-conscious girl and a chancel slippery with semen.

The colonel, who probably realized that this would be the closest he would come to active service, became more and more withdrawn and spent more time with his dog – with which he seemed to have greater empathy – than with the men. The dog, an elderly, dribbling Great Dane, had come with the territory. It quickly identified the colonel as top banana and adopted him as his master, assuming corresponding seniority in the mess. The dog was big enough to sit in an armchair with its rear end in the cushions and its front paws on the floor, defying any junior officer to evict it.

My position as Signals Officer was fraught with problems of protocol. I was attached to the battalion but was not a part of it. My job was to train regimental signallers and set up the telephone and wireless networks. And my first loyalty was supposed to be to Sigs not to these lowly foot soldiers.

My colleagues in the mess saw things differently. They expected me to take my turn on the duty roster like anyone else. I appealed to the senior Signals officer in the area for advice.

"Tell them to go to hell" he advised. "Give them an inch and they'll take a mile. We're above that kind of duty – we're Sigs after all. They have absolutely no right to ask you, it's all laid down in Regs, so just tell them to go to hell."

But the colonel had no patience with any protocol but his own.

"Lunan," he told me in his authoritative brogue. "As long as I'm your commanding officer I'll see to it that you perform your military duties as I understand them and . . . (pause) . . . that you go to chu-r-r-ch on Sundays."

These prairie lads, farmers for the most part, came from every possible ethnic background. They were there only because of conscription. They would much rather have been plowing, sowing and reaping. The officers and NCOs were all volunteers and they treated the men with cruel contempt. For example, the barracks were several miles from Niagara Falls, the nearest possible place to find a pub or a restaurant. Officers and NCOs usually had access to jeeps or trucks for the trip. They would sometimes refuse a lift back to barracks to some wretched hitchhiking zombie who had missed the last bus even if it meant him being late and consequently up on charge.

Few of the men had much schooling. As Sigs officer I was given my pick of them to form a platoon of signalmen which I would train to handle the telephone and wireless communication of the battalion. I was able to win their respect, largely by taking the trouble to pronounce their names correctly. They were good students and became proficient signalmen. Amongst other duties they manned the battalion switchboard which provided a telephone link between the different offices and outposts. Since it was unthinkable for a lowly signalman to listen in on the line and equally unthinkable to pull the plug on an unfinished conversation, a strict procedure was ordained. At intervals the signalman operator was supposed to come in on the line. If he heard no voices he was to say, "Finished, please?…Finished, please?…Finished, please?..." before disconnecting the line.

Of course, I did not confine my teachings to signal subjects. We had regular "current events" sessions to help fill some of the appalling gaps in their knowledge of the world around them and their place in it, not to mention what Canada was supposed to be fighting for. They were not the only ones who were in need of indoctrination. None of the young officers in the mess had heard of Tito until I mentioned him. Nobody knew about the Maquis, the French underground movement, or had the dimmest idea of the history of Hitlerism prior to Munich. And yet these young men could not wait to get into the fight. When they finally did, in response to an urgent appeal from the British for infantry officers in 1944, of the 673 like them who went overseas there were 465 casualties. The British – cynically, some felt – put them in command of forward platoons, inexperienced as they were, in the vanguard of the invasion of Normandy.

The most interesting and stimulating member of the mess for me was Sol Bond, a young doctor attached to the regiment as medical officer. We became good friends. The town of Niagara Falls replaced Sussex as the sex exchange and new liaisons were soon formed. Sol, who was a small man, not at all macho, but amusing, sophisticated and good company, quickly got himself a nice young lady and was received into the bosom of her family to be treated like a prince or, more likely, a future son-in-law. After all, a doctor would be quite a catch. Sol, more with amusement than cynicism, kept me informed while we waited for the other shoe to drop – the Jewish one. Of course, in due course he dropped the bombshell and the affair broke up in a tempest of tears.

Sol helped me both as a friend and a doctor. Like many couples whose marriages were not all they wished for, Phyllis and I began to think that a baby would somehow set things right. However, having deliberately avoided parenthood for several years we found it not so easy to reverse the trend. Sol advised that a first step would be for Phyllis to discuss the problem with her own doctor, although he warned me that I could be the culprit. Phyllis did consult Dr. Moe Braunstein, one of the earliest specialists in infertility. He diagnosed a problem with the fallopian tubes for which the treatment was to open them up by inflating them with air. Sol explained the diagnosis and treatment to me in detail, the next best thing to my being present with her during her ordeal. My contribution to the enterprise was made during my relatively infrequent forty-eight-hour leaves to Montreal, so it was an occasion for rejoicing, Sol included, when Phyllis phoned me in Niagara Falls one day in October to tell me she was finally pregnant.

Most of the senior officers – senior in age as well as rank – were reserve army men from the peacetime regiment who were finally getting their chance at the real thing. The adjutant, a feisty middle-aged fellow with a head of close-cropped steel wool, had very little to do. More and more often he retired to his quarters with a bottle. At one of the infrequent full-scale mess dinners, complete with Niagara Peninsula port, the adj passed out right after grace. He tipped forward and rested with his head on the table. The mess sergeant entered with two plates of soup. He put one in front of the colonel and then without hesitation ran his fingers through the steel wool and lifted the adj's head over to the bread and butter plate before putting the soup in place. The adj slept peacefully throughout the meal. Sol and I were the last to leave the table.

"We'd better get him to bed," Sol said.

We managed to get the adj more or less upright, supported between us with his arms around our necks.

"I bet he needs to pee."

We shuffled into the john where Sol unbuttoned the adj's fly (no zippers on battle dress trousers) and fished out his penis. Sure enough, the adj responded with a lengthy and powerful stream. When it stopped, Sol carefully shook off the drops then said, "Finished, please?…Finished, please?…Finished, please?..."

Sol was one of three Jews among the score or so officers in the mess. Among the officers was also a captain – a company commander on leave from the RCMP – who astonished us one evening by launching into an anti-Semitic diatribe.

"One thing for sure," he wound up, "you'll never find a goddam Jew in uniform."

"Captain Tomlinson," I said, "may I introduce you to..." I named in turn Sol and the other two Jewish officers who sat at the table. I had the impression that Tomlinson's gaffe only reinforced his attitude and that he had now added a Jew-lover to his hate list.

My regimental life came to an unexpected end one day when I was called in to the colonel's office.

"They seem to want you in Ottawa, Lunan," he told me. "Do you know what it's all about?"

He clearly thought it unusual for the HQ brass to reach out its long arm and pluck a lowly Signals lieutenant from the sticks. I was as puzzled as he was but I followed orders to report immediately to Captain Frank Park of the Wartime Information Board in Ottawa.

Forty
Canadian Affairs

The posting to Ottawa, seconded from the army to the Wartime Information Board, was like winning a lottery without even buying a ticket. The group to which I now belonged had been drawn from the army, navy and air force to produce a magazine, *Canadian Affairs*, and other publications for the armed services both at home and overseas. We would be fighting with pens, not swords.

Fred Poland, a newspaperman from Montreal and an old friend, had covered most of the important wartime conferences as an RCAF press relations officer and was now posted to Ottawa where he, too, became part of the armed forces information services team. I gladly accepted his invitation to share his apartment. Besides Fred, our team included Bob McKeown who was to the print media what his son of the same name later became to television: Donald MacDonald, a future leader of the Ontario CCF; Harold Acker, my old room-mate from Vimy Barracks; and a handful of other stimulating personalities under the quite unmilitary leadership of Captain Frank Park, a lawyer from New Brunswick. Frank had cultivated a wide circle of friends and acquaintances in government and senior bureaucratic and academic circles, giving us the feeling that, if we did not exactly have our hands on the levers of power, we were at least present in the control room. In the small-town Ottawa of the day, we regularly crossed paths with cabinet ministers, members of parliament and mandarins. More than once Fred Poland and I on our way to work would pass the Prime Minister tottering all alone to or from the House and snap him a salute to which he would respond with a tip of his Homburg.

We drew on this circle of notables for articles for *Canadian Affairs*. It is a tribute to Frank Park's diplomatic skills that they accepted uncomplainingly the sometimes radical rewriting we thought necessary to popularize their prose for our readership. All the graphics – the illustrations and animated statistical charts – we obtained from the Graphics Department of the National Film Board which still operated from its firetrap on Sussex Street.

We were in the privileged position of being insulated from authority by virtue of our "seconded" status – lost between the services who never gave us a thought except to send us our pay and the civil service (referred to by our lone permanent staffer as "tray-sury") whose claim on our souls we refused to acknowledge as they doggedly tried to rope and tie us in red tape. At weekly meetings of a Wartime Information Board committee we reported on our plans and progress as often as not as *faits accomplish*. In this way our team of six or eight people was able to put out a monthly publication with a well-researched article, a detailed discussion guide and a round-up of "Civvy Street" news, including answers to readers' questions. I doubt if we could have done this by following "tray-sury" guidelines.

It was a period of innocent euphoria during which iron curtains or cold wars would have been laughed off as the ravings of the hard-core right. The anti-war, nationalist elements in Quebec were fighting a losing rearguard action against progress. Their supreme hero, Marshall Pétain, faced a treason trial where it would be shown that, amongst his many pro-Nazi acts, he had congratulated Hitler for having slaughtered the Canadians at Dieppe. Nationalist René Chaloult deplored the flow of Quebec women away from farms and called on the government to warn farm mothers of the dangers awaiting their daughters in the wicked cities. Thanks in large part to labour leaders like Bob Haddow, Madeleine Parent, Kent Rowley, Lea Roback, Jack Shaw, Azelus Beaucage, C.S. Jackson and countless other toilers in the vineyards, the worst that befell these daughters of the soil was to learn independence and self-determination earning their living in a war plant and, where necessary, joining their sisters on the picket lines.

At *Canadian Affairs* our articles focused on the problems and opportunities of the coming peace – national health insurance, affordable housing for all, labour participation in political life, leisure and cultural facilities, community centres, citizens' rights and responsibilities – and, as a leit-motif, the holding high, unashamedly, of the beacon of One World of peace, prosperity and mutual aid which had been the justification for all the mayhem in the first place. It was an inspiring and gratifying time during which everything seemed to have come together for me, the writing, the political and social agenda, the hopes for a writing career not in the huckstering jungles.

At least once a month my work took me to Montreal where *Canadian Affairs* was printed and where, after a lengthy session putting the issue to bed, I would spend the night at home.

On one of these evenings Fred Rose turned up and invited himself to supper. He was by this time the Labour Progressive Party Member of Parliament and at the height of his popularity and political influence. He told a few sly anecdotes about fellow MPs and Ottawa mandarins who, it seemed, were eager to benefit from his powers of political analysis and prognostication. He then asked me about my job, who my co-workers were and my opinion of them, what I aimed to do after the war and so on. None of this struck me then as being a planned interrogation, rather the sort of casual, meandering conversation motivated more by politeness than by any deep interest in the answers. By this time I had started to write short stories and was nibbling at the edges of acceptance. Both *Harper's* and *The New Yorker* had sent encouraging notes inviting further submissions. I told Fred that I hoped to become a writer.

"You're in Ottawa. You should meet some of the Russians. You'll find them an interesting bunch. Lots to talk about. You know, they know bugger-all about Canada. They could use some help."

Until this point, the talk had been nothing more than casual chitchat as we sat with a drink while Phyllis prepared supper. Only long afterwards did I realize Rose had surely contrived the meeting for the precise purpose of recruiting me for the job. Did he believe I could interpret his vague words for the message he wished to convey? If so, he vastly overestimated my politically savvy.

I did agree wholeheartedly with one thing Rose said – the Russians certainly could use some help. I'd heard their Ambassador Gousev's speeches delivered with stiff Kremlin-style formality in almost unintelligible English. And the occasional contact I had had through Fred Poland with a couple of other embassy types made me feel they were ill at ease in Canada and could benefit from some well-intentioned indoctrination on Canadian life and customs.

This was the full extent of Fred Rose's conversation on the subject. I was intrigued with the thought of meeting some Russians. The Red Army had liberated Warsaw and was sweeping towards Berlin. Lester "Mike" Pearson, newly appointed Canadian Ambassador to Washington, made an eloquent speech in New York in support of international co-operation. Only days later the emotion passed from words to deeds at the Yalta meeting between Roosevelt, Churchill and Stalin. It was an environment in which it seemed natural and logical to give a helping hand to an ally who, if the truth be admitted, was doing more and at far greater cost to win the war than all the others combined. I readily agreed with Fred Rose's suggestion to meet the Russians and discuss matters of mutual interest. He said he would arrange for a meeting.

Forty-one
Fateful Decision

The meeting was arranged with a convoluted sense of caution. It was initiated by a phone call one evening from a young woman who asked me to meet her in the lobby of the Chateau Laurier Hotel and told me how to identify her. We left the hotel and began walking at a good clip along Sussex Street. A solitary man ahead was walking at a much slower pace. As we came abreast he said "Hello." It was like a relay race. One moment I was walking down the street with one companion; the next moment I had picked up a replacement while the first went ahead without breaking stride.

That is how I met Colonel Rogov – not that I knew his name or that he was a colonel. I was not impressed. A few inches over five feet tall, shabbily and rather oddly dressed, he certainly did not look like a military man. His un-Canadian pants, wide enough and long enough to hide his shoes, made me think of a *New Yorker* report that you could easily pick out the Russian secret servicemen in a crowd because they wore their fedoras undented. It seemed like an elaborate way to meet someone, especially since I had several times met Pavlov and Sokolov from the Soviet Embassy in our neighbour Jack Ralph's apartment and at various other places in the ordinary course of Ottawa life. We walked a short distance together to a parked car and got in the back seat. The driver set off at a fast clip in the direction of Rockcliffe Park where we were soon charging around, Russian style, at sixty miles an hour until I yelled at the driver to slow down. After a brief and somewhat stilted conversation, during which Rogov, who introduced himself as Jan, asked me a number of questions about my work and plans for the future, he handed me an envelope. Read it and then be sure to destroy it, he said.

This was not what I had expected – clearly no social encounter. I felt the sheepishness of someone who sees the point of the joke only after everyone else has burst out laughing. Shades of the Danish anal thermometer! Well, I had figuratively put it in my mouth; this must be the way they do things. They had had very little exposure to Canadian life and plenty of reason to look for enemies behind every bush. I would wait and see what was in the envelope.

Their sense of caution was greater than their intelligence as the driver demonstrated. He circled back more or less to our starting point and stopped in mid block.

"Why are we stopping here?"

"You get out now."

"Like hell I do…unless you want to draw attention to yourself. I'm going to have to walk either half a block back in the direction we came from, or ahead in the direction you're going. Neither makes any sense."

This was the first of several meetings the details of which, I must admit, would have vanished beyond recall except that they have been recorded for history in the archives of the Gouzenko case. I quickly realized that Rogov had no interest in or sympathy with me as a writer, nor in anything I might have to say about Canadian society and its relationship to Soviet affairs and to the future of the "One World" for which we were hoping and planning. The envelope Rogov gave me made it plain that I was to be simply an intermediary between him and a group of three people. I was being asked to relay to them requests for specific information on a variety of scientific subjects mostly in the fields of radio and electronics. I was barely acquainted with those mentioned – Durnford Smith, Israel Halperin and Edward Mazerall – having only recently joined a current affairs discussion group to which they, too, appeared to belong. Their names must, therefore, have been given to Rogov by someone else, presumably Fred Rose.

During the next few weeks I had the chance to get to know these men better. I found three gifted people orbiting in the upper reaches of contemporary scientific knowledge but down to earth on social and humanitarian issues. Halperin, for example, had always been ready to help victims of Naziism or anti-Semitic discrimination. He made no secret of his liberal views. His generosity of spirit ricocheted in a way he could not have foreseen. When Klaus Fuchs was sent by the British to be interned in Canada as an enemy alien, albeit a proven anti-Nazi, Halperin was asked by a brother-in-law who in turn had been asked by Fuchs' sister, to do what he could to help. He sent Fuchs some magazines and, although he never met him, put his name in his address book which the RCMP later found. So Halperin's name was irretrievably coupled with that of Fuchs – who would soon be known to the world as "the man who stole the atom bomb."

Like most scientists, and even like many statesmen and politicians, as later became clear, they saw scientific knowledge as international, inching ahead incrementally by the contributions of scientists around the globe. Science operated synergistically, the two of one person's imagination plus the two of another's ingenuity adding up to the five or even the twenty-five of an experimental breakthrough. Amongst scientists of the period the possibility of an atom bomb was an open secret. The basic physics were well known and had been developed mostly by non-American scientists. As early as 1943, Associated Press reported from Stockholm that Danish scientist Dr. Niels Bohr had arrived in London with data for a new invention for an atomic explosive weapon. The Germans, everybody assumed, were amongst the leaders in the field. And even the Russians, who had yet to demonstrate to a skeptical world their leadership in space technology, were known to have their Peter Kapitza and Abraham Joffees, old hands at juggling atoms. Halperin gave me the impression that he thought that the secrecy surrounding much scientific work to be a bureaucratic smokescreen. But this did not mean that he took his secrecy oath lightly. When I got around to asking him if he were able to offer the Russians anything they might find useful in their war effort, he suggested that I obtain information on the Valcartier ballistics program from his chief in my official capacity. My original assumption, since his name came to me from Fred Rose via Rogov, was that he was predisposed to helping the Russians. I soon came to realize that he was an unwitting victim who had no intention of becoming involved in what after all could be construed as technically illegal even if he was in general supportive of the Russians as allies and in favour of the sharing of scientific knowledge. This assessment explains why I acted as I later did.

Smith and Mazerall both had the chance before the Royal Commission and at their trials to speak for themselves and to explain their motives, all of which is a matter of record. My impression of both men was that they were ready to supply information, but only at their own discretion (that is, only information which was readily available or about to be made available). Some of this was being deliberately withheld from the Russians. Far from damaging Canada, my motive – and I assumed it must have been theirs also – was to help Canada by helping our most powerful and effective ally and thereby shortening the war.

Of course, I was thinking of the Soviet Union as an ally and not the vicious enemy the cold warriors would soon have us believe it to be. Both Smith and Mazerall seemed to be of the opinion that the Canadian scientific establishment had underestimated the Russians. They both hoped for a reciprocal exchange of scientific information from which Canada would benefit. I heard of two incidents from them in support of this. Canada was thought to be in the lead in the development of magnetrons, advanced electronic devices of vital importance in the development of radar. But an article in a Soviet scientific publication turned up showing the Russians to be more advanced than Canada in this field as early as 1943. Again, when a group of Canadian microwave specialists went to Moscow on an exchange visit they took with them as an exhibit a piece of superseded electronic equipment from the program then under development, an item they had never been able to get to work particularly well. On arrival in Moscow, they were annoyed at being stowed away incommunicado in a hotel for several days. When they were finally released by their Russian counterparts, they were shown their own equipment fine-tuned to a state of performance they had never thought possible.

I had not been prepared for the strange behaviour of Rogov – the code names, the elaborate meeting arrangements, the lack of any truly human rapport – but I put this down to the Russians' well-known paranoia, a strange mixture of arrogance and inferiority complex, bred of decades of fending off capitalist hostility, real or imagined. At no time did I feel beholden to Rogov. When he encouraged me to stay in the army, I laughed. No way, I told him, I'm a writer. In spite of the Kafkaesque script, I felt in control – even sorry – for this mechanical little man. Still, I was alarmed when on our second meeting he asked me for a photograph of myself and a biography, neither of which I gave him. I went to see Fred Rose.

"What gives with these guys? They're treating us like puppets. They pull strings and we dance?"

"Mmnnyecch." This is the closest I can come phonetically to Fred's reaction, but it cannot convey the frustration and aggravation it expressed. "Yeah, sometimes they act as though we're Romanians," he said. He persuaded me that we were in control of the situation, not to be intimidated and to use my own judgment.

Another, much more disturbing development was Rogov's sudden offer of money as "expenses." Shades of Noah Torno and the LaFlèche campaign. I told him there were no expenses as far as I was concerned, not even taxi fares. All the meetings were within walking distance. He was most persistent that I should be reimbursed and that I should accept money for the others. It was apparent that, in their unilateral way, the Russians believed that they were calling the shots. I refused the envelope Rogov pushed at me. But, for Rogov, what had been done could not be undone.

Years later, some of my advertising associates made a trip to the Soviet Union for the purpose of photographing Russian children wearing Canadian designed clothes. They were booked by the state-run agency Intourist on a round trip taking in Moscow, Leningrad and Kiev.

However, they found that they had all the shots they could possibly use without going to Leningrad and wanted to cancel that leg of the trip – but, oh no, Leningrad was ordained; impossible to cancel. It was this sort of bureaucratic thinking that faced Rogov. The money had been drawn, assigned, entered and irrevocably recorded.

Who knows what happened to it? But misappropriation of funds was not unknown among the embassy employees. Naturally, the subject came up at the Royal Commission enquiry. [I quote from the record:]

When asked about money:

A. [Rogov] was always bringing up the question of expenses and he did mention the question of taxi rides but it was from our point of view a preposterous suggestion and I simply ignored it.
Q. When you say "from our point of view" whose point of view do you refer to?
A. Mine and Smith's and Mazerall's
Q. Did you discuss this with them?
A. Yes, I did.
Q. With the three of them?
A. No.
Q. With whom?
A. With each at one time or another, and I discussed the question of expenses.
Q. Tell us what you said to them.
A. I told them that if they were involved in any expenses there was an offer for those expenses to be covered. Each one of them, however, said there was no such possibility of expenses, the question did not arise for them.
Q. From what you say, I take it they did not want to take any money.
A. Correct.
Q. What was their motive to do what they did?
A. Their motives would be idealistic or political.
Q. What do you mean by political?
A. That they felt they were serving a valid political motive in doing this.
Q. What do you mean by political?
A. I cannot describe for them their motives.
Q. What do you understand they meant by political?
A. I used the word myself.
Q. What did you use the word for?
A. That certainly there would be some motivation for doing this type of work, and it would have to be one involving ideals.

The commissioners referred to "denials" in their report but also said "the possibility must be considered" that money changed hands, and having considered the possibility went on to claim emphatically that it had been paid. They knew about the rumours of thefts of money by embassy personnel but they chose to ignore them in the interests of painting the worst possible picture. In fairness to the commissioners, it should be pointed out that the report was largely written by Arnold Smith, a senior, strongly anti-Soviet member of External Affairs, and was as much a cold-war polemic as a factual report.

My judgment eventually led me to abdicate my role as intermediary. Rogov was not interested in my assessment of Canadian or international affairs and I was not qualified to appraise information of a scientific nature, or to discuss or evaluate any reciprocal information coming from Rogov. Nor, for that matter, was I prepared to pressure or influence the others to do anything against their own judgment. I had had only three meetings with Mazerall by mid-summer, due to pressure of work on both sides and, as later became clear, Mazerall's growing reluctance. I decided it would be better to let Smith deal directly with Rogov and accordingly made arrangements for them to meet.

I found out later that Fred Rose admitted that he had overestimated my political savvy, had attributed to me more knowledge and insight than I really had, and had been mistaken in not discussing the whole proposal in greater detail from the very beginning. And supposing he had? Would it have changed the outcome? It's a big "if." To paraphrase Good Queen Bess, if my aunt had been clustered and not cleft she would have been my uncle.

It is difficult to reconstruct this critical period in memory as it appeared at the time in the context of the existing political environment, and not as the sterilized version of a half-century later. Moreover, there is a self-preserving human tendency to expunge painful memories. To try to get at the truth I went back to the official record and reread my remarks to the royal commissioners in reply to their invitation to explain my motives. I cannot think how I could have explained them better, except for a few lapses in syntax – and even that stands up remarkably well for impromptu remarks delivered under great stress to a hostile audience. Here are some excerpts:

> It is difficult in retrospect to analyze one's motivations and try to recontruct just what did take place. However, although I connected up this meeting [first meeting with Rogov] with Rose I had no preconceived idea of what it was going to be and not until after I had left Rogov…and had had an opportunity to look at the document did I begin to understand the nature of it. Naturally, I did not

go there with a completely empty head. The conversation I had with him at the meeting had a lot to do with me as a writer and I was not averse to writing commentaries which I felt to be a true and fair comment on the Canadian political scene. I did not go there with any fixed or firm loyalty to the Russians. I went there very much as a Canadian who was acknowledgedly a communist in sympathy and a well-wisher for the Soviet Union. I thought often and I still do think that sometimes they show a very superficial knowledge of the Canadian way of life…My first feeling, which of course afterwards changed, was that anything I wrote in that connection would help in some little way to improve their appreciation and analysis of Canadian life. Well, of course, I had only to read the typewritten instructions...to understand the full nature of this rendezvous. That is the first time that I fully realized that this was not by any means a casual meeting, that it involved three other people. I felt that I would at least see them and find out what they knew about it and what their attitude was to the thing. It would be very easy for me to claim very strong and unswerving idealistic motivation, but things did not happen that simply. I began to think very seriously of this position and I reviewed what I had done in the light of my political ideas and my political principles or, if you like, my Communist leanings. It seemed to me that, even before, I had been put in the position I found myself [in] – in the position where I had to wrestle with my ideology. I was a member of a committee which tried to help Canadians coming back from Spain who had fought there in the International Brigade. This was, from the prevalent Canadian public opinion, a very unpopular task, but in retrospect it seems to me that it was a worthwhile thing and perhaps I…had been a little ahead of public opinion in seeing the Spanish war in the light in which we did see it and that ultimately nobody would deny that Franco was a fascist tool in Spain and that to close one's eyes to these things would only mean war and loss for Canada.

I followed up this reasoning and it seemed to me that much of this time I have been faced with a very difficult decision in which I had to put my principles into action and that I had been right in retrospect. Then I was proud of the position I had taken.

The Quebec Committee for Allied Victory is another example. Against any feelings for my own security I joined and took a prominent part in the organization which tried to advocate the necessity of very close cooperation in the interests not only of Canada but of all people in fighting against the Axis. Here again, I think that much of the opinion we voiced at that time has since been justified. I felt that I was true to my real convictions and feelings in doing this, although because of the branding of this work as communistic I lost my job, for one thing. While it is true that when I suddenly found myself in the position with this man Rogov it far outweighed any battle with my motives and my convictions that I [had] had...

War was developing and it had become firmly established not only in my own mind but, I think in many other people's, that the Soviet Union was a very important ally. The beginnings of a much more advanced form of international cooperation were being formed. The Big Three and sometimes the Big Five were coming together. The whole principle of cooperation by the United Nations was beginning to be put into…practice.

Plans for a subsequent organization, the United Nations Organization, had already been laid and I felt that it was both a very necessary part of the need to defeat Hitler and I necessarily felt afterwards that our friendship and cooperation with Russia was tremendously important.

As I say, it was only after a great struggle on my part that I could bring myself eventually to accept this kind of work as something which would in the long run – I was conscious that it would be in the long run – advance the whole cause of international cooperation.

I certainly did not think of it in terms of cheating Canada out of anything. I felt that it was, as I say, that we were perhaps making a very slight contribution or giving a little push to this international cooperation which was the basis of my political ideology.

As the thing went on I do not say and I cannot claim that I unshakingly held to that. After a certain point I was determined to remove myself from this particular work as well as I could although I think I [had] vastly underestimated the position I was in and it was not particularly easy for me suddenly to withdraw.

There were two things which tended to keep me in these lines. One was the fact that I believed I would have an opportunity to write…these commentaries, and in fact I did write one. The other was the question of reciprocity of discussion between people I was dealing with…and the Russians. This was discussed almost right from the beginning, I think, between myself and Rogov, and it was one of the first questions each of the other people put.

…Subsequently, when the news of the atom bomb broke, I began to see how important some of the questions I had been asked were, and I certainly did not tie up the question of uranium with anything quite so devastating.

There was also in my mind at the time a feeling that scientific subjects were bound to become international and subsequently the discussions of great numbers of scientists all over the world following the atom bomb raid tended to bear out my belief and balanced off to some extent my own misgivings.

I would also like to say that in the light of the discussions at the United Nations Organization in London, I found myself still confident that the nations of the world who had fought and beaten Hitler would inevitably draw together within this organization for the peace of the entire world. I feel that Canada's part in the United Nations Organization is a very worthy one. I happened to be in London at the time and I did not feel any sharp contradiction within myself when I viewed the workings of that organization.

> I doubt whether I could keep any self-respect at all unless I truly believed in these things and that the very fast pace of world history in this new period in which we find ourselves will catch up to and surpass the results of this thinking on my part and the actions that it led to.
>
> I would also like to say that I had no idea of the scope and extent of this work. I was amazed when it first became clear to me during my interrogation. I never thought of myself as being more than just one person in a small group of five.
>
> I do not offer this in any sense as an excuse for my work, but I was striving to square myself with my ideals without a full knowledge of the position in which I really found myself.

So what exactly did I do for the Russians? In keeping with Rogov's cloak-and-dagger instructions (read and destroy), I kept no records of our meetings. There were half-a-dozen – perhaps as many as eight – of these contacts over a period of several months ending around the time the first atomic bomb fell on Hiroshima. I was not asked to supply any information that I personally had access to – simply because I had nothing of scientific, military or economic interest to offer. My function was that of a go-between or mailman. The Russians would tell me what they were interested in, and I would pass on the request for information to people such as Halperin and Mazerall. The information usually covered such subjects as the state of the development of radar or microwave technology and associated advances in pure science. Sometimes I would receive a reply from the Canadian scientists which I would then pass on to the Russians at the next meeting. Often, the scientists would simply say, no, they wouldn't or couldn't pass on the information – which was fine with me. There was, for example, one request for a sample of U-235, the key isotope in enriched uranium. That request fell on deaf ears.

At one point, the Russians did ask me to stay on in the Canadian Army in the hope that I would eventually rise in rank to a position in which I myself might have access to useful information. But as an aspiring writer, the idea of remaining in the military filled me with horror. I refused.

The one contribution I did make was to write a lengthy (and, in retrospect, a somewhat pompous) dissertation on the differences between our free and democratic way of life and their buttoned-down, regimented style of centralized government. No doubt, it went straight into the Soviet Embassy's official shredder.

Forty-two
Redhanded

On August 7th, I was going over the manuscript of an article entitled Science in the Peace which, as editor of Canadian Affairs, I had commissioned from Dr. Raymond Boyer, National Chairman of the Canadian Association of Scientific Workers, when the radio blared the news of the Hiroshima atom bomb. The casual theoretical explanations of atomic properties with Halperin and Rogov's interest in the uranium isotope U-235 suddenly assumed shattering significance. It must have had an equally stimulating effect on the plans of a certain cipher clerk in the Soviet embassy on Charlotte Street in Ottawa who a month later would make his famous exit with a shirtful of documents. Although formal peace was yet to come, the dropping of the two atom bombs on Japan had produced an unanticipated Japanese surrender and ushered in the atomic age. Even if Igor Gouzenko had not been under the gun of an impending recall to Moscow, someone having already arrived in June to be trained as his replacement, the uncertainties of the new era would make it imperative for him to act quickly to implement his plan to defect.

And then that bomb dropped. When Fred Rose gave me the news in September that "one of the Ruskies has flown the coop," I realized at once that life would never be the same again – not for me, not for Phyllis, not for our three-month-old daughter burbling away in her crib. Unlike Fred, who seemed unable to face the fact that he was about to be unseated as the left-wing political oracle consulted by Norman Robertson, First Secretary at the Department of External Affairs, on the hidden significance of international affairs, I clearly saw prison bars in the future, and God knows what agonies for Phyllis. Somebody who happened to have been with Fred when he got the news from the Russians told me later that he had been deeply shocked by it, paling and trembling. By the time he got around to telling me, he had regained his composure, but had swung over in the opposite direction, down-playing the development and maintaining that nothing would ever come of it. His political intuition, as it turned out, was not too far out of sync with that of Mackenzie King who was reluctant to trigger an international brouhaha. Do nothing – this was the extent of his advice.

It had been some time since I had seen Rogov, who had not kept the last appointment. In my mind, I had abandoned all contact, not without a great sense of relief, and was deep in my editorial duties at *Canadian Affairs* which had entered an exciting "planning-for-peace" phase leading, I so naively thought, to the one world of international understanding and co-operation for which we believed we had been fighting.

The pressure of work kept me often late at the office where writing, free from telephone interruptions, was easier. On one evening in October, I left the office and walked along a deserted Sparks Street towards Confederation Square. I suddenly had a feeling of being followed. I turned abruptly and walked back to a clothing store, ostensibly to look in the window. The door to the store was well set back from the sidewalk, and there, trying to hide in the alcove, were two men. When I appeared, seemingly blocking their exit, they broke cover, brushed past me and disappeared in the opposite direction at a fast clip. It was quite clear that, far from sweeping the defection under the rug, the authorities were nose down on the trail, even though the RCMP ("undereducated gumshoes" to borrow Richard Cleroux's phrase) were acting like bit players in a Peter Sellers Inspector Clouseau movie.

This incident was either not reported to Harvison or he misinterpreted it. How else could he have given himself this unwarranted pat on the back in his memoirs? "It was apparent," he wrote, ". . . that our investigators had carried out their widespread and difficult enquiries without breaking the wall of secrecy, a very creditable performance." It is probable, however, that the Russians did not admit to Fred Rose the full extent of the defection or the number and nature of the documents removed. I certainly had no idea of the magnitude of the affair until I sat opposite Harvison in that small room in the Justice Building.

The winding down of the armed services with all the problems of demobilization kept us busy at *Canadian Affairs*. I would spend weekends in Montreal happily *en famille*. As the weeks went by with no reaction from the authorities we began to think that Fred Rose's prediction was more than just wishful thinking. The unnerving thought of fighting the Japanese, for which I had volunteered, had disappeared on September 2nd with the formal Japanese surrender following the dropping of the A-bombs.

Weekdays I spent on the job in Ottawa, where Fred Poland, with the newspaperman's gregarious instincts, was never at a loss for evening diversions at the officers' club, film board showings, or elsewhere. I knew that he was acquainted with Pavlov of the Soviet embassy because he had introduced me to him somewhere or other. So when Fred proposed that we go to the Soviet embassy bash on November 7, celebrating the 28th anniversary of the revolution, I assumed he had been invited by Pavlov.

Just as we arrived and were about to join the crowd eyeing the mounds of caviar at the buffet tables we were stopped with a few others at the foot of the wide embassy staircase where a party of uniformed Soviet officials was coming down for the formal presentations.

I recognized Colonel Nicolai Zabotin, Military Attache, from his photographs – tall, charismatic. Behind him and a step above him, which still did not bring him up to Zabotin's height, came Rogov, not very military-looking even in uniform. Seeing me, he recoiled. For a moment he seemed about to go back up the stairs, but he quickly readjusted his collapsed diplomatic features and passed in front of me without a glance. He, of course, was well aware of Gouzenko's defection. Seeing me, if not cheerfully at least normally at large and taking part in a social event, must have puzzled his programmed mind and suggested God knows what horrible possibilities.

The Canadian government expelled Rogov and the other embassy personnel involved in the affair in February 1946. Rogov's boss, Colonel Nicolai Zabotin, did not wait for the expulsion order. He disappeared without notice in December 1945. As head of the enterprise it was assumed that he was liquidated. There are differing versions of how and where this took place. The true version, I am sure, is the one given to me by Fred Rose as we conversed unseen by each other through the barred windows of adjacent cells in Bordeaux jail, sharing a contraband mickey of rye, on the evening of the day he had been sentenced to six years in the penitentiary and I to three months for contempt of court.

"If it's any satisfaction to you," he said, "they shot the guy as soon as he landed at Vladivostok."

Forty-three
The Horseman

Earlier in this book, I quoted Inspector Harvison during his interrogation of me asking the question, "How could someone with your background and education get mixed up with people like this?"

I hope I have answered Harvison's question, at least as it relates to Jews and people with foreign names. But it seems that he had other questions on his mind, disturbing questions which he raised in his memoirs published years after our encounter. The lapse of time, or maybe a careless ghost-writer, may account for the factual errors in his chapter on Gouzenko. I can best deal with these in a review I wrote of his book *The Horsemen*:

Book Review

Clifford W. Harvison retired from the RCMP as Commissioner in 1963, but continued to act as a consultant on security matters to industry and governments. He died in 1968, but not before completing his memoirs, published under the title The Horsemen. In this candid and revealing work he makes clear the enormous gulf in thinking that yawned between us and his puzzlement over what makes people who have the background and education to "take advantage" of society choose instead to cock their snoots at established authority.

Harvison had no higher education except police training and indoctrination. There is no mention of any contact with or interest in literature, music or the arts. While still at school he dreamed of joining his older brother in the trenches of World War I and coming home covered with medals and glory to join the Royal North West Mounted Police. His home environment sounds somewhat jingoistic by today's standards: his father, an Englishman, was a lifelong feisty defender of Empire, Military Glory, King, Flag and Country. There was also a wandering uncle of undefined affiliation who breezed in from time to time with stimulating tales of "bringing a quick end to over-exuberant disturbances." This was the ground from which Harvison sprouted.

As it turned out, he did not get to go to World War I which ended before he was old enough to enlist. He saw the signs of hard times to come. He left school to take odd jobs, recognizing that the pay was poor and the hours long because "the unions were not yet strong enough to correct these conditions." These glimmerings of independent social awareness were quickly extinguished, however. In October 1919 at the age of 19 he was provisionally accepted by the Royal North West Mounted Police, the last recruit to join before the force became the Royal Canadian Mounted Police.

There followed three months of harsh boot camp training with the emphasis on riot control. Horses and riders were relentlessly programmed to ride into "mobs" and to ignore every diversion including gunshots. The government, he tells us, was acutely concerned with the threat of riots and disturbances, hence the training was more like that of a cavalry unit to be used as reserves when and if the local police could not keep the peace and maintain order.

The government had good reason to be concerned. Troops were coming home at the rate of thousands a month to face rising unemployment, with wages for the lucky ones of only twelve or fifteen dollars a week at a time when the money would buy less than half what it had bought before the war. Furthermore, the success of the Russian revolution was clearly giving food for thought to the labour movement.

Against this background, Harvison's training was especially rigorous because a few months earlier the Royal North West Mounted Police had been called on to break the Winnipeg General Strike. This strike, which started on May 15th, 1919, had such overwhelming support – 11,000 workers voting in favour to only 500 against – that even the Winnipeg police had voted to strike although they were ordered by the strike committee to stay on the job. The authorities had planned to use returned soldiers as strike breakers but had badly miscalculated; a majority of the veterans instead of condemning the strike adopted a resolution declaring full sympathy with the strikers and their two main objectives, namely, the right of collective bargaining and a living wage. The impasse was resolved on Bloody Sunday, June 21st, when the RNWMP, supported by a handful of "Specials" galloped on horseback into the crowd on Winnipeg Avenue, flailing baseball bats. They then reformed ranks and rode back, firing three volleys of revolver shots into the crowd, killing two people and wounding at least thirty.

Far from being bearded, bomb-throwing Bolsheviks, the strike leaders – Russell, Johns, Armstrong, Pritchard, Heaps – grew up in the tradition of British socialism and were acknowledged, even by the "concerned" authorities, to have done their utmost to uphold discipline amongst the strikers and to prevent violence. The violence, many who were there said, was provoked by the police themselves.

Whatever hindsight might conclude about the merits of the strike, Harvison tells us that the prevailing view of the authorities at the time was that it and similar eruptions of labour unrest were the products of the seditious plotting of foreign agitators. The sheer number of strikers was seen not as the expression of legitimate grievances but rather as proof of how dangerously influential "revolutionary" leaders had become. Harvison successfully absorbed this indoctrination – what he would term "brain-washing" when writing about communists – and won the right to wear the coveted red serge.

Describing his long and distinguished career, much of it spent in so-called anti-subversive activities, he never once refers to the intervention of the (so aptly-named) Force against strikers, demonstrators or protest marchers – no fractured skulls, no bloodied faces, no trampled children, no corpses. Any such use of the Force, he hints, was a sacred obligation to combat the seditious plotting of a handful of Russian-trained reds. Even his distaste for foreign-sounding names can perhaps be traced to these early days. The Mounties arrested the entire Winnipeg strike leadership in the early hours of June 17th, 1919, later releasing all but the four who happened to have non-Anglo-Saxon names – Charitonoff, Almazoff, Devyatken and Schoppelrel.

Even allowing that Harvison acted professionally and properly in the Gouzenko affair, simply taking advantage of the much expanded mandate which the government had bestowed on him, his memoirs still raise disturbing questions about how the police see themselves in relation to society and how they interpret their function in a democracy. He struggles with himself to understand the motivation of otherwise intelligent people to submit to "brainwashing" in communist cells and the abandoning of "normal codes of honour and decency." He suggests that coming to independent conclusions that conflict with those of the authorities is simply "arrogant." (He cannot have heard of Peter Abelard, an eleventh century subversive, who declared: "Constant questioning is the first key to wisdom. For through doubt we are led to enquiry, and by enquiry we discern the truth.") He appears not to have understood that simply by opening their eyes people might independently conclude that child labour was evil, certain industrial employment conditions were unsafe or unhealthy, that workers who felt themselves to be exploited could try to solve their problems without waiting for a local Lenin to lead them to the promised land – just as honest humans in previous generations had objected to hanging children for theft, jailing people for debt, keeping slaves, or denying the vote to women, all of which had had the hearty approval of the authorities of the times.

And what constitutes "a normal code of honour and decency?" One of his actions while he was top man in British Columbia raises doubts about his competence to judge. Jack Ralph in 1945 was Director of Distribution for the National Film Board under John Grierson. Although never charged with any offence, he was guilty, in the eyes of the witch hunters, merely by association with this alleged hotbed of radicals, and perhaps also by the fact that he was a friend of Fred Poland and of me and lived in the same building in Ottawa.

In any event he was fired and blacklisted just like the victims of McCarthy in the U.S. He and his wife Isabel moved to England where their talents and experience were soon rewarded. Jack found a job organizing the film section of the Festival of Britain in 1951; Isabel went to work for a government agency, The Central Office of Information. In 1952, Jack was invested by the King with the MBE (Member of the Order of the British Empire) in recognition of outstanding services. Isabel was not so lucky. The RCMP interceded with her boss, a confirmed red-baiter, and she was summarily fired. Her marriage having broken up, she returned to her original home in British Columbia where she was qualified as a teacher. Her first job was in a mining town high in the Selkirk Mountains. Social and living conditions were so bad that previous incumbents had all fled one after another in disgust. Isabel was welcomed as a saviour. Ah, but remote as the place was, it was not beyond the reach of Harvison who was now the Force's top man in British Columbia. Isabel suddenly found herself ostracized. Backs were turned on her in the street. The District Inspector of Schools appeared out of nowhere to pass judgment on her competence to teach. The upshot in Isabel's own words: "He came to my class three times in that last term. He was a Conservative, an austere, exacting man who later became the Chief Inspector for the whole province. But he recognized persecution when he saw it. He gave me an excellent report which I used to get myself a permanent position in Burnaby. Help, I discovered sometimes comes in the most unexpected disguise."

As might be expected, Harvison's recollection of my interrogation differed from mine. He seems to have rated the behaviour of the detainees, like Shugar, who almost literally spat in his eye as normal – exactly what he would have expected of brain-washed Bolsheviks. He rated my performance as the act of someone with a "martyr complex."

"So you know what to do?" he asked at the end of the last session.

I replied: "You don't have to worry about me. I know how to handle myself."

I was talking to myself as much as to him, steeling myself to "face the music," "not let the side down" and "give a good account of myself." He apparently interpreted my words to mean that I was bent on self-immolation. His psychological expertise, of which he was so proud, had failed to suggest to him that I might be ready to acknowledge overwhelming evidence against me without necessarily playing his game by bearing witness against others.

As it turned out, I "declined" to testify, as I euphemistically put it, many times in at least three trials and had a year added to my five-year penitentiary sentence for contempt of court (not three times three months plus six years as erroneously reported by him) in addition to the three months served in Bordeaux Jail. These refusals to testify, Harvison assumed, were made under pressure and only confirmed Harvison's opinion that I was "burdened with a martyr complex – an urge towards self-destruction in the fight for some lost cause."

Either he had his tongue in his cheek or was being obtuse when he called the complaints about the conditions of detention in RCMP Rockcliffe Barracks "fantastic." Why, he asks disingenuously, should anyone complain about comfortable rooms and good and plentiful food prepared by nutritionists? The commissioners tried to help the RCMP out by throwing in an aside in their report to the effect that none of the accused had complained to them about the conditions of their detention in the Rockcliffe barracks – but without adding that they brushed aside any reference to what had gone on before as having nothing whatsoever to do with them. Harvison's son, Wes, with whom be admits he shared information, probably in contravention of his oath of office, came back to it later in an interview reported by John Sawatsky in Gouzenko, The Untold Story. Both father and son ignored the real reason for the complaints – the bright lights twenty-four hours a day, flashlight arousals from sleep and, above all, the refusal of this four-star hotel to allow its guests contact with wives and lawyers. He expresses indignation at what he calls the "rape-of-justice" sensationalism of the "legitimate press" – as distinct, one assumes, from the illegitimate press, whoever they may be.

The inspector is delicately selective in his memoirs. He mauls "gross, tough and unscrupulous" labour leader Hal Banks, but in describing the famous Munsinger sex scandal case, he carefully avoids naming the central figure, Associate Minister of National Defence, Pierre Sevigny, without whose involvement it would have been just a routine police court story.

Harrison defends the sharing of information with allies as long as they are "friendly." This includes, one gathers, giving lengthy lists of so-called subversives, based on hearsay and unsubstantiated information, to the FBI. These lists, it turned out, fingered many citizens, even MPs, whose crimes had been to dissent from established, right-wing or police-approved positions, had exercised their right of freedom of speech to read left-wing journals or had had the effrontery to work too zealously for world peace or ecological sanity. Later, at the insistence of the Americans, the "subversive" list was expanded to include academics, homosexuals, feminists, students, blacks and aboriginals. Harvison could not write about his own enthusiastic campaign against homosexuals – practising criminals in his judgment – because the campaign was still under wraps.

Harvison discusses crime and police methods at some length. Writing in the sixties, he deplores the falling off of respect for the police. But did he think that only striking workers on picket lines object to unnecessary police violence, racism, unprovoked shootings of blacks and native Canadians, the tendency of the police to close ranks, cover up, commit perjury and "lose" embarrassing or compromising files to avoid public disclosure and responsibility?

To remedy the situation, Harvison calls for still stricter police action and the granting of a freer rein to the police. He recommends forcing accused persons to testify, and to make wire-tapping, interference with the mails, electronic eavesdropping and entrapment routine investigatory tools.

On reading these observations in *The Horsemen* I was reminded of an incident in the Black Maria transporting prisoners from Bordeaux Jail to the Montreal courts in 1946. I was handcuffed to Gerson, another of the accused, and we were talking about the case. A man in the seat ahead twisted around to look at us.

"You sons of bitches," he said. "The cops grabbed me off the street in Ottawa and I was sloughed up in a house somewhere for two days. Bastards beat the shit out of me...thought I was one of you guys. Assholes...they didn't even apologize." Although his language was violent, he was not really mad at us. He seemed to find it quite normal that police would act like that.

Forty-four
Established Authority

What Harvison liked to call brainwashing began when I attended lectures, quite voluntarily, by Communist leaders Stanley Ryerson, Emery Samuel and, occasionally, Sam Carr, and did some of the recommended reading. Harvison probably knew about these because they were sometimes held at 3610 Oxenden which I later learned he had been keeping an eye on. He probably had a stool-pigeon in the audience.

As a newcomer to Canada who knew very little about Canadian history, I was astonished to learn about the foundation of thievery and brutality on which the great Canadian institutions like the Hudson's Bay Company and the railroads had been erected. I have no idea what history Harvison was taught at police school at Regina, other than the history of the Force. It seems quite likely that very little was said about the larcenous background of the power structure which the Force serves. In any case, he would probably say, with justification, that my version of history and his are at odds. As Mark Twain said, the ink of history is "fluid prejudice."

For example, Carl Wittke in *A History of Canada* included four brief references to Donald A. Smith in its four-hundred-odd pages, and praised him as a "dauntless spirit." Gustavus Myers who wrote "to invest the past with the colour of legitimacy is a marked characteristic of conventional history" sees it differently. His more searching reading of the record revealed to me the truth, or as close to it as one is likely to come, so long as one does not flaunt the flag like a matador to turn aside harmlessly the horned reality. In his book *The History of Canadian Wealth* Myers records in depressing detail how the same Donald A. Smith was one of a handful of colonizing entrepreneurs who expropriated Canada's natural riches for their own profit. The story is one of fraud, deceit, brutal exploitation of aboriginals, settlers and labourers, and theft from the public purse. It would be difficult to credit were it not for the painstaking documentation through references to debates in the House of Commons, Select Committee reports, trial transcripts, Royal Commission reports, contemporary newspaper editorials, biographies and memoirs of participants.

Myers tells how Smith, a young Scottish immigrant, started with the Hudson's Bay Company in 1838, rose to become Chief Executive Officer, spread out into banking, land, mines, forests and railroads (he hammered in the famous last spike of the trans-Canada railway) and wound up as Canada's wealthiest capitalist, heaped with honours and raised to the peerage as 1st Baron Strathcona and Mount Royal. It was to serve the interests of Smith and his associates as they expanded their activities westwards that the mounted police organization was formed. Naturally, people were not always pleased to be exploited, shoved aside or expropriated for the profit of Smith and friends, so persuasion was sometimes needed.

While this grand larceny which put the public in debt for generations was proceeding unchecked, petty theft, sacrilege and insubordination by the lower orders were punished with barbaric cruelty. In 1849, a year in which the future Lord Strathcona was hitting his stride, ten-year-old Peter Charbonneau, serving seven years in Kingston Penitentiary, was lashed fifty-seven times in eight-and-a-half months for offences such as staring, winking and laughing; Alec Lafleur, eleven years old, was given the lash on Christmas Eve 1844 for speaking French; twelve-year-old Elizabeth Breen was flogged five times in four months. An element of chivalry could be discerned – for an offence for which a man might receive fifty lashes on the bare back, a woman received only twenty-five.

Much of Parliament's time in the late nineteenth and early twentieth centuries was spent attacking or defending the shady dealings, pork-barrelling, nepotism and influence peddling of Strathcona, his cousin George Stephen and most of the prominent members of the entrepreneurial *élite*, depending on whether or not they shared in the spoils. In 1886 during a speech in the House of Commons, MP John Charlton described the group as "plunderers gathered to the prey…In secret an empire has been bartered away." By 1891 it had become a national scandal, triggering that good Canadian reaction: a royal commission. The results brought international dishonour on Canada.

The *London Despatch* commented: "Yes, some have been punished – the small fry who were not in a position to steal much. But the conspicuous thieves…where are they? Living on their stealings, some of them even blazing with decorations bestowed upon them by the Queen – quite comfortably either in Canada or the United States."

Were these the people whose concepts of "loyalty, honour and decency" we are to emulate? Of course, all this was a long time ago; things are different today. They have indeed improved, thanks to a more sophisticated public and more open media which make secret dealings and cover-ups more difficult to conceal. But contemporary "established authority" had little to do with the improvement. The police, hangmen and jailers of the times went about their jobs uncomplainingly, even enthusiastically. The improvement in social conditions we enjoy was not brought about by them, but by people who "knew better" – dissenters from established authority, readers of the illegitimate as well as of the legitimate press. These were social sins in Harvison's eyes.

I was not in Canada during the worst days of the Depression but I soon learned about it, not from communists but from people who had survived its most bitter times, the starvation, the hopelessness, the humiliation of begging to feed their children and, in some cases, the bullets and billies to the skull the police dutifully dealt out. The inspector, on the other hand, believed that anyone who was lucky enough to have escaped such hardships by virtue of education, social status, employment or whatever should ignore the alleged injustices to the less fortunate and "take advantage" of their privileged position. For my part, my reading of Canadian history, considered in the context of Section 98 and the Padlock Law, merely confirmed my skepticism about "established authority."

It is, of course, the obligation – the *raison d'être* – of the police to stand up for "established authority," which usually does know best how to protect its interest, even when that may conflict with the interests of society at large. The question is: To what extent does class or political bias, greed or compulsive fear, not to mention stupidity, cloud the authorities' observation and dictate their strategy?

Established authority found much to admire in the methods of Mussolini and Hitler, especially in their methods of dealing with upstart labour. Rt. Hon. Lord Lloyd, a British Foreign Office spokesman who articulated Tory attitudes in the years leading up to Munich, was another authoritative voice it were better to ignore. An admirer of the "wise" Portuguese dictator Salazar and of Mussolini whose "genius" had created the Italian fascist system, Lord Lloyd praised the two rocks on which it was founded: one, getting religion out of politics, which should not be concerned with morals; and, two, bringing labour into line by a code based on the fascist Italian Labour Charter. Mackenzie King consulted his late mother and his dog on matters of state. The list is endless.

Viscount Rothermere, proprietor of the mass circulation British newspaper, the *Daily Mail*, presumably qualifies as "established authority." Although not an elected official (but then neither were Sir Nevile Henderson, Lord Lloyd or Lord Halifax) he poured out political advice to the government, all the more effective for its inspired yellow-press rhetoric. Rothermere supported "the necessary repressive measures of fascism." In his opinion Czechoslovakia had a "baleful and fraudulent existence." The Czechs themselves were "a race notorious for petty meanness," a description similar to that of Hitler, his friend and pen pal, who called the Czechs "a miserable pygmy race." The League of Nations was "a truncated and perverted instrument"; collective security "a myth." Rothermere was especially enthusiastic about the Nazi Labour Camps that provided young men with "the finest imaginable physical and social discipline." Our own General A.G.L. McNaughton, Canadian Chief of Staff, was already ahead of him in 1932 when he herded single unemployed men during the Depression into remote labour camps.

Even British Intelligence could make mistakes. It was convinced Hitler would attack Hungary, not Holland. The military variety of "established authority" is replete with disasters throughout history. Thousands of Americans were slaughtered on the beach on D-Day following the Omaha landing in Normandy when the supporting naval force mistakenly moved east instead of west and was hours late in supplying the supporting bombardment. The slaughter of British troops at Arnheim need not have taken place if Field Marshall Bernard Montgomery had listened to Dutch underground leader Marinus Kelkman on the strength of German panzer forces instead of ignoring him. The Hong Kong garrison in 1941 was abandoned to fight a hopeless action and kept deliberately unaware that a British signal denying them the needed reinforcements had fallen into Japanese hands. Chief Justice of the Supreme Court of Canada Sir Lyman Duff concluded that the action was "neither ill-conceived nor badly managed" and Canada should be proud of it. This helped Mackenzie King, but what did it do for "established authority"?

Churchill himself – according to his principal private secretary and close confidant, John Colville – said in June 1941 that a German attack on Russia was certain and that Russia would assuredly be defeated, proving that established authority can be both right and wrong within the space of a few words.

This helps to explain why some individuals, myself included, would have the effrontery to gainsay these sacred cows, to see past the striped pants, winged collars, top hats, braid, blinkers and brass buttons to the moral and intellectual poverty beneath.

PART THREE
FROM ALLY TO ENEMY

Forty-five
The Corby Papers

We still do not know in detail what went on in the weeks between September 5, 1945 when Igor Gouzenko walked out of the Soviet Embassy in Ottawa, and the following February 15 when the first arrests were made. For an important part of this time, from November 10 to December 31, entries in King's diary are missing. This is the only period of comparable length and importance for which his musings and confidences are not on public record.

We do know, however, that the British and Americans were drawn into the investigation from the start. In fact, since the RCMP were out of their depth, it was the British who master-minded the initial investigation. Two British intelligence experts were sent to Ottawa to work with Norman Robertson and Hume Wrong of the Department of External Affairs on "the Corby Case" – so-called because the Gouzenko documents were kept in a Corby whisky carton in Robertson's office. We know that King travelled to Washington and then to London in connection with the case. King went to Washington on September 30 to give Truman the news. Truman apparently showed little surprise. A week earlier there had been a meeting of his cabinet to discuss White House recommendations to Congress on the atom bomb. The *Ottawa Citizen* Washington correspondent reported that it had "seeped out" that Secretary of State Henry Wallace had argued in favour of the bomb secret being given to Britain, Canada and Russia, and had received some support for the idea. Secretary of War Henry Lewis Stimson favoured letting the United Nations handle the matter. The U.S. Army and Navy, as might be expected, were against sharing. In England, Sir Stafford Cripps had been even more emphatic on the need to share: "It is idle to imagine that the atom bomb could be preserved as a secret. It is not only the best policy to try and avoid war…it is absolutely vital and essential that we should not allow this new form of destruction to be let loose on the world." Perhaps as a result of the cabinet meeting, there was no "precious secret" as far as Truman was concerned.

Truman must also have been aware that scientists were in almost unanimous agreement that atomic weapons must be controlled by a world authority. Sir James Chadwick, one of the bomb's distinguished midwives, told a Washington news conference that many of his own people had been unwilling to work on the bomb for fear they might be creating a planet-destroying monster. On October 17, Dr. Robert Oppenheimer, testifying before Congress, made an eloquent plea for international control: "Six years ago the development of the bomb was considered visionary – why can't we apply the same effort to bring about a similar miracle for world peace?" Failure to do this, the Association of Los Alamos Scientists warned, "will lead to an unending war more savage than the last."

As a result of their discussions, King agreed with Truman that Canada, the U.S. and the U.K. should take united action on the Gouzenko affair. While in Washington, King also had an interview with British Ambassador Lord Halifax which became the subject of a testy diary entry. Halifax had seated King with the sun in his eyes while his own face was in shadow.

King's next stop was London, where his discussions with Prime Minister Clement Attlee took place against a backdrop of growing conflict between East and West. Tiffs were erupting in the allied love-in. While bickering over procedure at a Big Five parley of foreign ministers, Ernie Bevan of Britain had accused the Soviet's Molotov of "Hitlerism." Bitterness and anger prevailed. Other indications of changing attitudes on both sides of the Atlantic were beginning to appear. General George Marshall hinted that helping the Russians had been only one reason for opening a second front; the other was to defeat Germany before she got the atom bomb. As the love affair cooled, Anthony Eden wondered publicly whether there had ever been any fundamental unity between the Allies.

During this difficult time for the aging Mackenzie King he repeatedly confided his misgivings to his diary.

"I doubt the wisdom of attempting any general enquiry by a royal commission until we get some evidence other than that of Gouzenko's," he wrote on October 22nd. (The setting up of a royal commission had been proposed by E.K. Williams, who was to become its chief counsel.)

Harvison could not resist taking a swipe at the Prime Minister in his memoirs when he accused him of having no stomach for pursuing the case. In his opinion, Mackenzie King cared only about his retirement and his place in history. It is true that more than once King mentioned his fear of trouble with the Russians and he appeared to think that they were poised ready to swarm across Canadian territory to get at the Americans.

While King was still in London he read Truman's Navy Day speech of October 27th. This was the new president's first major speech to the American people and came like a bucket of ice water in the face to anyone who still believed in peacetime allied solidarity. Truman threw out all the high-minded concepts of Franklin D. Roosevelt as embodied in the Teheran and Yalta accords, and confirmed by Truman himself the previous August at Potsdam. In its place he proposed to substitute the world leadership of the United States, with sole possession of the "atomic secret." The only human being to press the dreaded "A" button – not once but twice, wiping out 126,000 souls – had now decided that he would not share this powerful political "hammer," as he is reported to have called it, and certainly not with the Russians. He repudiated existing agreements on the grounds that "after past wars, the unity among allies, forged by their common peril, has tended to wear out as the danger passed."

This theme of ally-into-enemy was to be repeated often during the next months after the Gouzenko affair became public knowledge. The first trial – that of Alan Nunn May – took place in England, not in Canada. The charge was breaching the Official Secrets Act in a manner "which was calculated to be or might be directly or indirectly useful to an enemy." And the Crown Prosecutor won a ruling from the bench that the state involved (the USSR) might well be a potential enemy. Similarly at the trial of Fred Rose in Canada, Crown Prosecutor Philippe Brais parried any talk of allies with the statement "History has shown that allies of yesterday have often become the enemies of tomorrow." Yes, especially when a plan is unfolding to make them so. At the appeal hearing of Mazerall, another of the accused, Justice Laidlaw asked Crown Prosecutor Cartwright what made it prejudicial to the state to communicate information to Russia, considering the Soviet Union was an ally. Chief Justice Robertson went further: "It is the best thing in the world to keep Russia advised of what we are doing over here – secret or otherwise. What must be decided is, was Mazerall's purpose...a prejudicial purpose." It then boiled down to legal hair splitting.

Less than two weeks after his Navy Day speech, Truman met in Washington with Attlee and King to agree on a united front. As far as the atomic bomb question was concerned, a joint statement of the three heads of government, as distinct from the governments themselves, bought time by shunting it to a UN commission. King returned to Ottawa so buoyed up that he made the diary entry: "There is no doubt that my association with these men and the atomic bomb problem has given me a place in world recognition that even years of war themselves did not begin to give." It was certainly a more macho role than choreographing a conscription pas de deux.

Forty-six
The Fulton Declaration

It is not hard to piece together the script which emerged from all these comings and goings during the five months preceding February 4, the date on which leaked information by US radio commentator Drew Pearson to the American public forced King's hand into ordering the arrests of twelve suspects a few days later. From the day the case broke, the media emphasis was on the atomic bomb. "Ottawa Hints A-Bomb Data Was Chief Aim of Plotters" was the headline to an early Montreal Star report. At a time when the Royal Commission was being conspicuously tight-lipped with information, and thereby contributing to wild press speculation, American media were already reporting "authoritative" news about an alleged atom bomb plot. The New York Times, even before the Royal Commission had issued a single report, informed its readers that Soviet agents in Canada had been told to put special emphasis on the atomic bomb. This had no foundation, as King admitted in the House of Commons on March 18, and this was further acknowledged in the Commission's final report which stated: "No one in Canada could have revealed how to make an atomic bomb…there is no suggestion in the evidence that anyone who had any information on the subject made any disclosures."

The situation was analogous to a front-page report of an archbishop being caught in bed with a well-known prostitute followed two months later by a four-line denial on page 48. But it served a useful purpose in preparing the public for a major switch of policy, shortly to become known as the Cold War. Peace is bad for business, especially defence business. As the war had progressed towards certain victory, war production had started to decline. Peace loomed – with all its problems of unemployment, raised expectations amongst the electorate and a probable recession. It should have come as no shock to those like myself who were caught up in the euphoria of post-war "One World" expectations that our one-time friend and ally should suddenly become a dangerous enemy. We had seen enough hostility to the Russians even at the height of the war when they were being killed in their millions in the common cause. But I was shocked nevertheless, and still unaware of Stalin's share of responsibility for the ensuing Cold War.

The new Allied policy was officially launched by Winston Churchill with his famous Iron Curtain speech at Fulton, Missouri, with President Truman present, on March 5th, 1946 – one day after I first appeared in court; while eight so-called atom spies were still being held incommunicado in the RCMP Rockcliffe Barracks; and almost two weeks before the Canadian government admitted that the atom bomb plot had no foundation in fact.

The Cold War strategy had been in gestation for a long time before the Fulton speech. The spy case dropped out of the blue as an unbelievable piece of good luck. It seems likely that the Fulton speech was timed to coincide with it and was cleverly orchestrated to have the maximum synergistic effect – the one boosting the other in producing the climate of fear and suspicion which would lead to McCarthyism and all the Cold War obscenities to come.

Forty-seven
The Billiard Ball Gambit

It was not until many years later, after the publication of the books, memoirs and diaries of some of the key government figures, that the curtain was lifted on the bickering and nail-biting that had been going on behind the scenes in Ottawa. Hard-liners like Harvison (egged on, no doubt, by the FBI and Britain's MI5) quickly took advantage of the plum that had dropped so unexpectedly into their laps. Between September

1945, when Gouzenko had flown the coop, and the public announcement of the Royal Commission in February 1946, they had plenty of time to plan their strategy.

This strategy was based on the principle of three billiard balls – the police, the Royal Commission and the courts. When these balls are lined up, the energy delivered to the cue ball is transmitted to the second ball and so on down the line. Of course, to make this work, you have to make sure that nothing prevents a ball from being well and truly struck and that nothing gets in its path towards the next ball. Hence the elaborate provisions of the two orders-in-council – one on October 6th, 1945, empowering the police to arrest, interrogate and detain suspects incommunicado in such place and under such conditions as they chose, and making it all legal; another on February 5th, 1946, setting up the Royal Commission with the power to require witnesses to give evidence under oath without being obliged to read their depositions back to them, and giving the commissioners virtually unlimited latitude to conduct themselves in whatsoever manner they chose. And they chose not to be too choosy.

Minister of Justice Louis St. Laurent, sharing the militantly anti-communist attitude of his peers including Quebec Premier Maurice Duplessis and Cardinal Villeneuve was a reliable ally. Prime Minister Mackenzie King, on the other hand, dithered from the outset. Even though he was a hostage to the French-Canadian electorate, his political intuition kept jabbing at him. On September 24th, 1945, he mused in his diary about the large numbers of men and women who "have their hand out against society as it is constructed today, whereby there are certain leisure classes too largely controlling the government and industry, and a readiness to go any lengths in gaining for working men and women the fullest opportunities possible." Not unexpectedly, he displays some political insight. One even detects a vein of sympathy running through the hard-rock pragmatism.

When the story broke on February 15th, 1946, within hours of the anticipated arrests he wrote: "I can see where a great cry will be raised, having had a Commission sit in secret, and men and women arrested and detained under an Order-in-Council passed really under War Measures powers. I will be held up to the world as the very opposite of a democrat." He was agonizing more over the probable damage to his reputation than any breach of civil liberties.

Four days later, after the world press had praised "the initiative and courage of Canada," King's spirits surged upwards. He confided to his diary: "…few more courageous acts have ever been performed by leaders of the government than my own in the Russian intrigue against the

Christian world..." As his diaries show, in politics as in his youthful whoring, King's Christian conscience kicked in only after the event.

The RCMP had planned to make the initial arrests in dramatic style breaking down doors at 3:00 a.m. and arresting people in their beds. This must have come to King's attention, because in his diary entry for February 15th, he records his horror and notes that this potential RCMP boo-boo had been "caught in time" and the arrests put off until 7:00 a.m. But even the change of time was not enough to prevent an embarrassing error on the part of the RCMP. In an effort to arrest Squadron Leader Fred Poland, a posse of beefy officers got the street and building number right – but broke into the wrong apartment. Thinking it was a hold-up, the innocent householder, a member of the armed forces and no pushover, stood his ground slugging away while his wife and young daughters screamed in the background.

Before it was all over, the Ottawa police had been called and RCMP Sgt. Crouch had been given a beauty of a black eye to explain to his superiors and to take to court later to the merriment of all.

Under normal legal procedures, an accused is allowed access to a lawyer and is warned that anything he says may subsequently be used in evidence against him. Habeas corpus, the most sacred symbol of protection against the abusive power of the state, gives any prisoner the right to be produced in court and formally charged within a reasonable time. The Canada Evidence Act extends protection against self-incrimination to witnesses provided they do not perjure themselves. A common thief knows all about this – but not, alas, an educated well-read thirty-year-old whose only brush with the law had been the odd traffic ticket. Of course, some inner voice whispered that such protection surely must exist. I challenged Inspector Harvison to inform me of my rights. He bluntly said I had no rights except to answer questions.

The unprecedented decision to wipe out by order-in-council all the legal and constitutional safeguards against abuse of accused persons by the authorities was carefully planned. It included suspension of habeas corpus, the banning of access to lawyers, and of visits from wives or next-of-kin. This was calculated to obtain evidence that the authorities knew they would be unlikely to get if the accused had access to legal advice. Arnold Smith of External Affairs, who had a big hand in the legal conspiracy, said later that you had to admit it worked because when King bowed to pressure and, over his and the commissioners' protests, relented and allowed access to wives and lawyers, nobody else gave testimony and the commission was foiled.

Jack Pickersgill, who had been close to Mackenzie King throughout his public service career, admitted to second thoughts in retrospect about the refusal to allow lawyers, and thought it was the biggest mistake the King government ever made. The Hon. E. Davie Fulton, a former Tory cabinet minister, deplored that the government had been guilty of conduct that allowed people to point their fingers. Mackenzie King himself repeatedly agonized over the matter, not so much over abstract questions of justice and civil rights but rather over what it might do to his reputation and that of the Liberal Party.

Notwithstanding the fact that an air of great secrecy had been built up, the newspapers were full of allegations and speculation. These were couched in the usual passive tense with evasive attribution – "Those close to the investigation..." "Authoritative sources report..." "While the authorities are playing their cards close to their chests, it is believed that..."

The leaked information on which these stories were based could only have come from the officially tight-lipped authorities themselves in an effort to whip up a public hysteria to justify their unorthodox methods. In the absence of any hard facts about the alleged offences, the newspapers were free to speculate to their heart's content. On February 23rd the Montreal Star published an article by James A. Oastler under the front-page banner heading: "Treason Trials Loom For Accused Spies" with complete disregard for legal distinctions between enemies, allies or friendly powers. In fact, no treasonable actions were ever committed or charged, the offences all falling within the shadowy limits of the Official Secrets Act. The Montreal Star editors must have had misgivings about their headline because in the same issue they published an editorial urging readers to reserve judgment on the question of treason – a good example of having your cake and eating it, too. The technique was evidently working. On February 27th the paper reported that the RCMP were pleased with the public's cooperation. Citizens had been swamping them with phone calls reporting "suspicious" movements in their neighbourhoods to such an extent that officers had to be diverted from regular duties to investigate all the "tips" and reports.

While this atmosphere of secrecy and intrigue succeeded to some extent, it also made the press and the public impatient for the dénouement, and it allowed time for growing criticism, initially from the legal profession. The first lawyers to be hired, presumably by wives or friends of the accused, tried unsuccessfully to reach their clients on February 20th, as soon as they had figured out what had happened. They were told their clients could be held as long as federal authorities saw fit without recourse to the law. But, not to worry, they were told – "Your client is quite comfortable."

On February 25th, lawyer H. P. Hill of Ottawa, retained by the families of two of the detainees, was barred from access to his clients. In a statement to the press he said that there could be only two reasons for "such an extraordinary limitation on the principles of British justice" – (a) that the commissioners didn't want the detainees to have access to any legal instructions that might lead to their release, or (b) that the commissioners do not trust members of the local bar to keep their mouths shut. "The first of these reasons is a sad commentary on the way in which our individual liberties are gradually being encroached upon. The second reason betrays a disturbing lack of confidence in the legal profession in which the public must have confidence if our system of justice is to be maintained..."

A few days later, R. M. Willes Chitty KC, chairman of the Ontario Civil Liberties sub-committee of the Canadian Bar Association, termed the barring of lawyers "a disgraceful infringement of civil liberties." He said that the right of a man to obtain legal advice was granted at the signing of the Magna Carta and charged that the British North America Act was being violated by the government of Canada "for its own ends."

The wife of one of the detainees threw a stick on the fire on February 27th by making public the text of a stinging letter she had written to Mackenzie King which ended with the words: "I cannot see why Canada cannot deal with any situation that arises through her established democratic procedures without borrowing methods from the Gestapo." She complained that she had received no acknowledgment of the letter. King told the press that he had immediately turned it over to the Justice Department Apparently, department officials ignored it just as they had ignored every other request for information on her husband's whereabouts. King's inner thoughts were reserved for his diary: "I said I thought it was wrong that those who are suspected should be detained indefinitely and that some way should be found to shorten the enquiry and give them the full rights of protection which the law allows them."

Perhaps in response to the bad press this was creating, some wives were allowed to visit on March 5th, three weeks after the arrests. They were made to take an oath not to say a word about what they had seen or heard inside the barracks. However, visits were soon banned again on the grounds that some of the wives had not honoured their oaths of silence.

The lawyers now began to turn to writs of habeas corpus, the time-honoured safeguard against abuse of state power. The problem was: How do you get your client's agreement to such an important procedure if you can't even reach him on the telephone? A.W. Beament KC, acting for one of the detainees, wrote a letter to his client asking him to send him instructions via his wife who had been allowed to visit. The RCMP refused to deliver the letter. Beament protested to F. P. Varcoe, Deputy Minister of Justice. "...the refusal of the authorities to deliver this letter," he wrote, "and thus to prevent my client from giving me any instructions is simply a further denial of the most elementary right to justice." He got no reply.

Two other detainees tried the habeas corpus route. Squadron Leader Poland petitioned the court that his interrogation had finished, that he had not been allowed to see counsel and that further detention was unnecessary. Israel Halperin, another of the accused, also applied for a writ. This one was granted, probably as the result of a searing letter of protest he wrote to John Bracken, Leader of the Opposition, which was made public. Both men had been held incommunicado for well over a month. The granting of these writs was at best a face-saving device, since before the writs could have had any effect, and before their trials, both men were publicly declared guilty. It was during Poland's habeas corpus proceeding that another little game of the authorities was exposed. Each of the players – the Justice Department, the RCMP and the Royal Commission – took the position that it had nothing to do with the others. It was as though they did not exist. When Poland wrote to the RCMP brass from Rockcliffe Barracks complaining about being held incommunicado, Assistant Commissioner Gagnon dutifully replied in a letter to Poland. But this was never delivered; either the Royal Commissioners or their counsel gave orders for it to be withheld.

In spite of these goings-on, St. Laurent when fencing with critics in the House of Commons over the suspension of traditional civil rights blandly stated that the detained persons had access to habeas corpus had they wished, but he could not explain how persons held incommunicado could be expected to exercise this right, nor why, when they later were able to, the Crown should go to great lengths to obstruct the process.

Apart from brief reports of these habeas corpus proceedings, the press had very little to say about them. Not so Opposition Leader John Diefenbaker. "Suspects [are] entitled to be tried by law and not by administrative lawlessness," he thundered in the House on March 21st. "Magna Carta is part of our birthright. Habeas Corpus, the Bill of Rights, the petition of right, all are part of our tradition." Harvison thought this kind of talk was "rape-of-justice" sensationalism.

Nobody had foreseen the stubborn, intractable behaviour of some of the detainees who refused to be turned into billiard balls. Of these, Dr. David Shugar proved to be more than a match for the RCMP and the commissioners. For twenty-eight days Shugar challenged at every turn their legal right to detain him, even going on a four-day hunger strike to protest the refusal of the RCMP to allow his wife to visit him. For two weeks he was kept under constant guard in a small, stiflingly hot room in which a naked 200-watt bulb burned continuously. When he was eventually brought to court, he described the conditions of his incarceration as "not, in my opinion, any veiled or light form of the third degree." His ordeal cannot have been made any easier by the anti-Semitism of the RCMP, as expressed to me by Harvison and to Nightingale by Harvison's partner, Inspector M. F. Anthony, who told Nightingale, another of the accused, it was his duty to send those damned Jews back where they came from.

Criticism was coming not only from the people directly concerned. Joseph E. Davies, former United States Ambassador to Russia, tried to calm the hysteria and warned against the "present chaotic mistrust." The alternative, he said, will be "a gigantic race in armament factories and laboratories resulting in totally destructive war." He was right, of course, about the armaments race, which proved to be a bonanza for the military/industrial complex.

On the same day the media reported a statement by the Ottawa branch of the Canadian Association of Scientific Workers accusing the government of attempting to create an atmosphere of mistrust and hysteria. "We do not defend individuals who have knowingly provided unauthorized information to any foreign power. However, the entire incident is further proof of the validity of the Association's stand condemning the present secrecy between nations regarding scientific discoveries."

On February 26th, Stanley Knowles, CCF member of parliament, who had recently been in Moscow, tried to put in a moderating word by saying that he felt that the Russian people basically sought peace and, while an effort was required to achieve it, mutual understanding was possible.

On March 2nd, Justice Minister St. Laurent was put on the hot seat in the House of Commons by John Diefenbaker. The previous December, Diefenbaker had brought up the question of secret orders-in-council in connection with another matter entirely. He was outraged at the provisions of an order-in-council forcing people to testify without counsel at an investigation into Eldorado Mining and Refining Company Limited. He called it "an invasion of public and private rights unexampled anywhere since the days of the Star Chamber" and asked "Will he [St. Laurent] tell us how many more secret orders there are which have not been produced?" St. Laurent, a former corporation lawyer, like Kellock, and a master of legalistic reasoning was never stumped for an explanation. Although he must certainly have known of the existence of the order empowering the RCMP to act in the spy affair, he denied that any secret orders existed. (He afterwards said he had forgotten.)

He went on to defend such orders as being perfectly reasonable: "It is not true in fact that every order which says that there should not be counsel attending witnesses called to testify in an investigation is necessarily bad. Here the witnesses are called for the purpose of giving information. They have no traditional or constitutional rights to be represented by a lawyer. They do not require to have a lawyer with them when they are asked questions on which they are only being requested to give true answers. One does not need a lawyer for that purpose." Then he added: "If the orders go beyond that, if the orders deny defence counsel to someone being prosecuted, of course I would consider…that it would be an abridgment of his rights."

When St. Laurent's alleged lapse of memory was exposed, Diefenbaker pulled out all the oratorical stops in the House: "Here is a strange thing. The Minister says that on December 6th, 1945, he did not remember this order of September 1945 that swept aside Magna Carta and the Bill of Rights. He forgot it!…Is it not passing strange that these people are detained until such time as they say something which implicates them? They are then granted the right to have counsel; they are then permitted to face their trials."

Dief's salvo hit home; King even makes reference to St. Laurent's anxiety and sensitivity over the attack in his diary entry of March 18th.

By this time, however, the order-in-council had already achieved its purpose; the last of the detainees – Benning, Adams and Durnford Smith – had been despatched to the commissioners who would now, in more senses than one, take their cue from the RCMP.

Forty-eight
Star Chamber

Star Chamber – n. any tribunal, committee or the like, which proceeds by arbitrary or unfair methods.

The first person to use this term in connection with the Taschereau-Kellock Royal Commission was Prime Minister William Lyon Mackenzie King himself.

When Norman Robertson told him that the commissioners may not sit for a couple of days at a time when none of the detainees had as yet been named or released, he expressed alarm that the government might be faced with a writ of habeas corpus which would give grounds for "Star Chamber methods."

My appearance before the commissioners had many of the features one would associate with a star chamber – the secret location, the burly escorts trying not to look like policemen, the circuitous comings and goings via back stairs and service elevators, the stares of the Corporal Smith look-alikes in the ante-room, but most of all the hostile ambience.

The Canadian Press news agency, amongst the deluge of background colour that flooded the front pages for weeks, described Justice Kellock as "a good-looking, greying man, [with] a suave voice which immediately attracts attention." Far from sounding suave, Kellock behaved in a harsh and hostile manner. With a history of bullying witnesses like the exploited department store workers of the Dirty Thirties on behalf of his corporate clients, browbeating appeared to come naturally to him.

As soon as I was seated, I asked the commissioners if they would kindly inform me of my legal rights as a witness. Kellock motioned to the stenographer who immediately lifted his hands from his table and folded them in his lap. Then, safely off the record, Kellock told me I wasn't there to ask questions; he would ask all the questions; my job was simply to answer them. He clearly felt his sworn duty to uphold the Law to be better served by suppressing and denying time-honoured rights than by seeing that they were enforced. It was, in fact, carefully planned entrapment – the sort of procedure the good judges would have indignantly struck down had the police in normal, lawful proceedings tried to get away with.

The RCMP had played the cue ball by supplying the commissioners with a script in the form of a transcript of the police interrogation. The job was to get it into the Commission record virtually unchanged. We know from Harvison's memoirs that the RCMP were ensconced on the floor below the Commission room, and that they fraternized with the commissioners and counsel in the elevators and over lunch. From the comings and goings during the proceedings it was clear that they were available to coach the commissioners at every stage. When my testimony seemed to diverge from what the commissioners had been led to expect, they would adjourn briefly for off-the-record consultation with the RCMP and Justice Department officials. What they were in fact doing was preparing a masterly prosecution brief for use in court proceedings to follow, and who better able to do it than two of the most distinguished jurists of the day.

Most of the interrogation was conducted by Gerald Fauteux, KC, Counsel to the Commission. The physical set-up had the two commissioners seated at a long table, at one end of which, and at right angles to it, was a small table for the witness. At a similar table at the opposite end of the room sat the stenographer. The witness's table at which I sat was so small that Fauteux could approach to within a few inches. His manner was to move in close and punch the questions right into my face. This was particularly offensive because the man suffered from a strong halitosis. Kellock broke in at intervals to extract repetitions of particularly damaging answers. During most of the proceedings, Taschereau was silent, seemingly lost in thought. Once he spoke up to ask for clarification of some point. Kellock addressed him as he might a retarded child, and I was momentarily amused that everyone else present – Fauteux, the stenographer and myself – spoke up simultaneously to set Taschereau straight. Whether this was an early indication of the alcoholism that eventually forced Taschereau to slip, figuratively if not physically, off the Supreme Court bench into early retirement I cannot say.

The government's stance throughout provided advance justification for the billiard ball strategy, allowing the Royal Commissioners to claim, in effect: "We didn't say you were guilty of anything; all we did was to tell the courts what you told us; it's up to them to say whether you're guilty or not…and if you didn't know enough to ask for protection under the Canada Evidence Act or simply dummy up – tough apples."

Only after my deposition had been given did Kellock ask whether I now wished to have counsel. This belated offer allowed the commissioners to deny the charge that counsel had not been offered and to bamboozle King – as the Prime Minister's diary entry reveals. Smarting under the growing criticism, King had been uneasy about publishing the commissioner's interim report ahead of any trials but on March 2nd rationalized: "It was clear however that the persons mentioned have already been given a chance of counsel and do not intend to deny the information contained therein. At the same time there might be criticism on this score."

Even historians like Granatstein and Stafford who are in general supportive of the methods used and defend them as "extraordinary but completely legal," find much to criticize. They admit that the commissioners "sometimes dropped their impartiality and dealt with witnesses in a peremptory fashion"; that Commission counsel behaved more like prosecutors than lawyers whose job was to help the commissioners assemble the evidence. And they find the McCarthy-style fishing expeditions for names "less defensible, perhaps." The commissioners' nets, however, mostly came up empty of fish, as in David Shugar's interrogation:

Shugar: Can you explain to me why I am obliged to tell you the names?
Kellock: Because that is the law, that you are obliged to answer any question that is put to you.

Shugar: I thought any question pertaining to the subject under discussion.

Kellock: Well, we decide what questions pertaining to the subject under discussion. You do not need to worry about any question put to you by myself or my fellow commissioner; you are obliged to answer. So you will go ahead unless you want a rest, if you are tired.

Shugar: Well, I would like to state that my legal counsel informed me that I need not answer, that I was at liberty to refuse to answer questions.

Kellock: Well, I am telling you that such advice is not sound, that you are obliged to answer. So what do you say?

Shugar: I remember, sir when I was administered that oath at the beginning of this afternoon that the oath read "pertaining to this enquiry."

Kellock: That is so.

Shugar: In my opinion, sir, that question does not pertain to this enquiry.

Kellock: But you are not the judge of that, we are the judges, and I have already told you that the question put to you must be answered.

Shugar: If I had known that I was not to be the judge of that, I would have hesitated before taking the oath.

Shugar's defiance of their authority did not sit well with the commissioners. In characteristic judicial vein, they reported: "We were not impressed by the demeanour of Shugar or by his denials, which we do not accept." However, Shugar had the last word. Interviewed by the press on his acquittal on April 25th, he said: "You can say that I definitely wasn't impressed with their demeanour either." Two other occasions clearly show how the commissioners drew their robes back from anything that went before or might come after.

When the accused Durnford Smith appeared before them, the following exchange took place:

Smith: I have the feeling that what is actually happening is that I am being questioned by a prosecution without the advantage of legal advice.

Kellock: Well, that is not so. Your conduct is being investigated but there is no question of prosecution; there is no question of a charge.
Smith: But I have heard that all the other people appearing before this commission have been subsequently charged.
Kellock: Well, that is not before us.

When still another of the accused, Eric Adams, refused to answer questions without his lawyer, Commissioner Taschereau told him: "We cannot report against you if counsel has not been offered. You will have full opportunity of having counsel and giving all the evidence you wish before any charge can be made against you. You are just a witness and you have to answer the questions that are put to you."

By the time Israel Halperin appeared before the commissioners, their bluff had been called to the point that they finally blinked and allowed lawyers to appear. But the justices fared no better with the lawyers than they did with some of the recalcitrant witnesses, as happened with Halperin.

"Before you swear me, would you mind telling me who you are?" said Halperin.

When Taschereau told him that the commissioners had the power to compel him to testify, Halperin responded: "Does that include physical intimidation?" And he refused to be sworn in.

Kellock then came to his colleague's aid.

"Do you understand, witness, that by refusing to answer you commit an offence, which is contempt, for which you can be punished? You understand that, do you? It does not matter whether you understand it or not. I am telling you."

Halperin stood his ground, until his attorney, Senator Roebuck, was allowed to appear at his side to remark that "…the questioning that has already gone on makes it quite clear that this is an inquisition so far as the witness is concerned, not just an ordinary general enquiry under the Act."

One of the problems shared by the commissioners and their counsel was an extraordinary cultural, philosophical and political naïveté, an apparent unawareness of the many shades of political thought and legitimate dissent between their own cozy establishment beliefs and the Bolshevik heresies at the opposite pole. E. K. Williams, President of the Canadian Bar Association and one of the Commission counsel, got an unexpected lesson in liberal democracy towards the end of the sittings when he tried to get John Grierson to say that he was a communist, thereby, by association, tarring the National Film Board, of which Grierson was chairman, with the same brush.

When pressed to label himself, Grierson responded, "My political views are to be as progressive as is possible within the machinery of the constitution, that is, within the machinery of government . . . In the matter of political philosophy the issue is this: Those of us who have been trained and who are dyed-in-the-wool liberal democrats [by implication excluding Williams and the commissioners] say that there cannot be any economic freedom if there is no political freedom. On the other hand, those who believe in international socialism say that you cannot have any political freedom unless there is economic freedom."

"Would you say," asked Williams, "that the effect of all this is that you are not a member of the Communist Party?"

"Oh, no."

"That is, officially," continued Williams, "would you say that your inclinations were of the leftist variety?"

"Not at all...I do not think that way...I am concerned with the floating of all ideas. I mean, I get as much from Gobineau as I get from Marx."

On March 12th, close to a month after the establishment of the Royal Commission and with several uncharged suspects still being held incommunicado, Mackenzie King records his indignation – and that of St. Laurent – at the length of time the commissioners are taking and his astonishment at Kellock's proposing to adjourn the sittings for some days in order to keep a speaking engagement with the YMCA. A week later, King got his chance to explain himself in great detail in the House. In a lengthy speech, he was at pains to establish his agreement with his critics about the importance of "upholding justice and of having justice followed in every step…For that reason to the exclusion of all others, two Justices of the Supreme Court of Canada were selected. The government did not know where in Canada it could find two persons who could be more certain to uphold justice in every particular, or who should be more zealous in protecting the freedom and liberty of the subject than would two justices of the Supreme Court of Canada." He also expressed regret that the proceeding had gone on so long, and made the remarkable confession that "when the commission was appointed we hoped it might be a matter of only a few days."

Quite apart from their juridical qualifications, the people chosen for the job were no Johnnies-come-lately to the Canadian Establishment. Defence of the status quo was bred in their bones. Robert Taschereau was the son of Hon. Louis Alexandre Taschereau who was premier of Quebec from 1920 to 1936, and the grandson of a former Supreme Court judge, Jean-Thomas Taschereau. He was distinguished for being the sole dissenter from the Supreme Court ruling striking down the Padlock Law, arguing that freedom of expression was not an absolute right. John Robert Cartwright, the government's choice to prosecute the cases in the Ontario courts, had if anything an even more distinguished pedigree. He was descended from Hon. Richard Cartwright, a prominent merchant, judge and member of the legal council of Upper Canada who settled there in 1780. Roy Lindsay Kellock did not have such impeccable antecedents, but he had earned his high station through skilful and loyal service to corporate clients like the T. Eaton Company and as a clean-up man for successive governments in such enquiries as the Halifax Disorders immediately following VE Day.

More grief awaited King. On March 22nd, John Diefenbaker, justice critic for the Opposition, a staunch supporter of civil liberties and a lawyer to boot, spoke in the House, criticizing the government and accusing it of crawling in the ditches of expediency.

Worse still, Chubby Power, one of King's Quebec lieutenants and a senior cabinet minister, backed Diefenbaker up. "If this is to be the funeral of liberalism, I do not desire to be even an honorary pallbearer," he said. King wrote in his diary: "I myself share that view." But again he was concerned not so much for any breach of civil liberties as for the damage to his own reputation and that of the Liberal Party. He makes the peevish entry: "It is unfair that Counsel and the commissioners should let the Liberal Party get into the position where it may take a long time for the Party itself to be rid of the charge of having acted in a very arbitrary manner with respect to civil liberties."

And yet again, on April 7th, he tells his diary that the commissioners "have done irreparable harm to the Party, and my own name will not escape responsibility."

Whether or not they had done irreparable harm to the justice system was clearly not at issue, for three of the principal players rose to become Chief Justices of the Supreme Court of Canada in succession: Justice Robert Taschereau, 1963-67; J.R. Cartwright, Special Crown Prosecutor, 1967-70; and Gerard Fauteux, Commission Counsel, 1970-73. Kellock, the other royal commissioner, took himself out of contention by retiring early, in 1958, due to ill health.

Many years after the dust had settled and most of the principals had died, the Royal Commission procedure was summed up, in 1985, in a scholarly work, The Supreme Court of Canada by Snell and Vaughan:

> "The Commission worked in secrecy, and no public announcement of its existence was made until nine days after it had commenced work. All of its hearings were held in camera...The Commission operated in a quasi-

> judicial manner, but violated judicial norms and individual civil liberties. Much of the evidence heard was unsubstantiated and would not have stood up in a court of law; persons arbitrarily detained were denied the rights of habeas corpus and access to counsel. These practices were justified as being in the national interest, and are a reflection of the growing cold war atmosphere. It had been the government's decision to give the commission the power to detain people and refuse them the right to counsel. That two members of the highest court in the land could easily and repeatedly violate civil rights and judicial norms is as appalling as it is indefensible."

Legal opinions of this kind and the outrage expressed by both Opposition and Government Members of Parliament have not survived in most of the histories of the affair. Granatstein and Stafford imply that it was "the press and the Opposition" who turned their attention to what they dismiss as the "extraordinary, but completely legal procedures employed by the royal commission." Legal or not, they were certainly intended to be inquisitorial, for which future generations may well condemn the procedures, to judge by an October 1981 article in the Toronto Globe and Mail with the headline and lead:

> CANADIAN PROBE USED MCCARTHY METHODS, BUT IN PRIVATE.
>
> If Mr. Justice Robert Taschereau and Mr. Justice R.L. Kellock had conducted their enquiry in public, their names might have gone down in history as Canada's version of Senator Joseph McCarthy.

In a letter of rebuttal to the newspaper, Mr. Justice Kellock's son, Burton H. Kellock, called the article "false, misleading and defamatory," but maintained that the commissioners were under no obligation to inform witnesses of their rights; no duty rested on them to advise witnesses of their rights under the Canada Evidence Act [even, it would seem, when directly asked about their rights, as in my case]. He quoted legal authority that such a commission "may be and ought to be a searching investigation – an inquisition as distinct from the determination of an issue." In reporting this letter in their book The Gouzenko Transcripts, Granatstein and Bothwell add that Kellock also wrote that the commissioners were only doing their duty to get to the bottom of "treason." But nowhere does Kellock mention treason in his letter, perhaps because, as a judge's son, he had more respect than historians for the niceties of legal definitions.

Forty-nine
The Courts

My advice to anyone who is unlucky enough to be arrested and brought to court by a police escort is: Don't be conned by them into hiding your face or turning it away from the cameras on the grounds that they are protecting you from the press or any such nonsense. Assume a neutral, non-committal, if possible confident, expression and look directly at the press photographers. Otherwise they will assuredly catch you in a hangdog, guilty, shifty-eyed posture which will delight their editors and buttress the prosecution's case. You will have learned this by the time you have your mug shot taken later, which invariably looks less incriminating than that initial photograph, the one which survives in the archives.

I learned this on being hustled from Rockcliffe barracks to the old Ottawa police station and magistrates' court on Elgin Street where I was jammed into a corner for "protection" while Magistrate Glenn Strike disposed of his regular clientele of prostitutes and drunks, some of whom he greeted pleasantly by their first names. After the formal arraignment I was taken below to the stink and filth of the holding cells from where I was soon transferred to the nineteenth-century Carleton County Jail on Nicholas Street. And so began an agonizing year in which the Crown tried with growing desperation to pocket the balls that the commission had shot its way.

I would spend a week in this miniature Bastille before being released on bail of six thousand dollars. This was where the small-time offenders uselessly dribbled out their debt to society. Few were hardened criminals – rather, they were the abused, impoverished, school-drop-out detritus of society, intuitively suspicious of authority and well disposed to anyone like myself who had fallen afoul of their natural enemy. There was nothing to do except sleep or talk. You could not even walk comfortably because of the sleeping bodies stretched out across the cement floor of the corridor. Among those inside with me was a Lower-Town Irish lad in his late teens who had been caught rolling a young girl in the hay and had been turned in by her farmer father. He spoke lovingly of his mother's baked beans and instructed me in the use of an elastic band to maintain erection.

I did not know it at the time, but I would be leap-frogging through the courts with two of the others all the way to Kingston. One was Nick Minnelli who spent the day endlessly shuffling and reshuffling a deck of cards from which he could deal you any card you wished to name.

The other was Tommy D. Tommy had been given a life sentence at the age of seventeen for a child sex-murder, had served fifteen or more years and had been paroled. He had been rearrested for a breach of his strict parole provisions and was being held for a court appearance where he fully expected to be sent back to the penitentiary. In preparation for this he wore a parka with a hood which he tied tightly around his head with multiple knots so that only his pointed red nose and ferret eyes were visible. Then he had had someone tie the ends of the sleeves with his hands drawn up inside. In the evening, we were locked into barred slots in the wall in which the only furniture was a narrow cot. Lying on its bare woven metal surface I could touch the walls on both sides with my elbows. As the guard went from cell to cell at lockup he was followed by Tommy who made the sign of the cross to each of us with his handless flipper and intoned pax vobiscum.

The pax of getting out on bail, and finally home after several weeks, was short-lived. Several times I successfully dodged a subpoena to appear as a witness at the upcoming Fred Rose trial, once by hiding in a closet, but it was inevitably served on me in the end. I had made up my mind not to testify – not, as Harvison maintains, because of pressure of any kind, except that of my conscience. From now on the Crown would have to pack its own snowballs.

Rose's preliminary hearing started in Montreal before Justice René Théberge on March 21st, but I was not called as a witness until March 24th. The Crown used the first three days to make the most of the first public appearance of their star witness, Igor Gouzenko.

The Montreal Star reporter's breathless prose gives some idea of the melodramatic scene:

> "Against a background of six alert Mounties in a crowded and dramatically hushed courtroom today, Igor Gouzenko…told his story of espionage in Canada…Fair skinned, with dark brown hair, and intelligent but slightly stolid features, he obviously had had a recent haircut.

> Two moles dotted his left cheek at mouth and eye level. His hair was parted to the side and his hands, with fists half clenched, rested on the top of the witness box. His deepset eyes are dark blue.
> "His dress was immaculate. He wore a single-breasted light grey suit with built up shoulders, an immaculately white shirt and collar, and a yellow-circled maroon necktie. He is about 5' 7" tall and weighs about 150 pounds.
> "From early morning the courthouse steps and the corridors were black with humanity, all hoping to get in to No. 3 courtroom. The corridor leading to the courtroom was barred halfway down its length when Provincial Police utilized a number of benches to act as a barrier to the oncoming hordes...
> "All photographers were barred from the court room and sketches were taboo. Even lawyers were refused admittance until their indignation at being barred from their Palais de Justice won the day for them."

Hon. F. Philippe Brais, K.C., special prosecutor, handled his witness ("this boy," as he called him) with kid gloves. He appealed to the judge to allow the witness to sit down. (Rose had to stand throughout.) He gave him the greatest possible latitude to interpret Soviet policy and to reveal the inner workings of the Kremlin minds in free-wheeling speeches.

At one point in his evidence, the Montreal Star reported:

> "...Gouzenko spoke for a solid twenty-five minutes detailing the differences between Canadian democracy and Soviet life. No orator, he spoke slowly, picking his phrases…the crowd hung on every word. Counsel did not interrupt him, and they were dramatic minutes to everyone in this room."

During this time I was waiting on the gallery outside the courtroom, dividing my time between sitting on a hard bench and leaning over the gallery railing to watch the comings and goings below. But mostly I was trying to quell the panic in my gut and maintain enough saliva in my mouth to lubricate my tongue and vocal chords when the time came. At one point the terrible Scarface of the Red Squad came up the stairs and made for the courtroom door, no doubt to gloat. I stood in the doorway to bar his way. "What is the password?" I demanded. He didn't see the joke and almost threw me to the ground as he barged into court.

When my name was called I went into the court with the feeling that I was about to face the Inquisition. I glanced at the huge crucifix on the wall above the black-robed judge hunched down in his throne. All at once the adrenaline began to flow. This was enemy territory. I would need all my faculties sharp and ready for the fray, remembering that offence is the best defence. I faced Brais with all the confidence I could muster.

Brais, too, had entered enemy territory. He had discarded the kid gloves he had worn for Gouzenko. As the court cases unfolded, I was able to compare the styles of the two main prosecutors. John Cartwright in Ontario was the snake – dispassionate, cold, unobtrusively coiling for the strike and rarely missing. Brais was the pit terrier – barking, snarling, grabbing and chewing. After I was sworn, he led me through some biographical details during which I was able to get the Quebec Committee for Allied Victory wartime contribution and my RCMP-inspired firing into the record, but when it came to direct questions about Rogov, I balked. My position as a defendant was that I should do nothing that might incriminate me.

The judge reminded me that I had the protection of the court; that my evidence could not be used against me, to which I replied: "My own interests at the moment are so much involved, and I think I have been so much prejudiced along with the others by what has appeared in the press that I feel I cannot answer questions which might have a bearing on the possibility of my own guilt."

Nothing has been reported, Brais claimed, except what has been testified to in court.

"I am referring to reports that [RCMP] Commissioner Wood had reported through the Minister of Justice that certain things did not take place during the solitary confinement of myself and others. Those reports are totally untrue."

"That has nothing to do with this court," Brais said, retreating behind the billiard ball gambit.

Of course, I was held in contempt of court and spent the night in Bordeaux Jail. The following day I was recalled so that Brais "for the sake of form" could put his full series of questions to me even though he was unlikely to get answers. As reported by the Montreal Star, his purpose was to have me "confirm or deny certain statements attributed to [me] in the report of the Royal Commission at Ottawa." His language, convoluted at the best of times and larded with anti-communist polemics, grew more and more dense as he worked his way through the list. He was so carried away at one point that it must have taken him a full minute or more to come to the end of an elaborate question.

"Will you repeat the question, please?" I said.

For a moment I thought he was having a heart attack. The blood drained from his face and his mouth fell open. A ripple of laughter washed over the court. I spotted the artist Ernst Neumann in the audience grinning from ear to ear, and the sight of a friendly face made me feel a little better. The judge banged his gavel and adjourned the court to give Brais time to recover. The following day, when I was led away after again being held in contempt, Brais said he hadn't needed me anyway. He had only called me to give me a chance to say my piece.

No sooner was Rose disposed of in Montreal, and sent to trial, than I was back in court in Ottawa in my own preliminary hearing. Here, the only evidence presented was the billiard ball of my deposition to the Royal Commission. My lawyer at this point, Henry Cartwright, was a cousin of Special Crown Prosecutor John Cartwright. To avoid confusion I shall refer to them as "my Cartwright" and "their Cartwright." My Cartwright was genuinely shocked at the quasi-legal procedures being used and did his valiant best to put them in the spotlight. He put me on the stand and led me through some of the events when in RCMP custody and before the royal commissioners. This led to a number of confrontations with Lee Kelley, one of the Crown lawyers who was doggedly trying to establish the billiard ball ground rules which would prevail from then on.

On the question of access to counsel at the Royal Commission, Kelley read from the Commission transcript showing that Kellock had decided to tell the government I was guilty but no charges had been laid, so now was the time to ask for counsel if I so desired. Wait a minute, my Cartwright said, this offer was made only after the commissioners were through with him. Yes, Kelley countered, but the evidence was not being submitted as a confession, only as evidence taken by a royal commission. He held it was perfectly admissible unless objection to giving the evidence had been raised by the accused. Just asking about your rights and being told by a Justice of the Supreme Court of Canada that you didn't have any didn't count, it seemed. He then, to the astonishment of my Cartwright and the other lawyers present representing other accused, proposed that they should all be bound by an oath of secrecy not to say anything about the documentary evidence. In defiance of this ban, my Cartwright called a press conference later in the day at which he read some of the evidence. He also made public the text of the oath everyone appearing before the commission had been made to take, an oath not to divulge to anybody any of the evidence. This oath was to cause the Crown some awkward moments when I and others invoked it as a reason for not testifying. But it turned out to be a some-time oath that the commissioners could switch on and off whenever it suited them.

Two weeks later this oath became the subject of a fencing match with their Cartwright when I was called as a witness in the Halperin preliminary hearing. I cited the oath as a reason for not testifying, and flashed correspondence my Cartwright had supplied me with in support of my stand.

"Oaths are not to be taken lightly," I said. Their Cartwright replied that the commissioners could release me from the oath. This gave them "rather divine powers," commented Halperin's lawyer, R. M. W. Chitty.

Halperin had to wait till April 25th for Magistrate Strike's decision to commit him for trial, the same day that David Shugar, another of the accused, was freed for lack of evidence. This, the first acquittal, did not sit well with the authorities. Shugar's government pay had been suspended shortly after his arrest and he would never get his job back. It would be a long time before they called off the dogs.

Now it was my turn again – this time in the Mazerall trial. This trial is of special interest because it introduced evidence that the alleged material passed to the Russians could hardly be called secret. For example, two reports on radar range and distance indicators Mazerall was said to have provided had been available almost simultaneously at a Commonwealth conference in London, at which the Russians were present as guests. The Crown agreed that the information itself may have been of little value but – and here made clear what would more and more become the crux of the prosecution – agreement to provide unauthorized information is proof of conspiracy, regardless of the value of the information, or even if it were never supplied at all. This explains why the Crown preferred to lay conspiracy (rather than substantive) charges, and why, as in my case, they added conspiracy charges to the original charges. Conspiracy charges open up the admissibility of wide new areas of evidence and greatly increase the presumption of guilt. For example, at the trial of Fred Poland towards the end of the trials marathon the following year, when the Crown had obviously failed to convince a jury with extremely shaky and unsupported evidence, their Cartwright tried to convince the jury to convict him on the basis of the number of times the name Pavlov (one of those named from the Russian embassy) appeared in Poland's desk calendar. Poland had freely admitted knowing Pavlov and had made no secret of their meeting socially. Mazerall's lawyer, Royden A. Hughes, got an admission from Sgt. Bayfield of the RCMP that both he and Harvison had prepared reports for the commissioners on the backgrounds of the detainees and the results of the police interrogations – but, he added, he would be surprised if the commissioners had read them! His surprise could not have been greater than mine when, upon my refusal to testify when called, the trial judge, Chief Justice J.C. McRuer, declined to hold me in contempt of court and allowed me to leave the stand because of his belief in the "signal importance of preserving a fair and impartial administration of justice."

Long after the dust had settled, many of those involved in the trials admitted that little, if any, damaging secret information was passed. Justice McRuer sentenced Mazerall, "as a very painful duty," to four years imprisonment. He acknowledged that the information Mazerall passed to the Russians was mostly freely obtainable and that Mazerall could have given very much more of a secret nature had he been so inclined.

The chief Crown Prosecutor would later tell an interviewer, "Scrape away the rhetoric and look at what actually happened in court. The information wasn't of any value."

Fifty
A Red, Red Rose

And now it was back to Montreal for the Rose trial proper, for which the preliminary hearing had been only a rehearsal. I was beginning to adjust to the stress of repeated performances as a hostile witness. Court appearances had become like the airline pilot's four hours of boredom flying and two minutes of panic landing – the boredom of waiting outside the Court for a call that was days in coming, and the adrenaline rush on finally being called to the stand.

The boredom for the spectators inside the courtroom was relieved to some extent by the RCMP's handling of Gouzenko. He was accompanied by six plainclothes guards who spread out through the court with their backs to the proceedings as they watched the spectators for would-be assassins. Later, a sniper watch was set up for the "flash of a rifle" from an adjacent rooftop, aimed to take the life of the Crown's tip-off man. However, Justice Wilfrid Lazure, the trial judge, left no doubt who was in charge. A couple of times, when Gouzenko appeared about to launch into one of his speeches, Lazure stopped him. "Facts, not opinions, you understand me," he told him. He reined in Brais, too, from time to time, accusing him of wasting the court's time by trying to introduce documents which had no bearing on the trial. When Brais disagreed, he told him: Too bad; you happen to be the attorney; I am the judge. When Brais tried to introduce Mazerall's conviction as evidence, Lazure blocked it, ruling: "It is illegal evidence and only legal evidence will be allowed in this court." At one point he was so tired of the bickering between Crown and defence lawyers that he threatened to retire and let them make speeches to each other to their hearts' content.

For the whole of this time, I and other witnesses– including Gerson, Adams and Nightingale – had been cooling our heels on the gallery outside the courtroom. Nightingale asked me what I intended to do. I told him I would stick to my guns and refuse to testify. If that was the case, he said, he would do the same. Apparently the others came to the same decision.

When finally called to the stand, I respectfully told the judge that I preferred not to testify since it would be prejudicial to my own case still pending. To my surprise, Lazure said that in the ordinary way he would have committed me to jail for contempt of court but in view of the decision of Chief Justice McRuer in the Ontario Court he would not do so. He cannot have anticipated that the next three prosecution witnesses would also decline to testify. This resulted in what the Montreal Star reported as perhaps the stormiest session to date. Taken by surprise, Brais admitted he would have to change his plans and called for adjournment.

Three days later I was again called to the stand. The Crown seemed to be almost desperate to get my Royal Commission testimony into the record. Brais had made it clear at the start of the trial that his case against Rose was based on the Royal Commission findings. Again I refused to testify, and again Lazure declared me in contempt of court and said he did not want to put me in jail. But he ordered me to remain at the disposal of the court.

At the end of the trial, in what the Montreal Star reported as "an unexpected change of mind" Lazure sentenced each of us to three months in jail citing common law and quoting an Alberta Supreme Court precedent. One can only speculate on what went on behind the scene to persuade Lazure to change his mind.

Rose lost his appeal on December 20th. A by-election was held the following May to fill the parliamentary seat from which he had been evicted. The winner was Liberal Party candidate Maurice Hartt, who accused Duplessis of having tried to steal the election by financing an opposition Independent candidate for whom large numbers of votes had been cast by women in nuns' habits wearing open-toed shoes and with diamond rings on their fingers. Things had returned to normal in Montreal elections.

Fifty-one
Bordeaux, Vintage 1946

It was a beautiful early summer evening when Gerson, Adams, Nightingale and I were bundled off in the big Black Maria to Bordeaux Jail to serve our three month sentences for contempt of court. The street smells and sounds of Montreal were tantalizingly close through the narrow grilles of the van.

Montreal's Bordeaux Jail at the time was a cross between Gehenna and a Dickensian workhouse – filth, ignorance, cruelty and corruption stirred up with a crucifix. (Almost half a century later, in 1990, a Paris lawyer from an international human rights federation visited Bordeaux and likened it to a mediaeval European prison.) We were stripped, made to shower under a pipe in a windowless cement room. The only other occupant was a frail elderly man sitting on an upturned pail, gently sobbing. As far as we could make out from his almost incoherent French, he had been dumped there by his family. While we waited, a rat ran round and round the inside of a garbage bin trying frantically to escape. We were issued with crude boots, coarse tubular socks, and randomly chosen jailhouse garments of grey canvas – no underwear. Nightingale, who was a very tall man, was given a pair of pants that came down to mid-calf and had no crotch – air-conditioned, so to speak. He wore them uncomplainingly and with great dignity. We were given cotton paillasses and marched to a barn where we stuffed them with straw and were then assigned to our cells. There is no noise quite as conclusive as the slam of a solid steel cell door.

Bordeaux, like most prisons of its era, consisted of a series of wings radiating from a central domed hub from which the entire jail was controlled. The cells were arranged in tiers on the outside walls so that they looked out on a wedge of yard between each wing – but you had to stand on your stool to be able to see out of the tiny barred window set high in the wall. Access to the cells was by metal stairways and narrow galleries running the length of the wings. It was not unknown for an inmate who had had enough to "take a dive" from the topmost gallery. Separating each "range" was a wide white-tiled hall. This was the only part of the jail that was kept scrupulously clean. Swabbers worked from one end to the other of the hundred yards or so of floor and then, like bridge painters, started all over again.

Each cell had a metal cot bolted to the wall, a stool, a shelf to eat off, a wooden box of salt and a massively built china combination toilet/wash-basin. In spite of the fresh straw in the mattress, the bedbugs appeared in battalions every night. Complaints resulted in a fumigating gas attack – more unpleasant and probably more toxic than the bugs, which in any case were so deeply entrenched as to be immune to eviction. This would be home for three months.

As part of the admitting procedure we were paraded before the doctor. He was seated cross-legged, Buddha-like, leaning back in a swivel chair with his hands folded behind his head, in the best of moods as he dismissed requests for aspirins or medical aid of any kind. "Ha, ha. You make me laugh. What do you think this is – the Mount Royal Hotel?"

He was particularly amused at one youngster who appeared before him with his genitalia swollen to an enormous size by poison ivy and carried in the open in a kind of sling supported from his belt. Luckily, none of us had any need to appeal to His Hippocratic Highness during our stay.

The four of us were split up with little opportunity to meet and share a few civilized moments. When we discovered that the Salvation Army held volunteer hymn-singing sessions we decided to use these as a chance to get together for a chat. It was a shock to find quite a different face of this admirable organization from the kindly, patient, charitable one I had seen in the army. Our small congregation of broken-down rubbies, junkies and petty thieves met in a cheerless room furnished with cast-off folding chairs. The major in charge was a no-nonsense martinet who made it immediately plain that there would be no talking, that we were miserable sinners whose only chance for salvation was to get down on our knees before God, confess our sins and grovel for mercy. He made us feel that even to look composed and self-assured was in itself a sin. Evidently we were to look contrite and humble as befitted our shameful condition. He bellowed at Gerson to wipe the smirk off his face. Perhaps his Christian immune system had detected an incompatible foreign substance and was reflexively rejecting it. When he had tongue-lashed us into submission he led us with his calliope baritone in the songs. (Not "hymns" – a word which was unknown in these circles. Likewise, the word "magazine" was never used. Anything printed, regardless of format, was a "book.")

"When the roll is called up yonder, I'll be there."

We resorted to the time-honoured device of schoolboy choristers and other prisoners of authority, singing along with the group but mouthing our own words in illicit conversation. I was surprised to see how enthusiastically most of the others joined in. The songs shared with advertising jingles an appeal to primitive emotions disproportionate to the triteness of the words and music. The group appeared to have experienced a communal catharsis so that even the major came out of the session slightly mellowed.

We had the option of working and thus getting out of our cells for part of the day, or not working and staying locked in. There was no really useful work to be done. I was assigned to washing cell walls. I soon found that no one expected you actually to do the work so I had plenty of time to socialize with my neighbours. Nothing so endears one to a con as to be known to have thumbed one's nose at authority. They took me under their wing and briefed me on jailhouse etiquette, whom to avoid and how to protect myself.

One of the most useful of these new neighbours, because of his lengthy jailhouse experience, was Hank Wilson, a heroin addict. He pronounced it hair-oin, to rhyme with join. A man in his fifties, he had started working in racing stables as a thirteen-year-old at a time when racehorses were being routinely doped. Seeing what it did for the horses, he tried opium himself and, of course, quickly became addicted and remained so all his life. His veins were so scarred with needles that he sometimes had to inject into a vein in his scrotum, he told me. Hank had suffered a punctured palate from a fall during his jockey days with the result that he could supply very little suction to hold his store teeth in place. When he spoke, his lips would move freely but the teeth would float motionless in the middle of his mouth. He was a booster by trade – that is, a professional shoplifter. He had done a profitable business with American tourists whom he accosted in Dominion Square in Montreal with offers to obtain whatever piece of Royal Doulton or Wedgwood porcelain they desired. He filled the orders from various specialty and department stores, whose stocks he had studied, until they finally caught on to his little game. It was from Hank that I first heard the saying, repeated endlessly by the thieves and con men I later met: There's larceny in everyone's heart.

In order to feed his habit Hank had to boost an enormous quantity of merchandise. He was professionally equipped with a boosting coat, a voluminous affair with many deep concealed pockets in back and sides. With this he wore a loop of cord around the neck and hanging down on his chest. He would whip a suit off the rack, still on its hanger, hook it onto the loop, wrap his coat around him and make for the nearest exit. Of course, the time came when he was immediately recognized in all the big stores. Age, the blunting of his boosting reflexes and fear of enforced withdrawal had reduced him to a desperate raid on Eaton's small appliance department where he had grabbed a couple of boxes and carried them unconcealed to the store entrance. When he saw the store dick waiting for him on the sidewalk he handed him the boxes and ran. Hampered by his bulky boosting coat, he was quickly caught and sentenced to six months in Bordeaux. (A few months after my first visit to Bordeaux I returned briefly during the endless comings and goings of the trials. Hank was still there, but he had no recollection of ever having met me.)

Donald Perrault was a different kind of inmate. Well spoken, debonair even in prison garb, fluently bilingual, he seemed to be completely un-criminal and as out of place as we were in this hell-hole. He sought us out and was friendly, almost ingratiating, in his efforts to be of help. Perhaps he would have evaporated from my memory like most of the other inmates except for what happened to him later. Together with his brother and another accomplice he was hanged in that very same jail in 1949 for the murder of a policeman during an aborted bank holdup.

I quickly discovered that the jail was really being run by Johnny Young. Young was a leading criminal of the day with headquarters at the Italian Spaghetti House in East End Montreal. He was serving a short sentence of less than two years; otherwise he would have been in St. Vincent de Paul Penitentiary. He was built like a wrestler, a bull of a man. Clearly he inspired fear and respect not only in the underworld. Ostensibly in charge of my range was an innocuous little guard who, it turned out, was illiterate and unable to take an accurate prisoner count. Giving Young authority was one way to protect his job. So Young had a nicely furnished cell which was never locked, he ate well, had all the booze he wanted, and had the run of the place. In return he kept order and made a fair distribution of graft to the guards on his list.

This graft came from selling favours and privileges to the inmates. No sooner had we been convicted than guards – in uniform – were calling on our families with offers to deliver contraband food and chocolate bars to their loved ones. They promised a dollar of delivered value for every two dollars collected. Young held the reins of this enterprise.

The food in the prison made boarding school or army meals look like gourmet feasts – thin "scouse" (porridge) and bread for breakfast, a steel mugful of either pea soup (quite palatable) or "gasoline" soup (poisonous) with bread at midday, or sometimes ragout de boulettes – spheres of gristle with the texture of golf balls. Supper was always a piece of cheese, bread and johnnycake – an insufficiently baked mixture of pork fat and flour. This diet prompted me to try contraband channels. Sure enough, I was duly delivered a magnificent sandwich loaded with sliced pork fillet and lettuce. I opened it up to admire the meat but found that there was a third ingredient – several rat turds.

Young's cell was actually a room on the ground level of the wing opposite the one I was in. It was brightly lit and had a large window through which could be seen the inside of the room. One evening the word went around that there would be a "show" that night. The show consisted of an exhibition of buggery starring Young and a couple of young inmates.

When we had finally ground out our time, Young was there to wish us well and send us on our way. "Listen guys, if there's ever anything you need – broads, booze, whatever – just go to the Spaghetti House and mention my name. They'll look after you good." Unfortunately for Young, his political pals deserted him. After nineteen convictions, including a four-year term for sheltering the Perrault brothers, he was locked up for good in 1950 as Quebec's first habitual criminal.

The resourcefulness and solidarity of the Bordeaux subculture was unbelievable to a "square john" like me. One evening I witnessed the delivery of a pair of boots to an inmate in the so-called trial ward whose cell was perhaps one hundred and fifty feet away across the yard. He was to go to trial the next day and he had no shoes. Someone in my wing had volunteered a pair of boots. The delivery was made by unravelling prison socks to obtain a sufficient length of coarse yarn. This was attached to a primitive kite which was then cajoled hop by hop across the ground by means of repeated tugs at the string. After a couple of hours the kite finally came within reach of the opposite cellblock, establishing a positive if tenuous link. The boots were attached to the line and ever so gingerly hauled inch by inch across the dirt until they could be pulled in at the opposite side.

One day, in what Hank Wilson would have called a "salty" mood, I refused what seemed like an unreasonable order. I was immediately hustled to le donjon – the Hole – where I was relieved of my belt and shoes. The Hole was a subterranean series of cages, the front bars of which seemed to be the diameter of young trees. There was a minute barred window well out of reach in one wall. The cell was bare of any furniture or equipment. I found that I had at least one neighbour with whom I could communicate by shouting. He identified himself as a recently demobilized soldier who had returned unexpectedly to his New Brunswick farm home to find his wife shacked up with another man. His solution was prompt and final: he took a hunting rifle, shot the man dead and fled to Montreal where he was soon arrested. Figuring he had nothing to lose, he resisted the authorities at every turn, winding up in the hole on a bread and water diet. But he was eating okay, he told me. The night screw was a "queer" so he had been able to make a deal. The screw brought a big lunch every evening which he turned over to him in return for being allowed to perform fellatio on him through the bars.

"I just grab him by the ears and pull him on," he said. "He eats me while I eat his goddamn lunch."

Bordeaux Prison was where death penalties were carried out. Everybody was aware that Ovilda Samson was in the death cell and tension in the cell blocks mounted as the day of execution approached. Samson was an unfortunate man in his fifties who had killed two elderly women in what had seemed to be a pointless, motiveless crime.

On the eve of the execution my neighbour asked me if I was going to watch it.

"Watch it? How could I possibly do that?"

He produced a piece of glass that he had smoked with a candle to make a mirror. Unknown to me the gallows were less than thirty feet from our cells, occupying an iron gallery jutting out a storey above the ground in the space where two cellblocks converged at the dome. A door in the dome opened on to the gallery. The death cell was a few paces beyond the door.

My neighbour gave me a piece of the smoked glass. It gave a surprisingly good mirror image of the gallows when held through the bars at the proper angle. The rope was already in place, attached to a thick iron bar above what was only too clearly the trapdoor, the noose ready at head level and the rest of the rope looped up out of the way and tied with a string. The string would break with the weight of the falling body. The hangman, a conscientious man, had carefully calculated the length of rope based upon the victim's weight, and had stretched the rope by making a test drop with a sand bag of equivalent weight. He was careful about this because on a previous occasion he had failed to take into account the weight which a woman had gained while in the death cell and had pulled her head off by mistake.

A few minutes after midnight the gallows were flooded with light. The door to the dome opened revealing a small group, including a priest, surrounding a surprisingly serene-looking Samson. Shoeless, dressed in black pants and a collarless white shirt, arms tied behind his back, he took his place on the trap as though it had all been rehearsed. The hangman knelt and quickly bound his feet. He produced a black bag from nowhere, snapped it full of air, jammed it on Samson's head, put the noose around his neck, jerked it tight with the knot at his jaw, stooped again to insert a short metal rod into a hole at his feet, straightened up and stepped on the rod. It all took no more than a few seconds. The spring-loaded trap opened with a fearsome crash. For a split second Samson seemed to stand on air before dropping through the hole to wind up with a sickening thud below. Immediately the body began to shake convulsively and jack-knifed feet first back towards the trap then swung in huge arcs from side to side.

(So it's true . . . you literally swing.) The doctor who, with a couple of witnesses now appeared from a door below, fielded the body and steadied it. At intervals he applied a stethoscope to the chest, but it was not until fourteen minutes had elapsed that he could certify death.

The legal process which had started with Justice Louis Cousineau donning his three-cornered hat and black gloves as he sat high on the bench beneath the big crucifix intoning the words (in French, of course) " . . . and there be hanged by the neck until you are dead" was now complete. A hot-blooded killing had been expiated in cold blood.

My neighbour muttered, "Maudits cochons."

Fifty-two
Trials and Tribulations

The Bordeaux contempt jailings resulted in further resort to habeas corpus and further indications that the authorities had no intention of interpreting this right with any generosity. In proceedings on behalf of Adams, his lawyers argued that his sentence was illegal, null and void since it had been imposed under common law, whereas the fault attributed to Adams was subject to the criminal code. He should have been charged accordingly and given a chance to defend himself. The court, however, accepted the Crown's rebuttal that even if the judge had been wrong it didn't make any difference since Adams had no recourse to habeas corpus by way of remedy anyway. In his judgment refusing the writ, the judge said Adams had no way of knowing what questions might be put to him, so how could he know whether his answers might incriminate him? Apparently nobody had told the judge about the billiard ball gambit. The authorities were clearly anxious to head off this defence tactic. Three weeks later, Chief Justice Rinfret delivered an elaborate ruling refusing writs to Gerson and Nightingale, by which time they had served almost the entire three months of their contempt sentences.

During the summer months, while we mouldered behind steel doors, the Crown was regrouping to grapple with the increasing difficulties they were facing in court. Four of the trials still to come were those of Gerson, Nightingale, Adams and Poland. The Crown laid new conspiracy charges, ostensibly to speed matters up but in effect making it much easier to obtain convictions, and proposed to try the four jointly. The defence successfully challenged this gambit and the trials went ahead separately. Joseph Sedgwick K.C., arguing for separation of the defendants, which was granted, and for a change of venue, which was refused, told the court that the Royal Commission report was "an absolutely damning document that contained statements made maliciously…studded with statements that could not be backed up in a court of law."

Meanwhile Shugar, who had been acquitted more than four months earlier, was again committed for trial on new charges. The Montreal Gazette obligingly started a series of daily articles based on material drawn from the Royal Commission report, in which the guilt of all those yet to be tried was proclaimed before they came to trial – and, in some instances, on the very same days they were in court. Shugar, who had earned special vengeance for having been acquitted, was featured on four consecutive days. The crack of ball striking ball was becoming deafening.

Of the four alleged co-conspirators, only Gerson was found guilty. Adams, next in line, was acquitted, to the Crown's discomfiture. "Their Cartwright" admitted that it complicated his plans for Agatha Chapman, another of the accused. He had banked on a guilty verdict for Adams making it easier to show Chapman to be a co-conspirator and therefore also guilty. He asked for an adjournment saying he would have to refer the matter to St. Laurent who was out of the country. This was the first public acknowledgment that orders were coming from the very top. Whatever advice St. Laurent was able to give proved ineffective, because on November 27th Chapman was acquitted by a jury of her peers.

Meanwhile, things looked better for the Crown when Benning was found guilty and given five years on the very same day the Montreal Gazette ran the article on him. But even this conviction did not stand up on appeal and Benning was ultimately freed. Nightingale, next to be tried, did not have to go to appeal; a jury acquitted him in quick order.

The Crown still had not finished with their bête noire, Shugar. When his second trial came up on November 27th, the RCMP packed the courtroom with thirty additional officers, ostensibly to give these alleged recruits first-hand experience of court proceedings. But in spite of this banana republic scenario, Shugar was once again acquitted – acquitted but not forgiven. Now the whole multi-departmental weight of the government was brought to bear. He successfully sued Time news magazine and other publications for damages. Nevertheless he found himself blackballed as a scientist in Canada and threatened with the loss of his Canadian citizenship. He moved to a research post in France from which Canadian authorities managed to get him ousted, as they did also at his next stop at the University of Brussels. He then moved to Poland where he established an international reputation for his discoveries in the field of spontaneous mutations in DNA, one of the main driving forces of all life.

In 1988 at a ceremony in Toronto on the occasion of the 16th International Congress of Genetics, David Shugar was honoured by his international confreres for his extraordinary contribution to world science. But he has yet to receive anything remotely resembling an apology from the Government.

The last of the quartet of alleged co-conspirators, Poland, did not come to trial until the following January, when he, too, was acquitted, in spite of Cartwright's last-ditch efforts to link him with Pavlov of the Soviet embassy. The Ottawa Citizen, which had avoided the editorial hysteria of some of the other newspapers, used the acquittal to take a shot at the Royal Commission:

> ".. using his undoubted right, he [Poland] refused to be sworn or to answer questions or to give explanations. So, taking advantage of the clause in the Official Secrets Act which makes even an attempt to communicate with an agent – a glass of vodka in the Soviet Embassy could easily be construed as such an attempt – the commissioners decided that he had "completely failed" to rebut the presumption of guilt against him. Fortunately the court before which he was tried had other standards of judgment and made short work of such flimsy evidence."

The commissioners were to come in for still more criticism of their judgment and sense of fair play. In spite of the acquittals in open court, at trials conducted with due process of law, the Royal Commission report continued to circulate worldwide, listing all these people as guilty. Understandably, there were those who thought this to be presumptuous on the part of the commissioners, to say the least. To make matters worse, the commissioners proposed to go to a second printing without making any changes. One letter to the editor read in part:

> "Is it not a little strange that the commissioners do not object to this [second printing]. They can hardly be very enthusiastic to see broader circulation of public reminders that their unusual proceedings of judicial enquiry seem to have led them up four embarrassing blind alleys to date."

Shugar's defence lawyer, A.W. Beament, took the matter up in a letter to Rt. Hon. J.L. Ilsley, newly appointed Minister of Justice, asking that the report be amended to take the acquittals into account. The Ottawa Civil Liberties Association went further, urging compensation for those found not guilty. The Ottawa Citizen in an editorial on February 20th supported the CLU demand, commenting:

> "It is farcical for the government to trouble itself about human rights and freedoms abroad while neglecting them at home...The eyes of a fool are in the ends of the earth."

The commissioners finally bowed to pressure and included a note on the acquittals in subsequent printings. But they could not resist emasculating the note with their own little rider, which read:

> "It should not be assumed that in any case the evidence before the Royal Commission and that adduced in the criminal proceedings were the same."

This drew an editorial rebuke from the Ottawa Citizen, castigating the government for "ambiguity" in the wording of the rider. Paul Gardner, an inveterate writer of letters to the editor, wrote: "The innuendo seems clearly designed to save the Commission's face at the expense of the acquitted persons."

Fifty-three
My Turn

After all the court appearances as a hostile witness, in and out of the lockup, my own trial in November came as an anticlimax. Although I had been charged in Ontario and would be tried in Ottawa, it seemed logical to seek legal help in my hometown of Montreal. Lucien Gendron was recommended to me as one of the best defence lawyers available. After my first visit to his office, Gendron switched our meetings to the recreation room in his house in Outremont where he would address me as "Captain" and start the interviews with a large whisky and soda. He came on-side without equivocation and, between anecdotes drawn from his long trial experience, began to plan the destruction of the enemy – the prosecution. Although I had few hopes of an acquittal, I was encouraged to have such a committed advocate with a reassuring cynicism about the motives and methods of the Crown. The Crown, however, also rated Gendron highly. When he routinely applied for the privilege of appearing to plead in an Ontario court – a courtesy which could have been shown to a professional colleague – he was refused. We had to look for an Ontario lawyer.

Meanwhile, the Party was in disarray, its leaders desperately trying to dissociate themselves from the debacle. Sam Carr was fired from his Party job for the heinous offence of failing in his Communist Duty to answer to a subpoena from the Royal Commission. Tim Buck set himself up as a target for ridicule by calling the investigation a capitalist plot. The Montreal Star, not without justification, called his efforts to dissociate himself "odiferous." The Party, unofficially, of course, was using its influence to help raise defence money for the accused, but recoiled from intervening directly in hiring lawyers. Paradoxically, all the capable and experienced labour or left-wing lawyers were being passed over in favour of the big guns of the legal Establishment. On a lawyer hunt in Toronto I had a talk with A. A. MacLeod, a Labour-Progressive Party (former Communist Party) member of the Ontario Legislature at the time, who advised me to take a leaf out of Dimitroff's book. Turn the tables; come out fighting. Show them up for the reactionaries they are. He was referring to Georgi Dimitroff who had been accused by the Nazis in the thirties of complicity in setting fire to the Reichstag and who, acting as his own lawyer at his trial, had made a fool of Prosecutor Hermann Goering and had been acquitted. This was flattering, perhaps, but surely a more suitable role for Fred Rose, who had conspicuously kept his mouth shut at his own trial. Besides, it meant involving others who had their own ideas on how to defend themselves.

When my trial finally started I had three lawyers or more accurately, two-and-a-half – as disparate in temperament and approach as any three lawyers could be. Gendron, there under sufferance as a "friend of the court" was relegated to the role of off-stage prompter instead of star performer. Henry Cartwright, nominally in charge, whom I respected as the most honest, decent and civilized of the trio, and who had piloted the proceedings efficiently through the initial stages, wanted to conduct an honest, decent and civilized defence. This would mean putting me on the stand to explain my motives, misguided as he believed them to be, and throw myself on the mercy of the court. This was not quite the same approach that A.A. MacLeod had proposed to me in Toronto, but was even less appealing. Neither did it suit Gendron's confrontational style. He took the hint and withdrew from the case, whispering to me: "He has too much hair in his ears." I was determined not to make it any easier for the courts to rubber-stamp the commissioners' findings. When Henry Cartwright saw that I would not follow his script he, too, withdrew, leaving me with J. L. Cohen.

I had brought J.L. into the case at the very last moment on the strength of his reputation as a scrappy labour lawyer and fighter for left-wing causes. He had been counsel to the CIO in Canada; also one of the three members of the powerful National War Labour Board until the Mackenzie King Cabinet intervened to throw him out because of his uncompromising defence of union rights. In return for a large fee (which was quietly raised by contributions from friends and sympathizers) he agreed to take the case and to rendezvous with Phyllis and me in the Chateau Laurier Hotel in Ottawa a day or two ahead of the trial. My brother from the United States joined us to lend moral support and a fourth room was taken for a young woman from England who had just become J.L.'s secretary and had no idea what she was in for. The stage had been set for a Marx Brothers farce.

From then until the end of the trial a week later J.L. scarcely left the hotel room except to appear in court. All meals were ordered from room service. It was depressingly clear that we had an emotionally sick man on our hands. J.L. took to his bed each day in the early evening after a session with the room service menu. His taste ran to oysters on the half shell, filet mignon and meringues glacés. By the time the meal arrived he was propped up on pillows ready to hold court and maybe, just maybe, talk about the case. We soon found that part of his pre-bed session in the bathroom was the popping of a handful of downers. By dessert time he was already slipping away from us into his nighttime oblivion. If Phyllis and the secretary were present he would take one of their hands in each of his and hold on until he passed out and we would have to pry his fingers loose.

The following morning I would go to his room to get him up, banging on his door for as long as it took to rouse him. His first act was to pop the Benzedrine uppers which wound him up for the day ahead, then perform his elaborate toilette. He was a short man of normal build, except for his hard round belly that stuck out like an eight-month pregnancy, but he did things in a big way. By the time he had showered and shaved, gargled with gulps of mouthwash from a giant economy-size bottle, spat it more or less in the direction of the toilet and powdered himself in a cloud of talcum, the bathroom looked like a battlefield. The accidental intrusion of Phyllis or the secretary on this performance did not bother him at all.

On the first day of the trial, as he prepared to dress for court, I got a glimpse of what we were in for. All the lawyers I had seen so far had been dressed like identical penguins. J.L. had given more thought to his appearance. He wore an expensive-looking Oxford grey outfit with a swallow-tailed cutaway coat edged with silk braid over an embroidered, pleated white shirt. His pot was hammocked in a brocade waistcoat with satin buttons. If the judge would be giving marks for sartorial elegance, we'd be home free.

J.L. started things off in court by dropping a bombshell. Unknown to me he had subpoenaed Prime Minister Mackenzie King, Royal Commissioner Kellock, Commissioner Wood of the RCMP, Laurent Beaudry of External Affairs and RCMP Inspector Leopold. Undaunted by this challenge, the Establishment sent a mouthpiece from the Justice Department to inform the court that all of these people would be only too happy to appear. The trouble was that King would most reluctantly be prevented from testifying because of his oath of office. Beaudry was confined to hospital following surgery and couldn't be moved. Commissioner Wood was unaccountably out of town and Inspector Leopold had apparently just broken his leg. Lawyers or counsel in any way connected with the Royal Commissioners would likewise, with the best will in the world, as the court would surely understand, be unable to take the stand because their relationship to the Commission was that of lawyer and client with its inviolable confidentiality. J.L. took it like a lamb. His ploy got us some headlines, but nothing more. He next made a series of objections, all of which had been disposed of by other judges in previous hearings and were disallowed. One complaint I thought particularly well founded: the fact that the press had been printing damaging extracts from the commissioners' report, finding the accused guilty even while their trials were still underway. The Montreal Gazette in particular had been doing this from the days the trials started. Judge McDougall tut-tutted and made a stab at locking the stable door. He agreed it was deplorable; he admonished the press to use the greatest of care which he was sure they would do in future.

J.L. now seemed to have emptied his quiver. His position up to this point was that I was not properly before the court for all the reasons he had advanced, so that I had not yet entered a plea. I was now faced with the question: "How do you plead – guilty or not guilty?"

All turned to look at me, including J.L., who had been adamant that I should not plead but who was now looking at me as though he had no idea what I would say. What I said was: "If I am properly before this court, I plead not guilty."

J.L. barely cross-examined the key witness, who, of course, was Gouzenko. Igor was in better shape physically and emotionally than J.L. and had had ten months of coaching and rehearsal. The rhetoric froze on J.L.'s lips and at times he seemed to have completely lost the thread of the proceedings. Cartwright and the judge could scarcely hide their embarrassment. During an adjournment one of the Crown lawyers commiserated with me. "How did you ever get tied up with a guy like this? You'd be better off with nobody."

In situations of prolonged stress, time takes on a different dimension. The bruised ego welcomes the balm of even fifteen minutes of détente from confrontation no less than a whole night's respite from fate's battering. The sweet reality of sleep, helped no doubt by a stiff nightcap, wipes out tomorrow's imagined agony. Sufficient unto the day is the horror thereof. All the more distressing when something happens to disrupt one of these cease-fires. In the middle of one night Phyllis and I awoke to loud banging on our door. I opened the door to find J.L. there wielding a walking stick, one of his affectations. Seeing me, he moved off down the corridor to bang on another door. By the time the hotel security people, my brother and the secretary had cooled J.L. down and put him back to bed, we were able to figure out what had happened. There had really been very little for the secretary to do in the past few days, and even less for my brother. As two unattached people with time on their hands, they had not unnaturally taken to spending time together, to the point that J.L. had felt they had formed an unacceptable relationship, one he had probably mentally reserved for himself. He had expected his overnight raid to surprise them in bed but had got his room numbers confused.

The trial moved quickly to its inevitable conclusion on Friday with the judge's guilty verdict, with sentence deferred until the following Monday. Back at the hotel J.L. started to whimper, whether over my fate or his own performance was not clear. Fat tears trickled down his cheeks. "I'd give anything to trade places with you," he said. "At least, yours is an honorable offence."

What I had not known was that J.L. himself was awaiting trial on charges of indecent assault and beating one Elizabeth Guenard for which less than a month later he would receive a merciless tongue lashing from the judge and a sentence of six months in prison. When I read the newspaper account of his trial it reminded me of another case I had read about in Montreal a few years earlier. A well-known businessman, whose name the judge ordered the press not to reveal, had been found guilty of indecent attack on two girls aged five and seven. He was fined three hundred dollars and given time to pay. The judge didn't want the man's name to be known to spare his relatives embarrassment.

Incidentally, the defence lawyer had been Lucien Gendron.

Fifty-four
Impasse

No sooner had I been found guilty and was again out on bail pending appeal than I was called to testify at Halperin's trial, where once again I declined. This produced a new and interesting reaction from their Cartwright. The Crown would have to consider its course with regard to further action against me, he said, because there was some doubt about the magistrate's powers to punish me summarily for my refusal at this time to be sworn. He asked for an adjournment, saying "I cannot safely proceed." I had argued, as before, that my own case was still before the courts. Even though my trial had taken place, the appeal was still to be heard. Cartwright tried to get me to say what I would do once the appeal was heard, but I refused to commit myself. The trial was then adjourned for three months to allow the Crown to huddle in search of a solution.

I should explain that both Halperin and his lawyer made every possible effort to persuade me to testify. They probably felt confident that they could show that I had deceived and exploited him, that he was at the worst an innocent and naive victim of a conspiracy. They might well have convinced a jury. I felt, however, that they greatly underestimated the determination of the Crown to obtain convictions, and the enormous scope opened up to the prosecution under conspiracy charges to find him guilty even on the basis of a nodding acquaintanceship, all of which was amply proven in subsequent trials.

During a court recess as I was standing in the vestibule talking to Phyllis, Byron W. Howard, the go-fer on the Crown's team, came up to us and said that they couldn't condone my stand but had a sneaking respect for my tenacity just the same and that, in view of my existing sentence of five years, he was sure Cartwright was not going to press for additional punishment. When I was called to the stand I once again refused to testify, saying, amongst other things: "I have been consistently deprived of the normal advantages afforded individuals under the law…I was forced to make statements to the Royal Commission and I was convicted before I ever came to court."

Cartwright responded with a savage attack on my behaviour. The three- month huddle must have resolved any doubts about the contempt question, because he demanded the severe penalty which he said was within the judge's power to impose. County Court Judge McDougall, the same judge who had presided at my own trial, obliged him by sentencing me to one year, which he made plain would be extra to the five he had previously imposed. I grabbed Phyllis by the hand, said "Let's get out of here," and made for the door, closely followed by the bailiff.

The following day, an Ottawa Citizen headline read: "Halperin freed in surprise move by court." Judge McDougall said that careful consideration of the evidence failed to prove to his satisfaction that Halperin had been linked to any conspiracy. The documentary evidence was inadmissible since Halperin was not linked to a conspiracy by other evidence. The newspaper, keeping up its editorial attack on the whole Royal Commission procedure, called it a blunder to have issued the Commission report before trials, and concluded: "The case for a Parliamentary Committee enquiry is stronger than ever." But, of course, there never was any enquiry.

Fifty-five
Life in Limbo

During 1946, court appearances as witness or accused were scattered throughout the year like currants in a bun. The spaces between were rarely restful. The stress of trying to get settled with a lawyer, the inevitable servings of subpoena after subpoena, the constant vilification in the press, the knowledge that it could only end behind bars, gave the year a nightmarish quality. I happened to be on the train from Ottawa to Montreal on the day the Ottawa Citizen ran a large photograph on the front page of me wearing a hat. Wherever I looked in the coach, I'd see myself. I had taken my hat off in the train which is perhaps why nobody showed a flicker of recognition. A noisy, nearby foursome included an elderly man with a broad Scots accent. They were speculating on the origins of the accused and on what would happen to them.

"What would you do with the Scotchman, Mac?" one of them asked.

"Him? Och, I'd shoot him."

It was not the first time this thought had been expressed. A burly guard escorting me from the Carleton County Jail to Magistrates' Court early in the game showed me how effective the Commission publicity had been.

"I guess you'll be shot," he told me.

I had long since decided, with surprising accuracy, that five years – or a "fin" as I later learned to call it – was a likelier sentence, so this talk did not overly disturb me. Being paraded in handcuffs and under escort in police cars and paddy wagons, the object of curiosity wherever we went, was worse until we got used to it and learned how to deal with our escorts. I say we, because there were many occasions on which the Crown shifted groups of so-called co-conspirators from court to court, and several times we had to be rounded up from temporary residence in one jail or another where we were being held awaiting bail or at the court's pleasure pending contempt charges.

On one occasion, Gerson and I were among the vanload of prisoners being driven in the early morning from Bordeaux to the Montreal courthouse. We were handcuffed together. In mid trip, Gerson had an uncontrollable urge to urinate and became so manic in his demands to the single elderly guard on board to stop the bus that the man probably thought there was a mass escape underway. Finally he unlocked Gerson's handcuff and let him go to the back of the bus where he let go on the floor with a prodigious pee. When he came back to our seat, the guard was so much off-guard that he forgot to put the cuff back on. When we trooped into the courthouse elevator Gerson was holding his half of the cuffs to make it seem we were still locked together. A sharp-eyed Provincial policeman saw this, and we were the ones who were bawled out, not the jail guard.

We learned from some of our new acquaintances that for journeys of any length such as Montreal to Ottawa or Montreal to Kingston, the police had a meal allowance for each prisoner. This they kept for themselves until we challenged them. The first time, they reluctantly took us into a restaurant in handcuffs, to be gawked at by the lunch crowd. By way of revenge, I ordered a rib steak, rare, with two fried eggs on top, Australian style. On the last trip we made, we even managed to talk them into beer with our meal.

Eventually, the word seemed to have been passed that we were not like most of their customers and were not likely to cause them trouble. This probably saved the life of an elderly Provincial policeman who was sent with a young driver a year later, in 1948, to fetch Gerson and me from Kingston Penitentiary. We were to appear for identification at the last of the trials, that of Raymond Boyer, in Montreal. The drive on old Highway 2 was a pleasant relief from a cell; we ate well en route, and the cops were generous with cigarettes. All went well until we reached Montreal Island when the cop in the passenger seat started to groan and retch and then slumped in his seat, seeming to lose consciousness. The young driver clearly did not know what to do; it must have occurred to him that he was now outnumbered and he seemed determined to go non-stop to Montreal no matter what. We began to berate him. Had he no feeling for his own partner? What if the guy croaked? Don't forget, we were witnesses to the event and in our opinion the only decent thing to do was to get help without delay. We were approaching Pointe Claire on the Lakeshore, where I knew there was a fire station, and we convinced the driver to stop there. The sick man was carried inside, a doctor was called and the next hour was spent pumping out his stomach and bringing him round enough to be propped up in the front seat to continue to Montreal. During this time we walked around unmolested on the main street, being careful to keep within sight of the young driver. Just before we reached Provincial Police headquarters in Montreal, he pulled over and with many apologies handcuffed us for the benefit of his superiors on arrival. I clearly remember the arrival because we got out into a crowd of cops, including the infamous Capt. Benoit, with four-foot-long riot sticks. They were unnaturally merry and boisterous as they waited for the cars that would take them to some picket line or other where a few skulls needed cracking.

I realized that my boarding school and army experience would come in handy in the penitentiary. I felt I could handle the probable hardships, except for one problem: from time to time I suffered from sinusitis which could become so excruciatingly painful and disabling that only a powerful painkiller was of any help, something I knew I was not likely to get on the inside. In the late summer of 1946 during a lull in the trials some friends invited me for a weekend of fishing on Georgian Bay, hoping it would help me to unwind. The moment our cabin cruiser hit the swells and the wind hit my forehead the pain began and went on without let-up for the whole weekend. Back home, I went to see a nose specialist who produced a torrent of fluid from my sinuses by sticking a long probe so far up my nose that I thought he must have reached my scalp. He diagnosed the condition as a physical allergy, in my case an allergy to cold. There really wasn't much I could do about it, he told me. Some unexplained feedback mechanism must have taken over because not once in the five years I was inside did I ever suffer from sinusitis.

The year was not without its lighter moments, too. I was in a department store one morning, waiting at a counter with a number of other shoppers, when I saw Staff Sergeant René Noël of the RCMP, the officer who had arrested me at Dorval, standing in plain clothes at the edge of the crowd.

"Hi, Sergeant," I called out. "Don't tell me you're following me."

He looked very uncomfortable, came up to me and whispered that he had retired from the RCMP. He was now working for the store…you know, shoplifters, purse snatchers, men exposing themselves in elevators, that kind of thing. I'm afraid I broke his cover to any flashers who might have been in the crowd.

"You're a store dick," I said, so all could hear. "I can't believe it. What a come-down."

During the long days of boredom, hanging around outside courtrooms, especially during the Rose proceedings, anything that broke the tedium was welcome. One morning, the halls and corridors were full of laughter as the word circulated about what had happened in one of the courtrooms. A middle-aged prostitute, still quite drunk after a night in the cells, had called out to the judge from the prisoners' dock, "You old goat, what you need is a good fuck, and I'm just the one to give it to you."

When the year of purgatory drew to a close and the time came to descend into hell, Miriam Kennedy and her friend Ed Chapin invited Phyllis and me to a last supper at the Samovar night club with the thought, no doubt, of ending up on a cheerful and even celebratory note. Instead, the evening turned into a wake. I was thirty years old, Ed more than twice my age. As we broke up to go home, tears welled up in Ed's eyes. He proposed to take my place, do my time for me. I was still young, with my life ahead of me; his life was mostly behind him, he had nothing to lose. I really believe he was sincere. But he was wrong about his longevity. He stuck around for another thirty years.

Fifty-six
Igor Beaver

The picture presented to the public of the young Russian cipher clerk who had defected from his embassy in Ottawa with a shirtful of documents was that of a terrified, fair-haired youth warning the free world at great personal risk of a dastardly plot which would lead assuredly to renewed world war. T. F. Ahearn, president of the Ottawa Electric Railway Company, was so moved by Gouzenko's brave performance that he set up a $100,000 trust fund for him. A score of editorial writers heaped praise on his selfless act. Mackenzie King went out of his way to receive him personally and described the meeting in a glowing diary entry: "I wanted him to know that I appreciated his manliness, his courage and standing for the right...Told him the Government would keep an eye on them all [his wife and children] and to keep his faith strong." The cabinet rewarded him for his services by invoking a rarely used prerogative to make him an instant British subject by special Act of the Sovereign.

The Gouzenko reality as it evolved over the years was somewhat different. On first meeting Gouzenko, everyone noticed one thing – he spoke broken English with a thick accent. In court he spoke slowly with frequent pauses while he searched for a word. He and the RCMP had a problem understanding each other and as a result had difficulty getting things straight. In spite of this language deficiency, Gouzenko miraculously composed a document in his own handwriting, a month or so after his defection, in English which was at least as good as everyday newspaper English and pregnant with classical North American anti-red jargon. His English had improved remarkably under RCMP tutelage. Or could it have been coaching? Not that he wasn't a willing and resourceful pupil. He practised new words and phrases before each trial, adding to his testimony as the cases proceeded, producing new reasons and motives which fuelled the cold war fever. According to Harvison's son Wes, his father considered Gouzenko to be an ideal witness, acting out of conviction. But it would appear that the conviction was as much the result of a carefully crafted and well-rehearsed performance directed by the RCMP and Justice Department.

Attempts to discredit Gouzenko's alleged idealism and altruistic motives by Rose's lawyer, Joseph Cohen, and others during the trials were foiled as much by Gouzenko's skill as a witness as by the care taken by the Crown to lead him and by the courts to protect him from too insistent cross-examination. Opinions and "hearsay" evidence adduced by the defence were invariably ruled inadmissible, while page after page of the same kind of evidence from Gouzenko wound up in the record. The prosecution treated him like a born-again Christian who had seen the light as he proclaimed his new-found faith in democracy and castigated the Soviet devil. Defence Lawyer A. W. Beament in one trial even asked point blank: "Are you a Christian?" "Yes," Gouzenko replied. In response to Beament's astonishment that a person could be a Christian while also a member in good standing of the Young Communist League, Gouzenko snapped back: "There is nothing strange about that."

As the Cold War burgeoned so did Gouzenko's memory. After a year of gestation following his first court appearance he brought forth new allegations that there were actually eight spy rings operating in Canada. In his role as military strategist he recommended that Canada, in co-operation with the United States, fortify the Arctic without delay to meet the anticipated Soviet invasion. This was too much for the Ottawa Citizen, which poked fun at the all-knowing cipher clerk – spy expert, strategist, military engineer, statesman and diplomat.

Dizzy with success, Gouzenko, his ghost writers and the RCMP wound up with egg on their faces in April 1947 over an article in New World which alleged that monies donated by the public to the Canadian Aid to Russia Fund were misappropriated by the fund officials, who happened to be public figures of the highest integrity. This was clearly a malicious and unfounded falsehood for which Gouzenko was forced to make a public retraction.

The composite portrait of him painted by the policemen and their wives, journalists and others who were associated with him, sometimes as a painful but unavoidable duty, is that of a thoroughly unpleasant, obstreperous, paranoid, opinionated individual. No altruist he, but a resourceful egotist, determined to milk his defection for the last drop of fame and fortune. According to most of these people, his motives were entirely selfish and materialistic. He had no compunction in leaving his mother and sister in Russia to face the consequences of his defection, which he admitted would be drastic. He wanted money and lots of it. But when he had it he squandered it, going through more than one fortune and winding up borrowing shamelessly from friends and, finally, casual acquaintances who were never repaid. His personal habits were piggish. In restaurants he ordered three meals at a time which he ate with knife, fork and fingers indiscriminately.

Although Gouzenko's disclosure of the passing of information to Soviet embassy personnel by some Canadians, including myself, is beyond dispute, he was used by the Canadian, American and British authorities for a purpose that spread far beyond the hard facts of the case itself.

Historian Donald Avery, in a paper entitled Secrets Between Different Kinds of Friends analyses the policies and motives of the Canadian and United States governments in great detail and concludes:

> The evidence...suggests that winning the war and retaining the friendship of the Soviet Union were regarded as the most important considerations by both governments. This view was shared by the general public. Between 1943 and 1945 most North Americans regarded the USSR as a gallant ally. In Canada, for example, the National Council for Canadian-Soviet Friendship had branches in eighteen urban centres across the country and an executive which included Sir Ellsworth Flavelle as president and John David Eaton as vice-president. It is in this climate of opinion that the willingness of some Canadian scientists, "persons of

> marked ability and intelligence," to supply Colonel Zabotin with certain "secrets" must be considered, though not excused. The tragedy of these fellow travellers was that by the time the Royal Commission on Espionage was created in February 1946, the Soviet Union was neither an ally nor a friend.

Gouzenko was exploited not only internationally to fuel the cold war against the former friend and ally, but also domestically to justify an increasingly bitter attack on the Canadian labour movement. Some of the most effective labour leaders during the war, especially in the aircraft, electrical and shipbuilding industries, had been communists. Their support for all-out war had even led them sometimes into siding with an unpopular Labour Department in trying to persuade disgruntled union members not to strike. Once the pressures of war were lifted, the unions naturally went back to hard bargaining to have wartime wage ceilings removed and to share in the general prosperity. This resulted in widespread strikes across the industrial spectrum – textiles, breweries, meat packers, metal workers, copper and asbestos mines.

Another billiard ball gambit was formulated, this time by the owners: Gouzenko has shown that communists are out to destroy Canada; many unions are run by communists; therefore the unions are out to destroy Canada. Expose and root out the communists; lacking this leadership the unions will collapse; labour peace – i.e. a compliant work force – will once again prevail.

The Financial Post, in particular, went on the attack. Throughout 1946, article after article appeared: "How Communist Are Unions?" "Where is Red Strength?" "How to Recognize a Red." The articles were illustrated with photographs of labour leaders and quoted extensively from RCMP Inspector Leopold's stock-in-trade of "communist" books, secret oaths and revolutionary instructions, smacking quaintly of 1907 polemics. One article "How Communism Grows" featured a chart showing every community in Canada with the estimated number of people infected with the virus. Another article by Gilbert E. Jackson called "Let's Teach Communism to Everyone in Canada" had as its theme: Strikes and lawlessness are part of century-old Marxist strategy. He compared communists to Hitler's hoodlums.

Just who the real hoodlums were can be seen in one example from the lengthy Quebec textile workers' struggle with the millionaire owners, who a few years earlier had been described by E.E. McRuer, counsel to a Royal Commission investigating the textile industry as "this gang of high-placed crooks" whose careers were characterized by "inordinate barefaced lying, general fraud." Kent Rowley had been delegated by the Montreal Trades and Labour Council to organize the Montreal Cottons plant where, in 1946, the highest rate paid to a worker with twenty-five to thirty years service was 52 cents an hour. In the ensuing strike, Rowley was arrested and held without bail on the orders of Quebec Premier and Attorney General Maurice Duplessis for "sedition and conspiracy." When asked before sentencing whether he had anything to say, he replied: "Your Honour, I am here because of a conspiracy between Blair Gordon [Montreal Cottons owner] and Maurice Duplessis." The judge gave him six months in jail.

But they weren't finished with him yet. Four years later, the battle still unresolved, Rowley was again on the picket line at the Valleyfield plant where, in Rowley's own words: "Paul Benoit of the Quebec Provincial Police, who stands 6 feet 4 and weighs 250 pounds, came up to me and said – Are you going to go on picketing, Mr. Rowley? I told him, yes, because it's my right. He then told two cops who were standing by to grab me. One of them held me by one arm, his pal by the other and then Benoit took his night stick and smashed me over the head. I woke up in a cell in the Valleyfield jail."

Rowley's co-organizer Madeleine Parent says he told her Benoit later tried to enter his cell to give him another potentially fatal beating but was prevented from doing so by an outside doctor.

Gouzenko was probably unaware of the full extent of his contribution to the domestic cold war in which more often than not the owners yielded on questions of wages and conditions, but only after they had purged the unions of so-called trouble makers. He went his sad, anonymous way, digging his grave with his mouth, suing those who crossed him, pontificating to a vanishing audience, an embarrassment to his erstwhile friends. He lost his sight to the diabetes for which he had refused treatment, apparently because he feared assassination at the hands of the doctors. He died of a heart attack on June 25th, 1982, thirty-nine years to the day after arriving in Canada. He was quickly buried before news of his death reached the public.

PART FOUR

HOME ON THE RANGE

Fifty-seven
Fish

Stone walls do not a prison make,
Nor iron bars a cage;
Minds innocent and quiet take
That for an hermitage.
(Richard Lovelace, 1618-1658)

On April 16, 1947, Ottawa was buried in an unusually severe snow storm which made highways impassable. The Ontario Appeals Court had predictably denied my appeals both against conviction and sentence. As required, I had surrendered to the Carleton County Sheriff on the date of the appeal hearing, but because of the storm I could not be moved to Kingston Penitentiary when the decision came down. I therefore was forced to spend a few days in the Nicholas Street Jail – time which rankles to this day because, thanks to the knotty patterns of red tape, it did not count as time served. This would start only when I had passed through the fortress gates at Kingston.

The bad news was given to me in the jail office with Phyllis present, and we were told to say our final goodbyes. To me this was just another slow and excruciating step along a predictable path, but to Phyllis it appeared to come as a stunning shock, as though what she had all along supposed to be a nightmare from which she would eventually awake had suddenly become reality. She clung to me sobbing uncontrollably. The two elderly plain-clothes court officers in their shiny blue suits, to whom I had now become a "body dead/alive (check which)" on their delivery slip, were as unmoved as a couple of farmers picking up a superannuated cow for auction. They quickly separated us, handcuffed me and hustled me out to the rear seat of the waiting two-door car.

The April sun had quickly asserted itself after the storm, transforming the fields into piebald patches of brown and white so typical and evocative of Canadian spring, like a Goodridge Roberts landscape. Once outside the city, the officer in the front passenger seat leaned back, allowed I wasn't aiming to take off, and removed the handcuffs. It was the only remark either of them addressed to me for the whole trip. They resumed their desultory, mostly monosyllabic conversation for the rest of the journey, leaving me to my anguished thoughts of Phyllis as what was left of my comparative liberty trickled away, mocked by the reawakening of the countryside.

On arrival at the penitentiary my escorts obtained a receipt for one live body duly delivered. They left me in the charge of a disagreeable guard who had noticed the absence of leg irons and handcuffs and clearly disapproved of such soft treatment. He relieved me of my cigarettes, cash, wallet and keys then marched me across the prison yard to a room in a small building that I came to know as the Chief Keeper's Office. The only occupant was clearly a convict, to judge by his brown denim clothes with sewn-on number. Without once making eye contact he told me to strip naked. He sat me on a stool and within seconds doubled my nakedness by removing my hair with electric clippers, making four or five passes from back to front of my scalp. I was then told to get into a tin wash tub on the floor, looking for all the world like the Durham miners' baths except that this one was filled with a pinkish opaque fluid smelling of carbolic. I was required to splash the vile liquid over every square inch of my body with special attention to the hairy and recently hairy parts.

I learned that my so-called valuables would be returned to me upon my release, but that normally clothing was burned. However, if I insisted, it would be bagged and could be picked up by an approved relative. I later came to understand that few who went through this procedure had anything worth preserving. Those who came in with decent clothes would easily acquire replacements by the usual means, out of the proceeds of their first "score" after release. There would be nobody from the outside interested in picking up their bagged garments and in any case they would be provided with a free "front" (suit) and "kicks" (shoes) by the "joint" (prison) when they were "sprung" (released).

As I stood feeling shrivelled by the disinfectant a uniformed officer came into the room. He turned out to be the Chief Keeper, third in command of the prison and responsible for the guard personnel. He was a working-class Englishman to judge by his voice. He put me in mind as soon as he spoke of the bullying Hughes of S.H. Benson and the Mill Hill drill sergeant. I came to know him as one of a detested breed – the military-trained British jailers, hangovers from colonial days, known as "broncos" or, more often, "bronco bastards." Theirs not to reason why, theirs but to hang and flay. He had held the same job when the Archambault Royal Commission probed the goings-on behind the stone walls in 1937 but had declined its invitation to appear before it to answer to unsatisfactory reports made against him, choosing to go on vacation instead. In spite of his slight build, quiet manner and deafness – he wore a large, old-fashioned hearing aid on his chest – there was an air of menace about him, emphasized by the lead-loaded swagger stick he carried and by the barely audible tuneless whistle coming from his lipless mouth. Perhaps he had only come to see me out of curiosity, or to size me up, because apart from asking me my name he had nothing else to say.

Disinfected, disenfranchised and dehumanized, having forfeited my name for a number – 8994 – I was outfitted with longjohns, heavy blue pants and jacket (both pocketless), denim shirt and boots a size and a half too big, obliging me to lift my feet carefully like a vaudeville comedian so as not to trip over my own toes, and marched to the prison dome.

Here I joined four or five other newcomers – "fish" as I learned to describe them. The work day had just finished and the different shop gangs were filing through the dome in an endless line to disappear down one radiating wing and reappear emerging from the adjacent wing carrying aluminum mess trays holding their suppers. They would then peel off at the appropriate wing and clatter up the iron stairs and along the galleries to their cells on one of the four levels in each wing. In spite of the no-talking rule, the drumming of feet and the clanking of metal reverberating from the unrelieved stone, tile and steel surfaces gave me a discouraging foretaste of the cacophony of jailhouse life.

Our little group attracted much attention. In the absence of "stiffs" (newspapers – streng verboten in those days) and any access to crime news, "fish" were an important source of information about friends further back in the pipeline in police cells, jails or even still on the street. The senior guard who oversaw the whole dome proceedings squelched most attempts at communication with nothing more than scowls and gestures. He seemed to me to be a particularly unpleasant and threatening individual, not someone to trifle with. While I was busy trying to make myself invisible, a redheaded con appeared and walked briskly right up to me.

"Lunan?" he asked.

I looked for guidance at the guard, who simply glared.

"Oh, for Chris'sake," Redhead said. "It's okay. Come with me."

I followed him to the kitchen wicket where the meal trays were issued. Here I was given a tray containing a quarter of barbecued chicken, french fries, coleslaw, several doughnuts, apple sauce, cookies, chocolate bar, an apple and a big mug of coffee.

"I'm Red Beaver," he said. "You do know it's Pesach, don't you?"

The tiny minority of Jews in the joint were evidently aware of my various refusals to testify. This alone would have been enough to establish me in their eyes as "okay," but to have refused to testify against Jews made me doubly okay. Thanks to the rabbi's efforts they had been allowed to receive special Passover meals prepared by the local Jewish women and brought in by the rabbi. They had made me an honorary Jew for the occasion. Thus my first meal in the penitentiary was a delicious home-cooked Passover feast.

I discovered that Red Beaver and his brother Max, who was also doing time, sat atop the criminal hierarchy in Toronto, controlling a large part of the heroin ("H" or "horse") trade. They, and in fact most of the big-time professional thieves and con artists, treated me with respect. This was because they could not believe that anyone with the opportunities for enrichment which I had had could possibly have come out of it without a bundle of money hidden away somewhere. Doing it for idealistic reasons or from political motivation was obviously so much hogwash. They listened to my denials with knowing smiles as much as to say, this guy knows the score; no way he's going to jeopardize his stash by even admitting that it exists. It was a strange feeling to have such approval, but far better than for same reason being labelled a rat and having them against me.

The single-occupancy cells, barred across their entire width like cages in a zoo, looked out across a four-storey-high hallway to the arched barred windows of the outside wall of the cell block. Once locked in, you were visually isolated so that human communication was entirely by voice during the limited periods when it was allowed. Obviously, to compete with a hundred other voices you had to be able to produce a high decibel level and somehow filter out the reply from the surrounding din. It was a bedlam similar to a particularly frantic day on the stock-exchange floor, except that there were no gestures or signs to help decipher the shouted messages. Even communication with my immediate neighbour, to satisfy his curiosity about my offence and sentence, I found almost impossible.

There were other methods of communication, I later discovered. Each cell had a toilet, and each toilet was connected by waste pipes in the usual manner to a common sewage-collection system. This made it possible to "telephone" a friend in a distant cell by each emptying the water in the toilet bowl trap and talking into the bowl with a blanket over one's head. Sewer rats were also said to travel by the same route. I heard stories, too, of old-timers patiently training a pet mouse to scurry along the gallery to another cell with a string tied to its leg. The string would then be used to deliver or retrieve some article of contraband.

Once the final count for the day had been taken, the ranges were secured by a central locking system until the following morning. This did not mean, however, that you were free from surveillance. At intervals during the night the duty screw would make his rounds in thickly padded shoes – and he had better wear them because if his noisy footfall were to disturb the sleeping cons, the cry would go up, "Put that horse in the stable." His job was to check each cell with a flashlight to see, amongst other things, that you had your hands outside the blanket. Penitentiary regulations had been virtually unchanged since the nineteenth century. A Victorian, puritanical Christian moral code, with a strong streak of sadism, still underlay penal philosophy, making masturbation a punishable offence.

In the forties, there were comparatively few well-educated inmates. The occasional embezzling lawyer, drug-addicted professional or pederastic priest would turn up, but these were the days before widespread white-collar crime involving company executives, financial wizards and government officials, or at least before these criminals were being uncovered and occasionally brought to justice.

The penitentiary departments and shops were in charge of uniformed instructors, some of whom were reasonably qualified as tradesmen but because of laziness, incompetence or functional illiteracy made hopeless administrators. Accordingly, any inmate with simple clerical skills was much in demand to work as a clerk in one of the offices. Since the written word in all forms – materials requisitions, reports, requests – had to pass through the Warden's hands on its tortuous bureaucratic passage to Ottawa, the Warden himself had an interest in seeing that the clerical positions were adequately filled. As long as the bumf which crossed his desk was reasonably intelligible he could simply minute it in the margin and save himself the trouble of composing a document from scratch.

After no more than a few weeks in the main cellblock, I was one day summoned to the Stores department, which occupied offices immediately inside the main gate, and installed as clerk. At the same time I was told that I had been moved to a cell in a separate building within the walls that had once been the Prison for Women but had now become popularly known as the Old Man's Home. I did not immediately realize how lucky I was. The Old Man's Home did count a few old men among its twenty-four or so occupants, but the rest were men of all ages, mostly lifers or those with responsible jobs as kitchen, hospital or clerical help. There were a few who probably would have had difficulty getting along in the general prison population, including a former Canadian prisoner-of-war who had co-operated with the Gestapo against his comrades; a tiny old church janitor accused of child molestation; and an unfortunate soldier who had gone berserk in action and shot and killed several of his mates before unsuccessfully trying to kill himself, and who probably should not have been there at all.

My new neighbours, in addition to the three already mentioned, included the prison's oldest inhabitant who was in the eleventh year of his second life sentence for rape; a young pyromaniac who had burned down a dance hall with the loss of several lives; a Ukrainian miner who had been using his wife and daughter in a family whorehouse enterprise until the wife baulked and was fatally disciplined with an axe; a young married sailor with young children who had celebrated VE day too riotously in Halifax and woke up to find himself accused of raping a sixty-year-old woman for which he was doing twelve years; the past president of the Lebanese Society in Toronto who was taking the rap for a conscription deferment scam involving some prominent Liberals; a drunk who had murdered his mother; Eddie MacDonald, brother of the famous Mickie who had been a fellow fish with communist leader Tim Buck in 1932 and who was one of the very few convicts ever successfully to escape from Kingston Penitentiary; and my old friend Red Hunt.

This group, in whose company I would spend the best part of the next five years, in spite of its horrific background, was a microcosm of society at large. It exhibited the same loyalties, prejudices, humour, pettiness, insight, jealousies, tolerance, vanity, pride, selfishness and generosity as any other random assortment of citizens. And it was united in having a common enemy – anyone with brass buttons. They claimed that if their mug shots were displayed side by side with similar shots of the warden and staff, or for that matter any group of judges or politicians, a discerning eye would unhesitatingly pick out the latter as the criminals.

My new boss, Storekeeper Harold G., took my ill-fitting footwear as a personal affront, reflecting poorly on the prestige of his department. He could not understand why I had not objected to them. My reply was that if I had my way I would not be wearing them at all; they were a reflection of the prison authorities, not of me. I discovered that this position always infuriated them. It was a perfect piece of dumb insolence which placed me in the position of not complaining while at the same time pointing out the mean standards of the authorities from which I wished to disassociate myself. He escorted me to the Change Room and saw to it that I was decently outfitted with shoes that fitted, summer underwear and denim jacket and pants more suited to the steam-heated, indoor working environment than the heavy winter wear I had been issued (which was essential to anyone working outside, because no outerwear of any kind was supplied).

The final step of indoctrination was an appearance at noon in the Warden's court, held in the Chief Keeper's Hall adjacent to the Dome. Warden Allen – Little Hitler to the initiated – sat at a small desk well protected by a group of duty screws. Others lounged in the background prepared to heckle and jeer at whichever unfortunate up on charge on a "ducat" was vainly trying to explain himself. The principal piece of furniture in the room, apart from the warden's desk, was the leather-covered flogging bench with its ankle and wrist straps to hold the blindfolded, bare-bottomed victim immobile. Amongst the hecklers were a few keepers – senior screws, all of them big and brawny – who would be called on by the Warden to administer the floggings, using a heavy leather strap cunningly incised with a pattern which would flex open in the air then bite on the victim's bare buttocks and pull off pieces of skin.

Against this intimidating backdrop, the Warden soothingly explained that you were in good hands. Provided you behaved yourself, no harm would befall you. Just keep your nose clean, obey every order of every officer unhesitatingly and concentrate on doing your time. (It was said that one distraught newcomer faced with a long sentence blurted out that he would never be able to do all that time, to which the Warden had replied: "We're not asking you to do all of it. Just do as much as you can.") The Archambault Royal Commissioners had sat in on trials conducted in this same court and concluded that a prisoner had little chance of fair or impartial treatment since the Warden invariably took the word of the guard against that of the convict. They gave Warden Allan himself a reluctant passing grade, noting his limitations of education which in a more efficiently staffed prison would have prevented him from rising to the position of Warden.

Under these circumstances, gallows humour helped to sustain us cons. It was accepted that at times the bit would chafe. But complaining to another con about one's lot was taboo. Anyone who did so was usually invited to tell his troubles to Jesus, or was silently offered a joint bandana handkerchief to weep into. Cursing judges, cops and screws for being every kind of perjurer, liar and hypocrite – especially hypocrite – was okay.

But never, never show self-pity.

Fifty-eight
Old Man's Home

Life soon settled down to a not unfamiliar routine – work alternating with home, home in this case being the Old Man's Home, specifically a tiny room furnished with a narrow cot, a stool, a table and small locker. There was a barred window that could be opened, looking out on the prison grounds. There were no bars on the door, only an ornamental iron grille over the glass pane in an ordinary wooden domestic door that was locked by a simple passage lock. Unlike the main cells, there were no toilet facilities. This omission was partially offset by conniving with someone with access to the kitchen to fetch you an empty canned tomato tin from the garbage. One of my close neighbours, a gross, slightly retarded day labourer who had killed a fellow worker with a blow on the head with a shovel, used his tin for all toilet purposes. Those of us who were more fastidious, when overcome by the urge after lock-up, had to bang on the door to summon the screw to let us out to go to the common toilet. This was a converted cell equipped with a six-foot-long cast iron sink closely flanked by two seat-less toilets. Morning ablutions were performed at this sink under one of several cold-water taps, cheek by jowl – all too literally – with the occupants of the two toilets, and preferably not when the little old child molester was using the sink to wash the rag he used to cover his anal fistula. Washing tended to be perfunctory while drying was a token gesture, the issue towel being a threadbare kitchen dishtowel.

No matter what the physical conditions of imprisonment, the loss of freedom is the overwhelming, inescapable reality. This was softened somewhat within the walls of the Old Man's Home by the granting of a tiny measure of self-determination denied to the cons in the main cellblocks. For two hours in the evening our cells were unlocked. We were free to stay in them to study, brood or lapse into the vacant trance-like state which hardened cons can switch on as an escape from reality – or we could emerge to sample the social life of the common room. Here one of the main activities was pairing off with someone to tramp back and forth the length of the hall, doing a brisk military-style about-turn at each end. In this way, I came to know the life stories of many of my neighbours.

One of my walking companions was a distinguished looking white-haired gentleman who looked like a pillar of the church, which in fact he had been. He was a manufacturer who had invented the rubber-coated horseshoe. One Sunday, after attending church, he had walked to the home of his business partner and, when the man had answered the door, shot him dead. He then walked over to the police station and turned himself in. He felt absolutely no remorse for the act, perhaps because his partner was "only a Jew." He claimed he had discovered that the man had been defrauding him for years and had put the business into such financial straits that his wife had died from the stress. His act was a simple act of justice that God would surely condone.

Another and much more interesting companion, also elderly, was Herman Stutz, known as "Hoiman the Joiman" although actually he was Swiss. He was a lifelong alcoholic, which had cost him his toes and any chance of ever being employed again in Switzerland. Love of wine was the cause of both problems. While working as a night watchman in a large Swiss winery, he had helped himself to a few glasses from one of the huge vats and forgotten to close the spigot before passing out. Later, while doing his compulsory military service, he had again passed out, but this time on night sentry duty high in the mountains, and was lucky to have survived with only frostbite of the feet. In spite of his wasted life, Stutz was an educated man who loved to discuss philosophy, about which he was very well informed, as he staggered back and forth at my side. He was doing something like twelve years for attempted murder, the victim of a mix of family hostility, police insensitivity, judicial skepticism and Eastern Daylight Saving Time. He had been bumming, with the occasional odd job, in Hamilton.

His wife, from whom he was separated, amongst other reasons because she was a "hully ruller" who disapproved of his atheistic life style, also lived in Hamilton with his daughter with whom he was still on friendly terms. He had heard that people were being hired for the summer in the Niagara area and decided to go there. But first he had time for a few beers with an acquaintance who confided to him that he had stolen a revolver and was looking for help to peddle it.

This was too much for Stutz who was a drunk, not a thief. He went to the toilet then took his coat which he had hung on the coat rack and left. When he got to the station to catch his train, he discovered that it had left almost an hour ago, these being the days when railroad schedules used standard time the year round. Left with time on his hands, he decided to go to say goodbye to his daughter. Going up the steps to his wife's house he stumbled and fell noisily. Part of the clatter came from a .38 revolver which he realized his tavern pal must have put in his pocket unknown to him, and which had fallen on the porch floor when he stumbled. He found the look of terror on his wife's face when she saw the weapon so ridiculous that he grabbed the gun and fired two shots into the porch ceiling for want of suitably scathing words. With such an unlikely explanation Stutz was doomed. His wife rallied the Holy Rollers to help her blacken his character and the judge obliged them by handing out a twelve-year sentence for attempted murder.

"Nifty" was another entertaining walking companion. He was prominent in the Lebanese community and was of some importance to the Liberal Party because of his influence in getting out the vote. He would receive new immigrants from Lebanon at his home to explain the intricacies of life in Canada. After inviting them to wash (he knew that many of them would use the toilet bowl for the purpose, never having seen a basin with running water) he would give them dinner then tell them that there was no way they would ever get a job in Canada without having a certificate of education. Normally this was almost impossible for a newcomer to get, but he was prepared to bend the law and provide them with the necessary paper. He issued them with impressively phoney documents, for which, of course, he collected a handsome fee.

I believe that the money meant little to Nifty; it was the scam itself that gave him so much pleasure. He had endless stories of the pork-barrelling and influence peddling of his political pals and of the after-hours fun and games, both heterosexual and homosexual, reaching up to the highest levels. No doubt Nifty embellished the truth, but I knew enough about Ottawa to realize that he was familiar with the scene, and with names, and could not have been making it up entirely. He and his Liberal friends had been doing a profitable business selling conscription call-up deferments through their bureaucratic connections until someone fingered them. Nifty was left holding the bag. He worked his way through the upper reaches of the political Establishment all the way to Mackenzie King's green baize door in an effort to wiggle off the hook but the Prime Minister refused him entry. I saw Nifty leave at the end of his sentence in a long limousine that took up most of the security lock between the outer and inner gates of the prison.

Paddy the Wop was another character I took a turn with. It puzzled me at first that he showed no offence at the racist label – in fact he even introduced himself to me that way – until I came to understand the universal use of racist shorthand – Wop, Hebe, Hunky, Mick, Coon – to be used descriptively, as much for easy identification, as out of racial animus. Paddy was a confirmed heroin addict with a poor reputation arising from his willingness when in the throes of a habit on the outside to betray anyone in return for a fix. With a name like his, he puzzled me by saying he was a Cornishman until I realized that, like many Italians, he was a plasterer by trade, his specialty being cornice work.

The other diversion in the common room, besides walking, was cards. Betting was forbidden, so poker was out, except for a few days around Christmas when the screw looked the other way and large quantities of weed (tobacco) changed hands. Bridge was the game. It took me some time to get up the courage to play. I had not played for years and I could see that the players were very expert and very unforgiving. When I finally did become the fourth at a game, old Louie, a perennial kibitzer, attached himself to me as a self-appointed coach. He would examine my hand, nodding and grunting as he assessed its possibilities and breathing his disgusting breath right into my face. Louie was a lifer, an old style Mafia-type hit man who must have been terrible to face in his prime. Even in old age the violence lurked in his rheumy eyes. When the hand was dealt, Louie followed the bidding and play and obviously decided which card I should play. If for any reason I played a different card he would deliver a vicious jab of his elbow to my ribs. Luckily for me, the others objected to this fifth man in the game and Louie was forced to quit.

Among my regular partners was a small-town lawyer who had helped himself to a fortune in other people's savings. He had a sharp mind and was an excellent player but was physically weak and flabby and an in-turned foot gave him a limp. Nevertheless even the toughest of the cons steered clear of him. At any threat, challenge, even contradiction, he would erupt with warning animal sounds. You could almost see his hackles rise. The tough guys would deem him unworthy of a major confrontation and back off. I think of our bridge games sometimes today when I watch the territorial and tribal rituals of baboons or hyenas on television.

My more or less regular partner was a young man, Wally K., who had been sentenced while still in his teens for his part with two partners in a long series of bank holdups across Ontario and Quebec. In the inevitable showdown with the police one of the partners had been shot in the spine, was paralysed and was now doing his time in a wheel chair. Wally was of Polish origin. He was embittered by the fact that his mother was obliged to work as a maid in a hotel and by the feeling that he would always be treated as a second-class citizen and not the deserving person he felt himself to be. And so he took his destiny into his own hands. In spite of the money, sex and luxurious living of his short criminal career (traceable bills fearfully spent, loveless gymnastic beddings, sleazy out-of-the-way motels with twenty-four-hour-a-day security watches, meals in cardboard containers) something in his peasant genes made him dream of the day when he would be released to establish himself as a chicken farmer.

With all these privileges, perhaps the most important aspect of the Old Man's Home lay in the quality of the screws assigned to duty in it. They were nearly always older men approaching retirement. They gave the impression of being sick of the whole business, not looking to provoke trouble like so many of the younger ones, even sympathetic to our plight. We were a fearsome collection of murderers, rapists, armed robbers and arsonists but there were no troublemakers in our midst. Security was never a problem for the authorities, and these old-timer screws, locked in alone overnight with their grisly charges, took it all in their quiet stride. One of them carried around with him the smell of the cancer that was slowly killing him. He had evidently decided to continue to work and be paid to die rather than quit. Another, Westlake by name, sticks in my mind partly because of his patience and good nature during one horrible night when I was stricken with a rebellious gut which kept him going up and down the stairs all night in response to my frantic rapping on the door. I was happy to see my judgment of him as a decent, compassionate man confirmed by his son, who himself became an officer with Corrections Canada, in his recollections of his father and of his upbringing in Portsmouth Village, the guards' nearby ghetto.

Two other regulars at the Old Man's Home gave the lie to the Bronco Bastard label. Both were Cockneys, old Imperial soldiers, but quite unscrew-like in their behaviour. One of them gave me a clue to his tolerant attitude when he spoke of being torpedoed during World War I and clinging to the slanting deck of the sinking ship. The cry went up, "Swim for your lives, boys." But he couldn't swim. He was saved from drowning by a shipmate. The relived anguish in his eyes as he recalled the incident was much like that of Charlie Mac, one of my neighbours, who had been sentenced to hang for murdering his wife and had been reprieved only forty-eight hours before his date with the scaffold. The brush of death can have a cleansing effect.

Fifty-nine
The Stores

The Storekeeper, Harold G., had at one time been employed by a bank. Although a uniformed officer, his manner seemed to say that this was a temporary aberration from his pinstriped status that was his true persona. He was at the top of his salary scale, which meant that he was pulling down fifty-five dollars a week. He had two, later three assistant storekeepers in addition to his three convict helpers, so he had very little to do most of the time and became a familiar sight daydreaming, sometimes gently snoring at his roll-top desk. My job as typist clerk was the only one which he would have had to perform himself in the absence of a capable typist, so he must have been relieved to get somebody reliable. For my part, I wanted to keep busy, avoid boredom and exercise my brains. I poached on his territory on a widening salient and he gave ground uncomplainingly.

The two assistant storekeepers were Howard P. and Ross C. Ross was a bookkeeper, with none of the usual attributes of a screw. In fact, he was a cop-hater, based upon an experience in Montreal when he had run afoul of a Montreal French-speaking policeman during a traffic altercation, been roughed up and barely escaped arrest. His anti-French bias cancelled out any possible fraternal bond with fellow brass-buttons. He loved cars and routinely drove far in excess of the speed limit. He was a big man with an oddly flattened nose sprouting black hair, and a deeply grooved upper lip, all of which gave him a bison look and made him speak in a sniffly, nasal voice. He was the only one of the three who treated us as equal fellow workers. He more than once expressed sympathy for our plight and, even more subversively, criticized the mean-mindedness of some other guards. On one glorious occasion he and Howard, who clearly disliked each other, nearly came to blows. They stood whirling their fists at each other and snorting until Harold came out of his trance to intervene. Best of all, Ross always left a full package of tobacco prominently on his desk with the unspoken understanding that we could help ourselves. The tobacco was the cheapest roll-your-own variety which he brought back from his frequent trips to the United States but was none the less much appreciated. For our evening supply we would roll a cigarette stuffed with as much tobacco as we could pack into it and still get the paper to overlap enough to get the glue to hold. Harold rarely left his tobacco unattended. Howard never did.

The strong-arm cleaner when I arrived was a redheaded hillbilly named Clarence. Clarence came from the Rideau backwoods and was doing life for murder. He was one of the few people who had got away completely with a killing, that of his uncle, whose body was never found. But as a devout Catholic, Clarence could not stand the torture of his conscience and turned himself in three years after the case had been closed as insoluble. He led the police to a remote wooded site where they dug up the victim's remains and heard Clarence's confession. He told stories of a primitive, violent existence in which huge quantities of homemade corn liquor were consumed and sticks of dynamite inserted in holes drilled in a hated neighbour's firewood, sooner or later to blow his stove apart. Clarence was a fascinating mixture of Christian devoutness and jungle brutality. We lost him to the warden's residence, where in return for the work productivity of two or three servants, he was rewarded with good meals and the run of the place.

Clarence was succeeded by Henri B., a product of the Depression who had survived unbelievable abuse as a child with good humour and humanity, and from whom I heard at first hand about the pederasty of the good Christian Brothers of Alfred Reform School forty years before it became public knowledge.

Henri came from a French farming family in the Cornwall area. His happiest days were when he started school. His father would load Henri and his brother bareback on an old mare, give the horse a slap and see them off to school. But the Depression overwhelmed the family, forcing them to take up a slum existence in town. Here Henri's father soon turned to bootlegging, his suppliers being the Indians on the Cornwall Island reserve. His stock of moonshine was stored in a narrow alcove between two rooms of the house, safe from the cops and accessible only to eight-year-old Henri because of his slender build. For Henri, now an essential part of the enterprise, the battle was joined. The good guys were his father and brothers, the customers and the Indians from the reserve; the bad guys were the cops and police informers. Henri could remember the moans of a stool pigeon lying in the snow with his legs broken as a warning to others. Soon after, he became a chronic juvenile offender, was shipped off to the Christian Brothers at Alfred, Ontario, where – he claimed – he fought off the repeated sexual assaults and was rewarded by savage beatings, food deprivation and solitary confinement. After two unsuccessful escape attempts he finally succeeded in running away to join an older brother in Toronto in a life of petty crime.

It is hardly surprising that Henri had developed a careless attitude to the law, but at heart he was an entrepreneur rather than a thief. He and his brother eventually became steeplejacks and made a good living risking their lives coming and going like alpinists to carry out repair jobs on smokestacks, domes and steeples the thought of which would give most people vertigo. He admitted that they sometimes skimped on the work, banking on the owner's disinclination to climb up to inspect it, but he looked on this as a normal and permissible aspect of doing business: caveat emptor.

Henri was happily married and couldn't wait for a job to be finished so he could get back to his wife, his two dogs and his trailer home. This homing instinct contributed to his downfall. Late at night driving home from an out-of-town job, he noticed that he was almost out of gas. All the gas stations at the next small town were closed, so Henri did what came naturally and helped himself to gas. Fate ordained that a patrolling Ontario Provincial Police officer should pass at that very moment. Henri was doing time not so much for the relatively small theft as for the length of his juvenile record.

Henri was a thoughtful conversationalist and good company. We had another bond – our dislike and contempt for Howard. When Henri found out that I spoke a little French, he began to make brief insulting comments to me about Howard in the latter's presence. Howard suspected what was going on but must have realized that he was on thin ice if he tried to forbid Henri to lapse into his mother tongue. Henri was the instigator of the revenge we later took on Howard.

Matt A., the convict bookkeeper, arrived at Kingston for the second time shortly after me. He was welcomed back to the Stores where he had previously worked because of his accounting skills which were a mystery to Howard whose job ultimately depended on balanced books. Matt looked less impressively handsome in his fish haircut than he afterwards appeared, but he was clearly an intelligent, well-read person who helped make the daily grind more bearable. Boredom was the main problem – that and the stultifying atmosphere of bigotry and philistinism from which there was no escape.

Sixty
Red Hunt

It might be thought that, as one of the few educated inmates, I would find myself isolated and even avoided. This was not the case. Many of my neighbours in the Old Man's Home were, if not formally educated, men of considerable intelligence and intellectual curiosity. They began to consult me on all sorts of subjects and to bounce ideas and theories off me to get my reaction to them. This led to some interesting discussions in which I tactfully tried to disabuse them of their most stubbornly held fallacies. Some were harmless and unimportant. I remember a discussion with a farm boy on wood, on which he believed himself to be an expert. When I mentioned that the knottiest wood came from the heart of the log and explained why, he insisted I didn't know what I was talking about because in fact the clearest and best wood came from the centre – heartwood, the very name implied its superior quality. I lost all credibility with him. I merely had book knowledge, untrustworthy as everyone knows, whereas he had lifelong, hands-on familiarity with trees. On another occasion I heard references to what sounded like "morfodites," an apparently fascinating phenomenon which some of the cons claimed to have actually seen. It took me a while to realize they were talking about hermaphrodites. I am not sure they appreciated having the subject deglamourised by my supplying the correct word and explaining its origin from Hermes and Aphrodite.

Other discussions, however, raised matters which were not so trivial. Red Hunt began to seek me out for talk. Bit by bit I learned his horrifying story.

Red had been given a psychiatric discharge from the Canadian army at the age of nineteen, late in the war. Although from Windsor, Ontario, he had chosen to stay in Montreal. Here he had carried out a botched robbery at a nightclub during which he and a partner tied up the night watchman and a charwoman. As he tried to leave via the outside fire escape with his loot – much of it in coin – in a pillowcase over his shoulder, the bag broke and noisily scattered the money. He was soon caught and brought to court. As he remembered it, after a ten-minute trial he was sentenced to twenty years and the lash for robbery with violence. The trial was entirely in French, which he did not understand. He was not aware that he had entered any plea nor if he had even been represented by a lawyer. He later found out that the nightclub belonged to a protégé of Premier Maurice Duplessis, and that a club employee who had not been present at the robbery had given perjured testimony that Red had burned him with cigarettes. Red was locked up in St. Vincent de Paul Penitentiary where he lost no time earning a reputation as a troublemaker and was abused accordingly. Eventually the St. Vincent de Paul authorities tired of the maudit anglais and granted his plea to be sent to English-speaking Kingston Penitentiary. Of course, his reputation travelled with him in his dossier, so he was out of a French poêle into an English fire.

Thrown into solitary confinement in the segregation wing, he decided "to put on the bug act." He refused to wear any clothes except a belt around his waist. Perhaps they left him the belt in the hope that he would hang himself. He went on a hunger strike. He masturbated to the limit of his ability and always when in sight of a patrolling screw. His 175 lb weight went down to not much more than 100 lbs. One day a screw went into his cell, picked him up by the belt and carried him out like a bale of hay to a van in which he was driven to the "Bug Ward" – the psychiatric wing of Montreal Prison at Bordeaux.

A day or two later he was summoned to the psychiatrist's office and told to take a seat opposite the doctor who looked at him for a moment then said:

"What seems to be the trouble, John?"

Red told me that it was the first time in years that he had heard a sympathetic human voice. He burst into tears that poured out of him for several hours.

The doctor asked him if he would like to become his personal orderly – bring his coffee, wash his white coats and so on. Thus began Red's restoration to the human race. At the end of a year the doctor reminded Red that so long as he was at Bordeaux he was earning no remission of his sentence and that he was now well enough to go back to Kingston.

To see him as I first did, one would never have guessed at such a history. Over six feet tall, well built and almost aggressively clean in his kitchen whites, he had a friendly, humorous, good-natured disposition, quite the opposite of what one would have expected.

Red, however, was bitterly anti-Semitic. His father in Windsor had been the janitor of a movie house owned by a Jew. Part of his duties had been to dispose of the used sanitary napkins in the washrooms, some of which had been stuffed behind partitions instead of in the receptacles provided. This demeaning work was, of course, "the Jew's" fault. Then I found out that Red thought that jewellers were so named because they were all Jews. By catching him out in such a stupid misconception, I was able slowly to change his thinking and steer him into constructive channels. I made him see that what harm he had suffered, if any, at the hands of Jews was negligible compared to his own self-inflicted wounds and the revenge taken on him by the French and English authorities, that hostile and negative thoughts only played into the hands of his enemies – those who had denied him justice, perjured themselves and, as he discovered, destroyed the records of his trial, making it virtually impossible for him to have any legal recourse. They want you to behave like a madman, Red, I told him; it justifies their treatment of you. Don't play into their hands. Fight them on their own ground. I encouraged him to disentangle the documentation and bureaucratic double-dealing that kept him thrown on the ash heap. With the help of his brother he eventually obtained an affidavit from the sentencing judge effectively repudiating the trial and expressing his distress. In the end, Red did get out, but only after spending many years behind bars.

When finally released in the early fifties, Red started an enterprise called the John Hunt Society, echoes of the John Howard Society. Its objective was to "aid in the rehabilitation of a prisoner," namely, John Hunt. He claimed that he had cleared the idea with the police who for the life of them could find nothing illegal about it. He made small engraved brass nameplates which he mailed to priests, notaries and other easily obtained professional mailing lists. The voluntary contributions to the good cause poured in. Red invested the profits in a rubber stamp manufacturing business which he named Dismas, after the good thief crucified with Christ.

There is a sad postscript to this story. Many years later I was having dinner in a restaurant with some friends where I was introduced to another guest who did a double take at hearing my name.

"Do you know a fellow called John Hunt?" he asked.

"Yes, I do."

"He thinks you're Jesus Christ."

My new acquaintance was a case officer with Canadian Correctional Services. Red had come to his attention as a result of being involved, after all those years, with a young woman – always his Achilles heel – in a bank robbery.

Another of my neighbours but of a totally different stripe was Eddie MacDonald. Eddie was fascinated by words, the more polysyllabic the better. If he heard me use a word with which he was not familiar, he would ask me to define it and repeat it in several contexts until he had absorbed it into his own vocabulary. He would come to me with words he had read or heard elsewhere to run them through me for meaning and approval. He was a paradox to me because like Red he was a friendly, presentable, good-natured person but, unlike Red, he was a long-standing confirmed criminal from a well-known criminal family of three brothers whose loyalty to each other and solidarity against authority in all its guises was unshakeable. By a rare coincidence I saw him one day with his brother, the infamous Mickie MacDonald, in the Change Room when I was on my way to take my weekly shower. He introduced Mickie to me with obvious pride, but I had the feeling that he was also flaunting me to his brother as some sort of trophy. Eddie was useful to me in educating me in the refinements of prison life, when to press an advantage, when to pull back. He was also skilled at breaking the regulations without being caught.

The beds in the Old Man's Home were ancient cast iron cots with a high, tubular metal head-rail such as you might see in a photograph of Florence Nightingale at work in a Crimean hospital. I objected to this as making the task of bedmaking unnecessarily difficult. That's easily fixed, Eddie told me. His job as cleaner gave him the run of the building during the day. He went into my cell and smashed the cast iron uprights clean off, leaving me with a couch rather than a bed. He had correctly foreseen that nobody in authority would bother to do anything about it.

Why Eddie was in the privileged Old Man's Home is hard to say, unless it was to keep him away from his brother. He took full advantage of the situation. In those pre-television days radio was the sole distraction. The programs were fed to the different wings and buildings from a central receiver and strictly controlled as to duration and content. A loudspeaker in a large plywood box hung from the ceiling about twenty feet from my cell. Like it or not, I had to listen to all the popular evening programs – Fibber McGee and Molly, Jack Benny, Charlie McCarthy and the top ten pop songs until the words of "In My Adobe Hacienda" and "Tennessee Waltz" were engraved on my brain. And, of course, the hockey games. We prayed that the games would not go into overtime because precisely at the curfew hour the signal would be cut, regardless of the state of the game.

A small group of cons, however, did not rely on the PA system for their entertainment. They were the few with the knowledge and resourcefulness to make illicit radio receivers. Somehow they had gathered up the necessary raw materials – fragments of copper wire to make coils and a cat's whisker, and pieces of quartz for crystals – to make a "bug," a tiny crystal set half the size of a package of tobacco. Snuggled down under the blanket, the primitive earphone sandwiched between pillow and ear, using the metal bedspring as an antenna, the owner would pull in whatever the local station had to offer, including forbidden crime news.

There was another form of bug in wide circulation; we even used it openly in the Stores to boil water for tea. This was nothing more than a homemade wire element wound around a piece of wood to form a primitive immersion heater. The coil was connected to a short length of electric cable attached to two small nails. A proper electric plug, even if obtainable, would have been of no use because there were no electric outlets in the cells. The method was to push the nails into any available live electric cable to make contact with the current-bearing wires. This tricky and potentially hazardous operation was made still more critical because the bug had to be already carefully positioned in water in the only available container, a steel mug, without touching metal and producing a spectacular short circuit. We always knew when someone had plugged in his bug because the 40-watt cell bulb would dim to almost nothing and begin to flutter. Once in a while the whole cellblock would be blacked out as the out-dated electric system gave up the ghost. And on one memorable occasion the entire prison was blacked out as fuse after fuse blew all the way back to the main circuit breaker.

Eddie was not one to let the loudspeaker box go to waste. He had discovered that there was plenty of room inside to accommodate a sizeable "brew" for which there was always a source of raw materials – prunes, stolen sugar, bread for yeast, potatoes and even grain from a friend in the farm gang. Unfortunately, Eddie became too ambitious and emptied the big fire extinguisher to replace its contents with another brew. Sooner or later the smell gave things away. There followed a major shakedown of the building as a result of which all sorts of harmless and laboriously acquired comforts like lighters, unauthorized books and illegally hoarded tobacco were confiscated along with the radio and immersion bugs. And then the heat would be on, making life miserable for all, including the screws, until slowly things would revert to their normal, larcenous state.

Sixty-one
Jug Up

Food, next to security, was the one item that dominated everyone's thoughts, prison administration and cons alike. The administration had to walk a narrow line between risking public outrage at what might be construed as unwarranted soft treatment, and having to deal with a rebellious inmate population if rations were allowed to fall below a minimum standard of acceptability. Police can get away with handing out cold bologna sandwiches for the few days they are holding prisoners over. Provincial jails, where the inmates were doing at the most two years less a day, and most of them far less, could maintain life and a shaky truce with the inmates on a diet of porridge, pasta and potatoes.

My very first experience of jailhouse food came at the call of "jug up" in the old Carleton County Jail in Ottawa. The food was prepared by the wife of one of the prison guards who was said to feel like a mother to the poor boys in the cells upstairs. The morning porridge, more soup than porridge in consistency, came in a flat aluminum bowl about nine inches in diameter. I could not understand at first why the other inmates took their spoons and, holding them vertically, began to probe methodically every square inch of the bottom of the bowl. They were locating the generous spoonful of sugar which the good lady had dumped in each bowl so they could dredge up some sugar with each mouthful of "scouse."

In the army, the authorities wielded the threat of army discipline and military law to keep the lid on incipient food riots against what could be truly abominable food. Even in the officers' mess the elderly mess sergeant – farmer-turned-cook – could convert the best of raw materials into dispiriting meals, but we had the means and the opportunity to indulge our appetites elsewhere. Not so a penitentiary inmate. In the forties there were no inmate canteens. Even if there had been, there was no money with which to buy anything, especially if you were a smoker, which most were. Convict pay was a flat nickel a day, not including the sacred sabbath. You were charged for your weekly package of roll-your-own "weed," putting you technically in debt to the government.

Food, therefore, was of enormous importance. Considering the difficulties under which the Kitchen Steward had to work – the siphoning off of the cream of supplies for the screws, and the petty thefts at every stage of their passage from delivery to meal tray the meals were surprisingly good. At least I was never as hungry in the penitentiary as I was most of the time in prep school in England. You can be sure that no steaks from the sides of beef wound up on the cons' cast aluminum mess trays, but meat appeared often enough to provide relief from the ubiquitous beans, probably the most important single item of food. As a group the cons exhibited the food prejudices and preferences of their early social environment. Don't try to fob off on them any rabbit food, spinach or junk like that. For many of them, whose childhood food patterns were established during the Depression, beans were like soul food, consumed virtually daily. Consequently, the cons knew their beans and responded immediately to any falling off in quality or quantity. I must admit that, at their best, they were as good or better than any I have tasted elsewhere, including those I cook myself.

I was dramatically reminded of the cultural aspects of taste in food by one attempt to improve the appeal of the line meals. An experienced professional cook had been sentenced on a drug charge and, naturally, had been put to work in the kitchen. Evidently he decided that the bland food needed to be spiced up. When the next food requisition came to my desk to be typed, I saw spices and herbs on it for the first time – things like sage, oregano and cloves. The first result of his efforts turned up as a spaghetti sauce, but instead of subtly introducing the alien flavour a little at a time, he had used the oregano with such a heavy hand that he almost triggered the very riot he was trying to pre-empt.

The portions of food were determined by the kitchen cons who loaded the trays, operating like a primitive cafeteria. The only self-serve item, available in unlimited quantity, was the jail-baked sliced white bread. Some men would take half a loaf at a time. If you were exceptionally hungry you used it to make bean or mashed potato sandwiches, or if very hard pressed, salt sandwiches. These you ate before going to bed because, if you left them overnight, the bread dried up to a brittle crisp.

Food was used not only administratively to forestall riots, but also as punishment. An important disciplinary weapon, besides the loss of "good time," beatings and incarceration in the "hole" was the threat of being condemned to a restricted diet. No. 2 diet, for example, which could be given for twenty-one consecutive days, consisted of bread and water for breakfast, dinner and supper, with the addition of three ounces of oatmeal and eight ounces of potato at dinner. Presumably some departmental nutritional expert had carefully calculated how to impose the pain of semi-starvation without actually killing the victim.

The same expert, out of concern for the health and welfare of the inmates, had ordained the inclusion of fish and liver in the diet. Both items were almost universally detested. If anything could have provoked a food riot, fish and liver were it. Canadians in general in those days had no great love of fish, especially those Canadians living hundreds of miles from the ocean and the fresh fish so beloved by the British working class in their traditional fish and chips. The fish that they encountered in the joint confirmed what they had always believed fish to be – an obscenely stinking, inedible mess. The result was that hundreds of uneaten pounds were regularly thrown in the garbage. The kitchen screw knew this. He was genuinely trying to provide the best possible meals he could within the strictures of budget and bureaucracy, if only to keep the peace and protect his job. I was aware of this because all his requisitions and rationales crossed my clerk's desk in the Stores. He eventually succeeded in substituting canned sardines on fish days – one five-cent tin per inmate. Alas, these were still fish in the eyes of the cons. I happen to like sardines and when this inexplicable quirk of taste became known to my neighbours they removed the tins from their trays and left them for me to pick up. I had as many as eight tins at a time. Imagine how many sandwiches that makes.

Liver was another matter. On this the nutritionists could not be budged. Naturally the liver supplied was the cheapest available. It was served up as a mousey grey leathery slab, mostly tubes and membranes requiring the skill and patience of a surgeon to carve out morsels of edible tissue. Most of the liver, too, went into the garbage. I pictured a conscientious, but absentee, nutritionist unable to understand how men could be so perverse and ungrateful as to refuse a meal of succulent broiled liver made doubly delicious with their own prison-grown onions – the kind of meal people drooled over in expensive restaurants. Liver stayed on the menu.

The guards had their own dining room where they ate a subsidized midday meal. This was one of the perks, along with free uniforms and controlled rents in their residential ghetto at Portsmouth village, used to eke out their miserable wages. To most of them it was the big meal of the day. They ate very well, because after the best cuts from the sides of beef had gone up to the Warden's house, there were still plenty of steaks that never found their way on to the main line. Their food was prepared by convict cooks and we sometimes wondered how they escaped being poisoned, or at least having their food adulterated in the same manner as the Chinese cook in the university fraternity house who took his secret revenge on the bullying boys by peeing in the soup. I would not be at all surprised if they consumed a fair amount of spit, snot and semen along with their steak dinners.

They could, however, run into worse trouble with their other perk – free uniforms. These were made to measure in the prison Tailor Shop. An experienced pants maker can distort a piece of cloth by judicious cutting and ironing in such a way that the pants, seemingly a good fit, will soon begin to twist around the wearer's legs. It therefore was not wise for a screw to earn a bad reputation with the tailors. I was always struck by the childlike pride and pleasure the screws showed when they were called to the Stores to take delivery of a uniform. For new screws, it was probably their first made-to-measure garment – something they could not have aspired to in civilian life, any more than they could have afforded T-bone steaks. For those unlucky ones whose pants began to spiral around their legs in response to wear and body humidity, their anger and frustration when they came back to complain was correspondingly uninhibited

The three of us cons in the Stores always knew when there had been steak on the menu in the screws' dining hall. Howard would appear after the dinner break sucking and picking at his teeth while delivering a critique of the noonday offering – its place of origin on the carcass, its size, its tenderness or otherwise, its state of "done-ness." He liked his steaks very well-done, charred to a crust without a hint of pinkness or, God forbid, blood. If he had been acting this way to provoke us or tantalize us we would not have minded. We would have thought it behaviour natural to a screw. Reminiscing about unattainable meals, known as "burning the grease," was discouraged amongst the cons who thought it showed very poor taste. But in this as in so many other aspects of his behaviour, Howard had no insight into his tastelessness and mean-mindedness. He was just naturally obtuse and inconsiderate.

Howard was also a thief. My confrères did not hold being a thief against him. Amongst cons the term "a good thief" is a term of respect. But Howard was despised because he was such a petty and unacknowledged thief. His job was to receive incoming shipments, check packing slips and pass suppliers' invoices for payment by Ottawa. His tools of trade were old-style push pens with steel nibs, pots of red and blue ink and a hefty stapler. When he had finished with a supplier's invoice it was almost illegible through the red ink ticks, arrows and notations. He would then gather together all the related scraps of paper, including his laborious little sums and calculations, sort them into piles and staple them. Then he would staple the whole dossier together six or seven times, pounding on the stapler to drive it through the thick wad of paper, and toss it into his out basket with the sigh of a long-suffering man who had done his painful duty against all odds.

On a good day there would be a shipment of something susceptible to undetectable filching – for example, the spring bulbs for the prison grounds and the warden's garden. Daffodil bulbs come in clusters. He would break off one or two bulbs from each cluster and secrete them at the very back of his desk's centre drawer. There they would stay until any pang of conscience had dissipated, the bulbs had become kosher, and he took them home.

Another thieving opportunity came when he received and checked a shipment of tea. The tea came in 100-lb. tin-lined plywood chests. The third convict member of the stores staff was a cleaner-strongman-helper, part of whose job was to off-load from delivery trucks to a wheelbarrow at the main gate receiving area, then trundle loads within the prison walls to the various departments and storerooms. This helper's participation in the petty thefts was needed and, of course, was more than willingly given. The technique was to "accidentally drop" a chest of tea so as to break it enough to cause it to leak tea leaves. Theoretically this loss would be contaminated by contact with the ground. In reality, it was carefully collected into a container that just happened to be at hand. Tea chests are built to withstand long voyages by every means of transport and do not readily surrender their contents. The trick was to drop the chest forcibly on one corner. This sometimes took a few "accidental" drops but resulted in a steady supply of tea to the stores staff.

The amount of thievery varied with each change of convict helper: the bolder and more larcenous he was, the more was stolen. Later, when Howard's part of the job was taken over by a young honest guard whom we nicknamed Goodie Goodie Gumdrop, the procedure had become so routine that Goodie was quite unable to control the depredations of M., a particularly violent convict helper. The latter came from a well-to-do Toronto family but was what was in those days known as a psychopathic personality. He was big, unencumbered by conscience or personal loyalties, with a long history of violence and escapes from army and civilian lockups. He disliked me from the start – much too wimpy, egg-headed and law-abiding for his taste – and I later learned that he was waiting for a suitable opportunity to beat me up. Fortunately, he did not last long enough at the Stores for the opportunity to present itself. Included in our inventory of supplies in the office itself was a gallon flask of alcohol for the dentist's spirit lamp. This was issued a cupful at a time on request. M. had discovered it and for some time had been drawing off enough for a nightcap and replacing it with water. Inevitably the time came when the dentist could no longer get it to hold a light, putting an end to M.'s bar supplies, to his cushy job and to my impending nemesis.

Let no one say that Christian charity had been totally extinguished at Kingston Penitentiary in the forties. At Christmas, each con received a paper bag of goodies to help while away the twenty-three-and-a-half hours he spent locked up, there being no work on Christmas Day. The bag contained a handful of hard candy, a few cookies and, I seem to remember, an orange. The meal tray also was tarted up with a few extras like canned fruit and a doughnut. Some cons felt so insulted by the paper bag offering that they gave it away, not even deigning to use it as barter for some other commodity, such as weed.

When my first Christmas in the Stores rolled around, Matt and I were surprised to be called aside by Howard and in the most conspiratorial way offered three cookies each with Christmas greetings from himself and his wife. Since more cookies remained in the bag than the six he had given us, we concluded that he was cheating on his wife and was keeping the rest of the cookies for himself. We accepted the cookies two Christmases in a row but felt so demeaned by it that the third year we decided to refuse. We gave him profusely phoney thanks, told him we really couldn't accept such generosity and took our Yuletide pleasure from watching his benevolent expression revert to its usual flinty cast.

Howard also had his generous side. This was expressed on another occasion when he heard that a carload of cantaloupes that had spent too long en route from California had been withdrawn from distribution and left to rot on a siding. Rotten or not, they were good enough for cons in Howard's opinion. He decided to put his name in lights by talking the owners into turning them over to the penitentiary. This was too much for Harold, the Storekeeper, who, having seen a sample of the proposed delicacy, decided not to risk either a riot or an outbreak of food poisoning.

I personally ate better than most in the joint, at least as far as quantity goes. Through my friendship with Red Hunt, I had two trays – his and mine. After unbelievable hardships, Red had settled down to complete his long sentence and had a good job in the kitchen. To minimize stealing, the kitchen staff was given a good meal in mid-afternoon. Red was eating so well that he had no use for his supper tray so he simply gave it to me untouched. He, like the other kitchen workers, was allowed to take a mug of milk from the kitchen at the end of the workday. Red was tall and well-built, with a confident, friendly air. He was known to have had a troubled and violent past so no screw wanted to provoke him and rock the boat. He was, therefore, given the most perfunctory frisk when leaving the kitchen for his cell, and sometimes was not frisked at all. Rarely a day passed that did not see him leave with some edible contraband hidden just below the surface of the milk – a stolen steak, two or three eggs or a couple of pork chops. These he usually kept for himself but occasionally he would be so surfeited with goodies that he would pass his contraband on to me. In the last year of my sentence, when I had managed over the Storekeeper's objections, to get myself transferred to an open-air job in the vegetable garden, I was able to reciprocate by supplying Red with tomatoes, cucumbers and fresh lettuce.

Sixty-two
Revenge is Sweet

The Stores premises consisted of two levels, with the offices on the ground floor and supplies of various kinds on shelves upstairs. There was also a locked cupboard in which was stored the prison's supply of tobacco – pipe, cigarette and chewing. It was Howard's job to issue this weekly, for Saturday distribution to the cons. He would count and recount his inventory compulsively until he was finally satisfied it was all accounted for, then stack the packages, lock the cupboard and pocket the key.

Matt, Henri and I all had access to this floor – especially Henri, part of whose job was to fill requisitions from the shelves. Matt and I would make tea there and do weight lifting exercises with a piece of rail that had somehow been left there. One day when we all happened to be together upstairs – something we normally avoided because it would almost certainly arouse needless suspicion – Henri suggested we stick it into Howard once and for all. "Let's screw up his weed count," he said. The idea was appealing, but how?

Over the next few days Henri demonstrated exactly how. The weed cupboard was locked with a heavy padlock. Henri examined the keyway to estimate its size. Within a couple of days he had scrounged a piece of metal which, after a few filings and adjustments, could be slipped into the keyway. The next step was to smoke the metal with a candle, insert it in the padlock, gently wiggle it then withdraw it with the impression of the tumblers clearly visible. I have no idea how Henri got his hands on a file or where he did the work but a few days later the key was ready.

The weed came in packages of six. It had been agreed that we would take only a single package, the object of the exercise being to embarrass Howard, not to score for the sake of scoring. The key worked faultlessly. The final act of the drama was over in a few seconds and the evidence dispersed by concealing it in our socks where it eluded the light frisk of the gate guard.

The following weed day when the horror of the discovery of a shortage started to freeze Howard's veins as he time and time again vainly recounted his stock, it was hard for us to suppress our glee. We, of course, went about our business without the slightest sign that we were aware of his growing panic. He for his part was not yet ready to speak of his mortification, especially not in front of us. There was no way he could balance his books by making up the deficit himself. The weed was specially packaged for the joint; it was simply unobtainable elsewhere. He cannot have been looking forward to telling Harold, because among other reasons Harold had recently rebuked him for one of his daffodil bulb scores. Would Harold think that he had actually swiped the weed?

The days passed with not a word of any investigation being breathed in our presence although the paper must have been flying back and forth between Kingston and Ottawa. It was the resourceful Henri who had initiated the caper who also closed it. He had found the opportunity to riffle through the office filing cabinet until he came on a folder containing Harold's report on the incident, a report which cleared the convict staff of suspicion. Howard suffered no permanent damage to his career. Soon after he was promoted in rank to Storekeeper and posted elsewhere.

Sixty-three
The Day Kennedy Was Shot

Among the requisitions I would have to type were civilian clothing lists for female prisoners whose time was about to expire. These consisted of the absolute minimum for decency – one each: bra, panties; pair stockings; dress. The total cost usually ran to twelve or fourteen dollars. A matron from the women's prison across the street would pick up the authorization from the Stores in readiness to take the lucky inmate on a wild shopping spree downtown. One day a young blonde matron came in accompanied by a dark-haired girl we had not seen before. They made a beautiful pair, smiling and seemingly happy in each other's company, almost like lovers. Only the difference in uniforms betrayed the fact that the brunette was a con – Evelyn Dick, in fact, who had been at the centre of a made-to-measure tabloid crime story involving her husband's corpse minus legs, arms and head (How could you Missis Dick!), her dead baby found in a shoe box, and a plot to defraud the Hamilton streetcar company out of thousands of dollars by the sale of counterfeit tickets, for which Evelyn's father-in-law was now doing five years in the Old Man's Home. Dick had been sentenced to hang for murdering and dismembering her husband but the death penalty had been commuted. She was certainly nowhere near being released. There was no reason for her to be in the Stores. We could only assume that it was her good looks that had established her as matron's pet in preference to the Indian women and elderly strip-teasing Doukhobors who were kept securely locked up for fear of causing an embarrassing disturbance.

One of the inter-prison services provided by Dick's sister inmates was special laundry sent over from the main laundry in the men's prison. As every Shakespeare and operetta fan knows, laundry baskets are a natural medium for illicit, romantic communication. The laundry was therefore carefully searched going and coming for letters and contraband. Two or three of the cons with wives or girl friends across the road were usually foiled in their attempts to exchange love letters via the laundry hampers until they hit on an undetectable system: they exchanged pubic hairs. What could be more romantically fulfilling under the circumstances?

The prison messengers were two regular callers whom we came to know well as they checked in at the Stores counter coming and going on their errands. One drove a flatbed truck, the other a car. The truck driver had a reputation as a practical joker. He was said to engage an unsuspecting fellow screw in small talk while surreptitiously peeing on him. He was big enough to indulge this particular brand of wit.

The car driver, John Kennedy, I shall never forget. On one typical dreary afternoon we heard the familiar noise of a vehicle entering the adjoining security lock between the main gates, following by a loud bang like metal being unloaded.

"Shoot him again," Howard called out. He must have immediately bitten his tongue because the glass-panelled door to the Stores opened with a crash and I caught sight of a uniformed figure projected into the room at a forty-five degree angle to collapse on the cement floor. Within seconds all the screws had rushed out of the office, leaving Matt and me alone with an unconscious John Kennedy who was turning bright red, green and purple in quick succession.

"The son of a bitch is croaking," Matt said.

We loosened his collar and tie, undid his tunic and propped his head on his cap. There was no blood; we assumed he had had a heart attack. We soon found out otherwise. Two cons from the garage who had somehow got their hands on a revolver had managed to conceal themselves in the trunk of Kennedy's car. Once inside the first gate they had emerged from the trunk, ordered the main gate guards at gunpoint to open the outside gate and made to pull Kennedy from the driver's seat. Kennedy made the fatal mistake of suddenly reaching for the car keys, whereupon one of the cons shot him in the side, under his outstretched arm. The bullet pierced a lung. We had been witnessing him drowning in his own blood.

The two cons got away but were soon caught. Oscar Craft, an unstable man with a history of childhood abuse, who had done the shooting, never came back to the penitentiary. He finished his troubled days on the scaffold of the Frontenac County Jail in Kingston where, according to Howard, he died like a man.

There was an unpleasant though less drastic sequel to the crime for me, too. During the police investigation I was questioned along with the screws, Matt and also the con stationed at the main gate. I told them I had not seen the shooting, had simply seen Kennedy fall to the floor in the Stores. How little I had absorbed about jailhouse etiquette in all those years! Matt, and the other con who had actually witnessed the shooting, came down unequivocally on the go-boys' side and swore they had seen absolutely nothing. Matt was appalled at my ignorance, because now I was the only non-staff person who could possibly give evidence and, of course, the Crown subpoenaed me. Hostility against me immediately began to build.

The authorities normally counter this by a transfer to another distant penitentiary. I could see myself spending the rest of my time in a regular cell far away in Saskatchewan or the Maritimes, cut off from my visits, bridge games, extra meal trays and settled job. I saw no alternative but to write to the Warden that I felt my testimony to be totally unnecessary in view of the officers who had actually witnessed the event, that it was a hardship for me and left me no alternative but to refuse to testify, which he already knew I was capable of doing. In spite of this, I was handcuffed and shackled when the trial came up – the first time I had worn leg-irons – and held for the day in the courthouse lockup, expecting momentarily to be called for yet another gut-wrenching session of nose-thumbing at authority. The Crown, of course, had absolutely no need of my presence. Craft was quickly convicted without difficulty and without my testimony. The cons' hostility slowly dissipated, but even Matt withdrew into a more distant and less trusting relationship.

Sixty-four
Go Boys

I came perilously close to unwitting involvement in another caper which could have drawn unpleasant consequences both from the cons and from the authorities. Eddie MacDonald's cell was a few removed from mine, with the same view of the prison grounds. He showed me that he had rearranged his cell so that his bed was up against the window, with his head at the window end. He suggested I do the same. Why? Well, you never know, you might see something interesting, he told me. It seemed to me that this would be asking for trouble and unnecessarily jeopardize my small cache of illicitly stored weed, so I kept things as they were.

The following morning, an hour after work began, the prison bell began to toll, signalling an escape, an unheard of event in this maximum-security fortress. Howard reacted as though he had been stung. Abandoning his ink pots and stapler, he made for the door lusting for the hunt. Harold shouted: "Come back, Howard. Stop acting like a common screw." But a moment later, Harold himself sprang into action. He had realized that an escape would mean a heavy demand on the prison gasoline supply which it was his personal responsibility to maintain equal to all emergencies. It was a long time since we had seen him take his eight-foot dipstick marked off in gallons with which he periodically measured the contents of the tank. He now grabbed it and galloped off, praying that there would be enough gas to get the chase started. Off-duty screws now began assembling at the main gate. As an afterthought, Matt, Henri and I were lined up and thoroughly searched as though we might hold the key to this stunning event.

What had happened was that Eddie's brother, Mickie, along with Nick Minnelli, my card-sharper pal from the Nicholas Street Jail, and Ulysses Lauzon, Wally K.'s bank-hoisting partner, had pulled off a perfect, classic escape, complete with sawn bars, dummy decoys, roof-top travels, bed-sheet descents and a hook-and-rope scaling of the formidable, manned outside wall where a car waited to whisk them to oblivion. The rope had hung outside the wall since their departure in the small hours but it was not until the workday was well under way the following morning that someone had equated "rope" with "escape" and raised the alarm.

Eddie, of course, had been in on the plot. He had seen them make the short exposed trip from the cellblock wall to the cover of the lush vegetable patch growing right up to the foot of the perimeter wall, and thence up and over. This was his last glimpse of his brother who was never found. Lauzon's body later turned up in a ditch in Louisiana. Nick was the only one to be caught and returned many months later. He had been working as a card dealer in a casino in the States where he was picked up on an impaired driving charge.

Eddie clearly had been itching to share the secret with someone. While he had stopped short of telling me in so many words, the bed-moving suggestion would have been enough to throw suspicion on me if for any reason the attempt had failed. If on the other hand I had moved my bed, two such moves in neighbouring cells all of a sudden might well have warranted an official investigation of our possible complicity. For once my caution – or timidity – had paid off.

Escapes are commonplace today. In the forties there would be the occasional "go boy" who would wander away from an outside work gang usually to be caught within an hour or two, but the MacDonald/Lauzon/Minnelli escape was almost unprecedented – almost, but not quite. In 1923 a notorious "bad man," Red Ryan, had escaped from Kingston at a time when it was even more tightly secured. The notable aspect was not so much the escape and recapture three months later but his subsequent release as a born-again Christian. He had been able to hoodwink no less than Prime Minister R.B. "Iron Heel" Bennett himself about his repentance and rebirth and was rewarded with a parole. Hardly surprisingly he was shot to death in a holdup less than a year after his release.

Sixty-five
The Power of Prayer

My old commanding officer in the Edmonton Fusiliers – Colonel Strachan, VC – and the Commissioner of Penitentiaries saw eye to eye when it came to religion. Church attendance was compulsory and inescapable, as much part of your sentence as it was of your military duty. This stubborn belief in the power of religion to reform the most hardened characters still motivated the priest and minister to gather little groups of prospective penitents around them. These seemed to include a large proportion of the least savoury types – rapists, baby-fuckers, sneaky killers, including the miner-pimp who had axed his uncooperative wife. This man's cell was on the ground floor of the Old Man's Home where we had to pass in front of it several times daily. He had converted it into a shrine. The priest had probably supplied the pictures of Jesus on the Cross, and Mary, but the tinsel, artificial flowers, song birds, paper chains and blinking lights were his own contribution. He had a little prie-dieu on which to kneel as he bobbed and crossed himself, especially at those times of day when he knew there would be a patrolling screw passing his door. In spite of this conspicuous hypocrisy, the priest appeared to be working loyally for his release, and he was in fact granted a generous parole when compared with those of honest lifers like Charlie Mac who was consumed with deep, excruciating but unreligious remorse.

Discipline in God's house was if anything stricter than elsewhere, probably because here there were several hundred men in one body with all the potential for a riot which that implied. Consequently the congregation was surrounded by screws, with a couple patrolling up and down the aisles to nip in the bud any attempts at conversation, note passing or mutual masturbation.

I felt sorry for the minister, who lacked the bullying assurance of a Sally Ann major to impose his street-wise empathy on the audience. He behaved as though he was addressing a normal, civilized flock on the outside. He ignored not only the groans and heckling laughter of the cons but also the occasional noisy interruptions of the screws as they moved in on an offender.

I tried everything to avoid church attendance, short of playing into their hands by declaring myself an atheist or even an agnostic, which I had been warned not to do or suffer the consequences of having it recorded in my file, making me fair game for any sadistic screw. I did succeed in the end, although it took me close to four years, when I had moved to an outside job in the vegetable garden. The three of us who made up the gardening gang worked on our own, unsupervised. I was able to parlay this work status into a release from church parade.

The church premises served a more useful purpose later, in 1949, when movies, which had been discontinued after the 1932 riot, were reintroduced on Sunday afternoons. The "B" movies proved to be very popular, and the darkened church even more so, a cover for contraband trading, conspiracies of various kinds and even fellatio. The movies were managed by half the number of screws laid on for church. God, it appeared, was more in need of strong-arm help than the devil.

Sixty-six
Croakers and Shrinks

Among the facilities at the penitentiary was a primitive hospital, a cell block in miniature, where the prison doctor, Tommy Tweddell, performed Sunday morning operations assisted by a couple of convict orderlies. Tweddell was the son of a guard, was said to have been born in the prison at a time when there were still some staff apartments within the walls. Before taking up the prison appointment in addition to his private practice in Kingston he had had a distinguished career as a front-line military surgeon where he was said to have wielded a fearless but often spectacularly effective scalpel. Cons in need of really serious operations were sent to outside hospitals but routine operations like circumcisions and hemorrhoidectomies (ring jobs in the prison vernacular) were done by Tweddell in the prison hospital.

In 1947 he performed eighty-seven operations without benefit of X-rays. He also removed Stutz's toes when the old man became so frustrated at these useless appendages getting tangled in his socks that he threatened to cut them off himself. This was the only example I knew of non-essential or elective surgery, the attitude being that you gave only enough medical aid to keep the cons alive, just as you gave them only enough food.

This basically punitive measure, the withholding of corrective surgery, was self-defeating and cost the public untold money in frauds, thefts, legal and police costs and ultimately taxes. My co-worker Matt was a case in point. Matt had been born with a defective left arm, a not uncommon birth injury resulting in a short twisted limb and an underdeveloped hand with little mobility. It was the same kind of arm that Germany's Kaiser Wilhelm kept hidden inside his elaborate uniforms. Matt was a handsome, intelligent, educated man who could hold, and had held good jobs, but he had been uttering worthless cheques – paperhanging – for a decade and was now on his second lengthy sentence. Under the veneer of his criminality was a decent but deeply branded man. It took three years for him to tell me not only of his teenage torment, his blighted sex life and his job frustrations, but also his vain efforts to improve his disability – if not radically at least cosmetically. He had considered having the arm amputated but could find nobody who would agree to do it. He knew that there was a procedure available to straighten and tidy up the joints so that at least the arm would not stick out like a plucked chicken wing, but the cost was beyond his relatively modest con-artistry and certainly more than he could ever hope to earn clerking in a coal company office which was where he worked between his extended stays in prison. Tweddell, to his credit, took an interest in Matt's problem and tried to help him, but Ottawa vetoed any medical intervention.

Another example of Ottawa's obtuseness in rehabilitation matters, although only peripherally medical in nature, was told to me by the barber who gave me my twice-weekly shave. Henri G. was one of a half-dozen barbers plying their often gory trade in the cement hall which housed the Laundry, Change Room, Showers and Barber Line. You were supposed to go to the first barber whose chair became free. This was a potentially hazardous move since most of the barbers were "merchants" looking for some favour such as tobacco in return for a bloodless shave with a freshly stropped razor. Luckily I got Henri's chair for my very first shave. He turned out to be a passionate although uninformed socialist and was pleased to have someone who could tune in to the same wavelength.

The Chinese revolution was underway. To Henri's immense pleasure the Chinese were pushing the Americans out of the country. Henri lathered me then with my nose pinched between his thumb and forefinger waved the cutthroat razor over my face as he eulogized the Chinese and cursed the Yankee dogs. Henri had seniority over the other barbers. He claimed me as his customer and shaved me from then on until his release, and again after his reappearance a few weeks later. His problem was booze, although he was not a serious drunk. He was a professional barber unlike most of the other con barbers, and he had no trouble getting work as a barber. The problem was that a barber had to come to the job fully equipped with the tools of the trade – about seventy-five dollars worth at that time. Since the government gave Henri all of ten dollars when he hit the street he saw no alternative but to steal enough to buy the tools. The ten dollars he had already spent on Dutch courage. He was clearly a better barber than thief.

Rehabilitation, other than in the religious sense of confessing one's sins and seeking salvation in Jesus, was not in the penitentiary lexicon in those days. Yet on purely pragmatic grounds, surely seventy-five dollars would have been a tiny gamble when measured against the cost of imprisonment. Well, perhaps not the cash, which might have gone on beer – but at least a set of tools.

There was a general belief amongst the cons that it was best to stay clear of any contact with Tweddell or the prison hospital. This was partly a class prejudice against all "croakers" – and this one in particular who stood in for Hippocrates at the flogging bench. It also reflected the attitude of the authorities towards illness and physical complaints. These were assumed to be malingering unless the complainant was unconscious or bleeding freely.

The day-to-day administration of health care was in the hands of the nurse screw. Each afternoon after work, as the line went through the dome to pick up the evening meal trays, this nurse screw presided over the medicine cart, dispensed whatever medications had been prescribed and passed judgment on complaints. Headaches – no matter how excruciating – colds and minor cuts and abrasions went untreated. Even requests for aspirins were routinely refused. He seemed to take pleasure in turning down all requests with the exception of laxatives. The only medication at Kingston which was freely available without begging or stealing was Epsom salts. A steady supply of salts solution was always at hand in a big earthenware crock in the dome from which the cons could help themselves. I once saw one of them flood his porridge with it.

To refuse an aspirin to someone suffering from a sinus or migraine headache seems to be particularly mean-minded, but the authorities had enough experience with drug addicts, or "junkers," to be suspicious of all requests. Anyway, the nurse screw, who seemed to relish his reputation as one of the notable S.O.B's in a company of S.O.B's, never relented. One day he met his match at the hands of a Native man from Hamilton, a muscular but gentle and soft-spoken young man who had replaced the terrible M. at the Stores. Upon being refused an aspirin he seized the medicine cart and tossed it in the air, scattering pills and bottles all over the dome. A great cheer welled through the ranges as the news circulated. Strangely, nothing happened to him as a result, perhaps because his action had unveiled the coward within the bully.

Even if you did report sick and managed to get your name down for the hospital parade you did not necessarily see the doctor, who also had an outside practice. You had to pass through the needle eye of the same nurse screw, who made his own diagnoses and dispensed his own treatments. In close to five years I had my share of colds, fevers and headaches, but only twice was driven to report sick. I have forgotten the reason for the first occasion but I remember the treatment – penicillin – so presumably I had an infection of some kind. Our pseudo-doctor immediately prescribed the antibiotic. He had me pull my pants down and bend over. I got a glimpse of the syringe in his hand with a needle that seemed a good three inches long. He placed the syringe against the side of his knee then swung his leg to drive the needle for its full depth into my buttock.

DDT was another modern wonder that was dispensed with a heavy hand at Kingston in the forties. Howard seemed to have a particular liking for it. I have seen him dusted all over from eyelashes to shoelaces with the miracle powder as he dispensed it for use by the farm boss with, naturally, a little bonus laid aside for his own use.

My second trip to the hospital came about because of a burn. I was having my regular shower – not really a shower because there were no showerheads; the water came from a pipe as though from a tap. Without warning the water turned to live steam. Someone in the boiler room had opened the wrong valve. By the time I could jump out of the way I had been badly burned on the chest and all other anatomical high spots on the way down, including my penis. Everyone found this to be very funny, but no one thought it funnier than the nurse screw. He gave me some jelly to apply to the affected parts and nature, as nature usually does, took her course in her own sweet time.

The rumour circulated among the cons that Tweddell was a drunk. The convict hospital orderlies had let it be known that they had strong black coffee waiting for him on the Sunday mornings when he was to operate and kept sobering him up for as long as they could before he started his work. This was the kind of rumour which could have been a total invention, or based upon the slimmest of evidence. But I had reason to believe it to be true. On my last year, when I had managed to evade the compulsory church attendance, I spent the time quietly in my cell. The cell window looked out on the prison grounds, giving me an unobstructed view from the main gate almost to the entrance to the hospital annex. Several times I saw Tweddell walk the distance on a Sunday morning. On one morning, however, he staggered rather than walked and twice fell down. A few days later from my work post at the main gate I saw him leave the prison. His eyes were dazed and the side of his face was bruised and pock marked with half-healed abrasions. Soon afterwards we realized that he had disappeared from the scene altogether to be succeeded by a portly and gentle replacement.

In 1948, the federal government belatedly turned its attention to the mental health of the inmates. A psychiatric ward was built on the ground floor of the Old Man's Home and a part-time psychiatrist taken on staff. As an occupant of a cell two floors up in the same building I could see the progress of construction as I came and went daily to work. There were a half-dozen cells – same old steel bars and cement, of course but flooded with light from the outdoors – and a spacious common day room. I watched with interest the installation of a whirlpool bath for hydrotherapy, complete with heavy restraining cover with a hole for the patient's head. We were told that they would be equipped also to give electro-shock treatments.

Matt, who by now had had enough of Howard and the Stores, applied for and got the job of orderly when the Psychiatric Ward opened for business. It was from him that I got the news of what went on down on the ground floor and the reasons for some of the screams and bellowing that occasionally rent the air. Dr. C.M. Crawford, the psychiatrist, did not appear to be too familiar with some of his new tools, according to Matt. They had one patient, an elderly catatonic, who was the most seriously ill of the group. The doctor chose him to inaugurate the hydrotherapy program.

The bath was filled with water thermostatically controlled to the prescribed temperature, the old man was secured in the bath with his head through the hole in the cover and the pump was switched on to circulate the water. Exactly as prognosticated, the old man's rigid muscles relaxed and he appeared to go into a serene trance. He was left alone to enjoy the amniotic bliss. After what seemed a very short time Matt heard shouts and screams coming from the direction of the bath. The old man was hysterically trying to claw his way out of the bath. It took Matt a minute or two to realize what had happened. The only hot water supply to the bath was from an ordinary domestic water heater. Nobody had thought to match the bath's hot water requirements to a heater of sufficient capacity. The hot water had been quickly exhausted leaving the old man immersed in near freezing well water.

Since it was a bureaucratic impossibility to change the heater, the bath was abandoned. Old-timer Mike O'Hara said he couldn't see why they had to spend all that money on a fancy bath in the first place; in the old days they just used a stone trough filled with water to dunk unruly people in. He claimed the trough was in use when he first came to the prison, and that the empty trough still existed, although I never saw it myself.

The doctor turned his attention to his other hi-tech toy, the EEG machine. Matt and another orderly assisted at the treatments, mostly to try to restrain the victims. As Matt told it, the doctor was by nature conservative and was reluctant to use as much current as the owner's manual advocated, so he cut down on the recommended shocks. Even so, the results were horrifying. The patient, fully conscious, untranquilized and usually panic-stricken, would rise convulsively inches off the table, yelling and sometimes ejaculating.

A male psychiatric nurse named Sellers was hired to run the new facility. He was in sharp contrast to his opposite number in the hospital. Approachable and friendly in manner, he clearly knew his job and treated the inmates with compassion and humanity. This attitude probably stemmed from his religious conviction: he was a Jehovah's Witness. The superficial softness in his manner, unexpected in a screw, and something about the inflection in his voice belied his toughness of character and led to the false belief that he was a homosexual, in spite of the fact that he was a married man with a family. Matt came to respect him highly. Later when I had succeeded in becoming a gardener and could surreptitiously grow a few cucumbers, onions and cauliflowers for myself, I got the idea of making pickles. Matt, with Sellers' connivance, got me into the psychiatric ward kitchen long enough for me to cook up and bottle my harvest.

Matt's co-worker was Mac, a young man doing life for murder. He was a cheerful fellow, popular because of his prowess at bat in the Sunday afternoon ballgames that had been introduced in 1948. As with so many murderers, it was difficult to see the criminal in him, possibly because the uncontrollable temper which led him to kill had never been unleashed in my presence. I heard after my release that he had saved Sellers' life. One of the inmates had gone berserk and attacked Sellers with a knife, cutting him up severely. Mac's adrenaline surged to the occasion. After a ferocious battle in which he was badly cut up himself, he subdued and disarmed the attacker. For once the penitentiary moguls reacted humanely by commuting Mac's sentence.

Red Hunt, who was no stranger to bug wards and had learned the psychiatric jargon, loved to pull the doctor's leg. We were often together for a few minutes after work, waiting in the yard outside the Old Man's Home for Mike O'Hara to arrive, dragging his wagonload of evening meal trays from the kitchen. Occasionally the doctor would appear at the same time. "Watch this," Red would say. He would walk towards the doctor at a fast clip. The doctor would stop in his tracks, then back up slowly as Red approached. The conversation would go something like this:

"Hey, doc…it's okay, doc, I'm not going to hurt you."

"Aah…er…yes, what is it?"

"Well, doc, there's something I can't figure out and it's bugging the shit out of me. I mean, it's well established that we have two sides – or should I say lobes – to our brains, and the left controls the stuff on the right and vice versa...well, you know all this, I don't have to explain it. My question is – what happens with lefties? Are their brains ass backwards as well as their hands?"

This poured out of Red, walking backwards as the doctor doggedly made for the sanctuary and relative sanity of the bug ward.

The Old Man's Home housed still another health facility – the dentist's office. This occupied a hole in the wall off a landing on the stone stairway that we used daily on our way to work. It was not unusual to see a trail of blood leading from the dentist's door. The part-time dentist owned a prosperous bottling business in town and perhaps came to the prison only to keep his hand in – and a very muscular hand it was. His convict assistant, Nick, lived in the Old Man's Home and it was from him that I learned of the goings-on behind the source of that trail of blood. Nick described with admiration how the dentist would take the extractors in his huge hand, almost completely concealing the tool, and with one roll of the wrist remove the tooth – not always, according to Nick, the one the patient had in mind. The dentist would question Nick in advance about the patient's character and reputation. If the victim were a good guy, he would get an injection of novocaine; otherwise the syringe would contain distilled water.

I do not think they bothered with fillings. In any case, most of the cons were terrified of the drill and would far rather suffer the one-time pain of extraction. Some of them, whose teeth were beyond redemption, would beg the dentist to yank out the lot of them to save them from recurring toothaches. The dentist was only too happy to oblige, usually doing the whole job at one sitting. They would then endure a few weeks of gumming bread and porridge before appearing one day in identical, immaculate and pure white store teeth that transformed their looks if not their characters. The dentist's ministrations cost the government a princely $1.67 per con in 1947.

I had only one encounter with the dentist. I was well received, no doubt thanks to Nick, and suffered no harm at the doctor's hands, perhaps because he was intimidated by a mouthful of gold inlays and other signs of well-maintained even, if unattractive, teeth.

Sixty-seven
Outside But Still Inside

When I had served all but a year of my sentence, I applied to the Warden for permission to do the rest of my time in an outside job, specifically in the vegetable garden. It was generally believed that anyone doing five years or more had this privilege – presumably to put a little colour in his cheeks and a little muscle on his frame before being turned loose on society. The Storekeeper was not pleased at the prospect of having to go back to work and tried to block the move but the Warden overruled him. I had prepared the way for the request by enrolling in a correspondence course in horticulture given by the Ontario Agriculture College at Guelph, to which I was entitled under the provisions of the Veterans Affairs Act. I had found the course absorbing and instructive. Professor Shumacher seemed to have gone out of his way to supply lengthy, detailed answers to my many questions. I was eager to put my theoretical expertise to practical use.

The prison operated acres of farmland outside the walls. It was this land that produced virtually all the vegetables – potatoes, onions, corn, cabbages, tomatoes – consumed in the prison. All the necessary seedlings were produced in hotbeds in a half-acre garden plot inside the walls, together with additional crops of cucumbers, lettuce, beets and other vegetables. This operation was in the capable hands of Frank Kramarich, a peasant from Yugoslavia who had emigrated to Sudbury where he had somehow become involved in a killing – uncharacteristically, I felt, for he was a decent, quiet and law-abiding person. I had come to know him and like him after he had shyly approached me one day to ask my help in writing to his niece, Dragica, who was his only family contact. This was the start of a long correspondence during which I became almost a member of the family. I tried to keep myself out of the letters by chatting with him, asking him questions, reading Dragica's letters and eliciting as much from him as possible – not easy, because he was a taciturn, reserved person. He was not pleased when I broached the subject of helping him on the garden, feeling, I think, that I wasn't enough of a peasant either in physique or mentality. In any case, he already had a helper, a young Pole who would have been a market gardener if he had not been a thief.

I got the job in the end, starting one frosty morning in February. Instead of replacing the incumbent they added me to the gang, perhaps feeling I would be incapable of the same productivity. I joined the other two, escorted by the farm boss, at a steaming pile of horse manure that had just been dumped. They were already at work on the pile with manure forks.

"We'll have to get you a fork," the farm boss said. He looked at my pale face and clerk's hands. "Maybe we'd better start you off with a table fork."

The work was indeed hard, but exhilarating, and all the more satisfying for taking place just outside the Stores office window where Harold could see me happily at work. We built hotbeds in the centuries-old style, first tramping down a thick layer of manure on which we set up the wooden frames, packing walls of manure all around, then filling the frames with rich compost, the inheritance of the previous year. Frank knew how to control the temperature of the beds by adjusting the contact of the manure walls to admit more or less cold air and by gauging the openings of the glass lids. He would watch the weather anxiously from his cell window after lock-up, worrying that some quirk of temperature might cause preventable damage during the only hours when he was unable to run to the rescue.

Our score or so of frames produced a prodigious number of seedlings. Crate after crate of plants went out to the farm gang to reappear weeks later transformed into ton upon ton of vegetables for processing in the prison cannery. As a sideline, we supplied the warden's house and the prison grounds with flowers, then turned to mining the deep, rich soil of our half-acre garden, made prolific by generations of horse manure.

The garden was Frank's empire in which he held undisputed sway. The farm boss treated him with respect as a partner in the organization of the season's program. He made sure that Frank had everything he needed in the way of seeds and fertilizers then left the timing to him. We had ample running water including an overhead irrigation system. This gave me the idea of trying to grow watercress. The farm boss had never heard of it, so I was surprised when a few days later he made a special trip to the garden to present me with a packet of watercress seeds, which could not have been that easy to find.

We were exposed to the scrutiny of buildings on all sides and to the armed guard in the tower on the wall above us, but we could retreat from rain, or just to take five, into the cover of a tiny gazebo in the centre of the garden. Over the years Frank had squirreled away all the equipment he had managed to steal or barter to carry on his independent peasant existence. There were sharp knives which would have been serious contraband items elsewhere in the joint, supplies of salt and vinegar, pickle jars and a big oak barrel for Frank's delicious dill pickles which also served as our currency. We sat on boxes with hinged lids that had been used to store a private supply of ripening cantaloupes from the melon patch under the wall until the great escape had turned the patch into an unplanted no-man's-land. Frank was a hard taskmaster, but at least he shared the wealth with us.

Shortly after starting work in the garden my original five-year sentence expired. I still had a year to serve for contempt of court. My lawyer decided to challenge the sentence by habeas corpus proceedings. At about the same time a visitor in civilian clothes came into the garden enquiring for me. He introduced himself as MacLean, one of the Assistant Commissioners of Penitentiaries, concerned with accounting and administration as distinct from discipline and security. He must have become aware of my work in the Stores and presumably had found my attempts to unravel supply problems in simple English an agreeable change from the obscure, ambiguous prose he usually had to deal with. He thanked me sincerely for my contribution which, he assured me, had not been overlooked. He then wished me good luck with my habeas corpus application. I thanked him for his good wishes but told him he was incredibly naive if he thought for one minute that "they" would relent in their attitude; I would give him any odds that I would do every last second of my sentence. He seemed to be truly surprised, but, of course, I was right; the application was refused without my ever having been produced in court.

The scent of this habeas corpus application attracted the attention of one of the literary vultures who fed on the Gouzenko corpse. We were so used to working under the gun – literally – of the screw on the tower above us that we paid little attention to him. An old lifer, Honey Bucket Charlie, would come daily to the base of the tower to send up an empty latrine bucket in exchange for the used one that the screw let down on a rope. Occasionally we might feel generous and offer the screw lettuce or a tomato for his lunch. On this day, however, I heard my name being called. I looked up and saw two people leaning over the railing outside the turret – the screw and Andy O'Brien, sports writer, RCMP confidant and ghostwriter for Gouzenko. Even a prisoner has some rights. This was clearly an invasion of my right to privacy, connived at by the authorities in violation of the regulations. How else could a newspaperman penetrate one of the most secure locations of a maximum-security penitentiary, and one that just happened to be a few feet from me? And how could he have known I would be there, and call me by name? I do not believe Warden Allen would have allowed this without his superiors in the Justice Department ordering it. (When the time for my release came, he foiled the waiting reporters, without my asking him, by arranging for the car which met me to drive inside the gate to pick me up unmolested.)

Frank, always tight-lipped, seemed to become more and more withdrawn as the season progressed. He waged war on birds, and on cats, which he particularly hated for what their love-making could do overnight to a frame full of seedlings, and seemed to become more obsessed and paranoid as he defended his turf. He once caught a marauding cat, rubbed turpentine on its anus, put it in a sack and walked slowly around the garden swinging the sack over his head.

Two or three years earlier, before the establishment of the psychiatric wing, he had suffered a mild depression from which he seemed to have recovered. One day my co-helper and I were taking a break in the sun when we saw Frank coming across the garden towards us, in a straight line over the rows of vegetables, carrying a long-handled shovel in the air like a flag. As he came close we could see a vacant, trance-like look in his eyes. Trusting that the thread of our friendship would hold, I said, "Frank, don't you think we should go and see the doctor?" He nodded. I took his arm and walked him slowly to the Psychiatric Ward where Sellers admitted him without a word. It was the last we saw of poor Frank. He was sent to the Penetanguishene Hospital for the Criminally Insane. I often wondered afterwards who, if anyone, was writing to Dragica.

Sixty-eight
Sprung

In 1948 the Canadian penal system began to show signs of catching up with changing social attitudes. As far back as 1777, John Howard, whose name continues to be synonymous with a progressive, humanistic approach to punishment and rehabilitation, saw crime arising from the same source as disease, namely, from the terrible living conditions of the poor and underprivileged. In his book The State of Prisons in England and Wales, John Howard insisted that punishment, to be effective, must be seen to be morally justified both in the eyes of the prisoner and of the public. Show the prisoner humanity and you have a chance to make him a useful member of society. Property owners, however, who were the most common victims of crime, saw things differently. They saw crime as a social disease, typical of the poor because of their natural laziness and lack of moral sense. Over the years, while paying lip service to Howard's humanitarian approach, prison authorities imposed the most cruel and inhuman conditions on the inmates, men, women and children, all in the name of reform. Total silence, the banning of all human communication, even by a look or a smile; isolation from human contact to the point of being forced to attend divine service cooped like a laboratory monkey in a blinkered box; floggings and long periods of solitary confinement – all were piously employed to uphold the virtuous standards of society and show the wretched offender (who might, for example, have been overheard uttering a blasphemy or have shop-lifted a bun) that poverty does not pay.

Bureaucracy by its nature is in no hurry to change and penal bureaucrats are perhaps the most lead-footed of all. Of course, there have been enormous changes – some would say, too many – but up until the forties, Canadian penitentiaries were still largely guided by the principle enunciated by the Inspector of Penitentiaries in 1887 in his Annual Report "...religious instruction is found to be the most effective means to make known to the convicts the principles of morality and to lift them up from their moral degradation." And, of course, a bit of Christian scourging was held to do no harm.

The riot of 1932 at Kingston Penitentiary, the attempted murder by the authorities of communist leader Tim Buck in his cell and the subsequent publicity resulted in the Archambault Royal Commission which exposed the prison system as "barbarously out of date" and "needlessly cruel." Although the Commissioner's Report lay on the shelf for years unimplemented, some of its effect trickled down to us in 1949 when we were told that we could now spend our Sunday afternoons in the main exercise yard as participants or spectators in a program of organized sports. Bleachers were built, a ball diamond marked out, umpires elected and teams organized. We even had a boxing ring and the necessary landing pits for broad and high jumping. The cons organized their own softball league and fielded their best team, The Saints, to challenge visiting teams, including one made up of members of the Toronto Maple Leafs hockey players. The Saints issued a challenge to the screws, who accepted. One of their players was a particularly hated screw who went out of his way to charge the cons with every possible breach of regulations. The Saints were well on the way to winning when this screw came to bat and walloped a pitch clean over the wall and out of the prison grounds for a three-run homer. The frail appearance of sportsmanship which had prevailed up until then evaporated as the cons revelled in their time-honoured fans' prerogative to boo and insult the player, screw or no screw.

One of the most popular of the Saints players was a young man from Cornwall called Seguin, nicknamed Ziggy. He was not only an excellent player but a born clown who could keep the crowd entertained with his antics. For this reason alone I should probably have remembered him, but he, like Donald Perrault, supplied another reason. A few years later I saw a newspaper report that a certain Séguin, nick-named Ziggy, was to have been hanged early that morning in Cornwall but had stood the hangman up. Only minutes before his rendezvous at the gallows he had bitten on a concealed poison capsule to take charge of his own execution.

I had another Sunday afternoon diversion besides baseball. Sam Carr ("Kogan" of course, to Inspector Harvison) had finally been apprehended in New York, or had more likely given himself up to get it over with, and had started serving a six-year sentence in Kingston. I barely knew him, having seen him not more than four or five times over the years, usually in a crowd, but we began to sit together in the bleachers for an hour or two of conversation. Sam was a most entertaining companion, articulate, enormously well-informed and surprisingly free from anger or bitterness in spite of the fact that he had spent a large part of his life either on the run from authority or locked up in one of its Bastilles. He was a totally committed, professional revolutionary, absolutely without illusions about the nature of power – "theirs" or "ours." We rarely talked about the trials, rather about family matters and what little news we could gather about current events.

Sam also would occasionally talk about his experiences in the movement, his early training in the Soviet Union and his secret assignments in Spain and elsewhere. He told me of being sent in the early '30s as a trainee with an experienced commissar into the Ukrainian hinterland to lay the line down to the "muzhiks" (peasants). The villagers would be assembled and called to order by the commissar whose first step was to produce a big automatic pistol, wave it around then place it on the table in front of him. The meetings usually followed their democratic centralist course without opposition.

Sam told me also of the early days of the Communist Party in Canada when John Leopold of the RCMP had infiltrated the Party under the name of Esselwein, a coup which turns up in all the history books and which is still a source of great pride for the RCMP. What the books do not relate is that the Party was not fooled for long, according to Carr. Leopold was recognized as a plant. Taking a leaf out of Lenin's book, Tim Buck decided not to expose him on the grounds that it was safer to have him where he could be watched and programmed rather than operating as a loose cannon.

Leopold liked to fish. So did Sam and a couple of the other comrades. They would take a boat out on Lake Ontario, often going far from shore. Sam told me that he begged Tim to let him dump Leopold overboard and get rid of him once and for all, but Tim would not allow it. So it would appear that Leopold owed his life to Tim Buck, of all people, and lived to be the chief witness to put Buck, Carr and six others away in 1931 under Section 98 of the Canadian Criminal Code which had been enacted originally to prosecute the Winnipeg General Strike leaders.

It became increasingly clear to me that there was a gulf between the committed hard-line professional and the sincere but perhaps ambivalent, naive, idealistic amateur whose commitment was not to revolution but rather to a civilized upgrading of the human condition. We found less and less to talk about, especially as I was more and more absorbed by the evident crumbling of my marriage. Phyllis had struggled against all odds to make a living for herself and our daughter. She had worked her way up to an excellent job with a financial institution where she had many friends and well-wishers. Her visits to the prison had become less frequent; her letters more and more perfunctory.

The relationship had sustained me through the hard times. Now, it seemed to have run its course. Sam, who had lived his own family life mostly in absentia and did not appear to need the close presence of loving family members, was no help as a marriage counsellor. "Dump her," was all he could think of by way of consolation.

The last days of a long sentence bring a mixture of excitement and anxiety. Fantasies of unlimited hot water and soap, of rare roast beef and fresh blueberry pie, of glasses of Pommard chase after worried thoughts about employment and meeting the challenge of self-determination after years spent as little more than a zombie.

You know that you are about to be sprung when they measure you for your front and kicks. Because I had the illicit weed to "piece off" the con tailor, I was given my choice of a number of swatches and was assured of a good fit. I chose what looked like a brown flannel but turned out to be more like a horse blanket, with a loose, soft texture that barely held a crease. The tailor outdid himself by designing a garment in the height of "zoot suit" style which I am sure would have turned heads in admiration on Jarvis Street in Toronto. Luckily I did not have to take the train from Kingston where the conductor and refreshment vendor were known to be able to spot a con immediately by the cut of his joint suit and mischievously make his presence known. Thus attired, with ten dollars in my pocket and a knot in my stomach, I left the prison discretely by car, as already mentioned, to a new life and an uncertain future.

Sixty-nine
Freedom

Phyllis and her brother Henry had come to collect me. There were no hugs or kisses, no tears, no exultation, barely even smiles. They looked ill at ease as they were gawked at by the gate screws and by Howard who came out from the Stores, curious for a look, but ostensibly to say goodbye – or maybe au revoir. As for me, I just wanted to put as much distance as possible between me and those yard-thick, weeping limestone walls. The atmosphere in the car remained stilted, almost formal and impersonal, as we drove eastwards along the old Highway 2. It was not all that different from the trip all those years earlier that had delivered me inside – to an unknown fate.

I sat in front with Henry. He had had no car when I last had seen him – couldn't even drive – so I made conversation with him on cars and driving techniques. As we passed through town after town I felt a yen for some real food – a cup of decent coffee and a grilled cheese sandwich maybe. I could not understand Phyllis' reluctance to stop until I realized that she had the same discerning eye as the CPR conductors for a joint suit. She was not keen, it seemed, to be publicly associated with someone so attired. I had the sandwich anyway, but the death penalty had already been pronounced on the suit and would be executed within the next couple of days. This posed a financial problem as my entire wardrobe – suits, shoes and shirts had been liquidated during my absence.

We were headed for Phyllis' apartment in downtown Montreal. When we got there they let me out on the sidewalk a short distance from the apartment house door while they went to park the car. A little six-year-old girl playing on the sidewalk looked at me, then came running towards me, arms outstretched, shouting "Daddy, Daddy." She jumped into my arms. I wept. My dearest daughter, what have I done to you!

Clearly the marriage was finished. Phyllis allowed that I could stay under the same roof. Sexually and in all other intimate aspects the marriage was over. It had really been finished for six years – all the years I was in prison and for a whole year before that when my libido had succumbed to the unremitting daily stress of the trials. Could the marriage be rescued? I decided it could not, unless at the expense of capitulating to her program for the future which began to sound like conversion to acceptable bourgeois status. My brother Douglas who had stood by me loyally during my trial felt the same way. He paid a visit to Montreal in a vain attempt to collect his interest in the form of an admission that I had learned my lesson and would behave myself from now on. Sorry. That would be like testifying against friends. Phyllis and I settled into an armed truce.

Soon after this, a group of old friends, including Miriam Kennedy and Ed Chapin who had tearfully bade me farewell at the Samovar night club five years earlier, threw a welcome home party for me at Ed's basement apartment. Phyllis came with me in a far-from-happy mood in contrast to the love-in atmosphere of the gathering. Among those present was Miriam Taylor, an old comrade I had run into from time to time over the years. In mid-evening, seeing Phyllis' grim mood, Miriam said to her, "Phyllis, if you're not having a good time I'd be glad to drive you home." Phyllis immediately agreed and they left.

Half an hour later, Miriam returned. As she came into the room we locked eyes. I cannot say the earth moved; that would come later. I felt as though I had been zapped by some ineffable beam of energy – whether from her eyes or from some celestial source I couldn't tell and really didn't care – which suffused me with joy and miraculously turned the cold, synthetic fluid in my veins into the hot blood of love. Miriam walked over to my chair without a word, sat in my lap and we locked not eyes but arms, mouths, hearts and souls in a lengthy embrace to the shocked silence of our friends. Communists in those days were as sexually uninhibited and promiscuous as conventional society, maybe more so, but you were supposed to be discreet about it, as befitted the virtuous, almost puritanical face the Party liked to show to the public.

Miriam, I learned, had left her husband of fourteen years several months previously and set up housekeeping with her two young sons and a grand piano in a walk-up flat in what she liked to call "the slums of Westmount." She was living on the alimony she received plus the fifty dollars a week she earned on her first job ever, working for Grete d'Hont, her erstwhile decorator. In spite of the passionate prologue to our affair, it took some weeks to convince her that I was serious. Also, I had to conclude the unfinished business of Phyllis. This ended, unhappily, in a violent scene climaxed by me and my meagre effects landing up in a pile outside the apartment door.

Miriam was never short of dates or aspiring suitors but our courtship continued on its hide-and-seek way, with me sometimes taking her home from parties to which she had been escorted by someone else. By this time I had taken over Ed Chapin's basement apartment, and it was there, finally, on a lumpy studio couch that the earth moved.

Unknown to either of us, Miriam and I had been circling in interlocking orbits for years before we came close enough to collide. While I was hacking out advertising copy and slogans in London she was attending art school there, and probably walking the same streets, riding the same buses and lunching at the same bistros. Later in Montreal we became anonymous neighbours on Oxenden Avenue. She might even have called the police from time to time to quell our Saturday night excesses at the infamous 3610 across the street from her. Her time in London was spent with fellow students of all persuasions who debated endlessly and openly the political subjects which would have been taboo in conventional Montreal circles. The Spanish war was in a critical stage at the time. Her good friend Hazen Sise stopped by to say hasta la vista before joining Dr. Norman Bethune in Spain as his sidekick and ambulance driver. Now married, Miriam returned to life in Montreal with her political juices already flowing freely.

When I sounded out the possibilities of work in an ad agency with a former colleague, he refused to see me at the agency itself. Instead, we met in a tavern where he made it plain that it took courage to be seen in my company. In his opinion there was not the remotest chance of any reputable agency ever giving me a job. Luckily for me, Sol Pomerance whom I knew from my QCAV days, had transformed his trades union publicity office into a regular commercial advertising agency. He made me a job offer which I was delighted to accept.

Next to her grand piano, the inanimate object Miriam loved most was her little baby-blue Morris Minor affectionately known as "The Bluebird of Happiness." I was invited to use the car, but first I needed a permit. We went together to the License Bureau where I began to fill out an application form at the counter. Among the questions was one: Have you ever been convicted of an indictable offence? Oh, God. If I put "yes" will they always be on my back? But if I put "no" that in itself would be an offence. I'd better come clean. No sooner had I written "yes" than I felt a tap on my shoulder. I turned to face a burly character who shook his head, reached for the application, tore it up and handed me a new one. Presumably he was a plain-clothes police officer. But was he there especially for me? Or was he just a political hack with a casual attitude to the law who impartially dispensed his flexible interpretation of the regulations? I shall never know.

In the years following, nothing happened to make me feel I was under close surveillance. Clients, if they found out about me, seemed to do so on their own and not from the RCMP. The few who did seemed to take the knowledge in their stride. The only harassment came from the media, in search of "where are they now" stories, and from the odd poison-pen letter.

It wasn't easy for us to marry since we first had to get our divorces. The only way for a Quebec resident to do that was by means of a private bill passed by the Canadian Senate on the grounds of adultery. This meant a lot of money in lawyers' fees, the hiring of private eyes and the farce of a formal hearing on faked evidence. Even then, since there were no civil marriages in Quebec, we had to find a clergyman who would consent to a marriage in which not one but both parties were divorced. But married we finally became.

This made Miriam the target of one of the poison-pen letters. She had left the employ of Grete d'Hont and started her own interior design business. On the recommendation of an antique dealer who was supplying the wealthy Bronfman family with museum-quality antiques, she was engaged by Mrs. Sam Bronfman as her interior decorator. One day, after looking over a proposed colour scheme Mrs. Bronfman said to her, "You must have an enemy. Take a look at this." She showed her a typed, unsigned letter.

"Are you aware," it read, "that you are employing the wife of a dangerous communist, a traitor and ex-convict?"

Miriam immediately recognized the typewriter as the one she had so often used herself and saw the letter for what it was – d'Hont's attempt at revenge for her perceived defection. Mrs. Bronfman would not release the letter, but Miriam reported the incident to a lawyer friend who confronted d'Hont's scandalized husband and extracted a promise that it would never happen again.

My, but things had fallen into place. I had Miriam. I had a job. But what about politics?

I had been released into a political environment far different from the one I had known five years earlier. The heady "One World" post-war expectations of 1945 had been replaced by the Cold War and, in the eyes of the Party ideologues, by a resumption of the war between capitalism and communism that had been only temporarily interrupted by World War II. Miriam and friends were working under new slogans on new issues. Peace was the main theme of this period as it was for communist parties world-wide under the urging of Stalin. The Canadian Peace Congress, which had been launched in 1949 under the Chairmanship of Rev. James G. Endicott, being careful to dissociate itself publicly from any Party programs other than achieving peace, succeeded in collecting hundreds of thousands of signatures on Ban the Bomb petitions, in spite of the fact that the Party's influence had been drastically reduced as a result of the Gouzenko debacle.

I merged imperceptibly into these activities, discreetly avoiding the limelight more out of concern for the negative effect my involvement might have on them rather than on me. I joined a writer's group which turned out to be more of a seminar on socialist realism conducted by the only non-writer in the group, a didactic young woman who had had the supreme experience of mastering her subject at a Marxist school in the United States. The poet Milton Acorn, working-class down to his boots, which he kept planted in the cushions while he sat on the arm of Miriam's sofa, clearly disapproved of my presence. I discovered later that he had taken me to be Hugh MacLennan incognito – not, in his view, suitably proletarian.

Inevitably, living with Miriam, I was drawn more and more into her sphere of political activity. I became so much a part of the scene that someone in the higher leadership, hard up for a suitable straw man I suppose, proposed that I become the Labour Progressive Party candidate in a federal by-election in conservative Westmount-St. Antoine riding. This was an offer not too hard to refuse, but I went to work with Miriam in support of Louise Harvey who had accepted the nomination. This meant combing the poorest slum areas of the riding for votes, often facing a more hostile reception than in the middle-class districts. One evening Miriam, canvassing alone, was nabbed by the police who came in response to the supposed proletarian householder's telephone summons, and spent the night in the slammer. Her crime: canvassing without a permit.

I found that I could not altogether leave the penitentiary behind. One day as I walked on St Catherine Street during my lunch break I saw a familiar figure coming towards me. Only one person had that toe-less stagger. Sure enough, it was old Stutzie. He was not drunk but seemed dazed. He brightened when he saw me, a rare friendly face I am sure. We talked for a few minutes but both of us realized that it could be no more than ships passing in the night.

Another encounter grew into a lengthier association. In the course of her work Miriam had found a Danish cabinet-maker in the process of starting his own company. To have some income until the business began to show a profit he had taken a job at the Mount Royal Hotel, in charge of furniture maintenance and repairs. He told Miriam, with some amusement, about a tall, redheaded guy who had applied for a job as a repairman, claiming to have the necessary experience. He handed him a tack hammer and some tacks and asked him to show how he would use it. It was obvious that it was the first time the man had ever handled a tack hammer but he hired him anyway, mostly because of his persistence and pleasant personality. Of course, this was Red Hunt.

When Red soon after tracked me down in the phone book and called, we invited him to dinner. From then on we kept in touch from time to time while he went about getting his life together. While still working at the hotel he decided to do the honourable thing and marry the girl he had made pregnant. As an employee he was given the use of a salon for the wedding breakfast. He was still on parole and under the wing of the John Howard Society who sent their local honorary chairman and his wife as guests of honour for the occasion. Red had invited us to attend but had not told us that we would also be treated as head table guests of honour.

Unfortunately we arrived rather late. The door to the salon was opened by a middle-aged waiter in hotel uniform. We saw that the guests were already seated and all eyes were on us. The waiter glanced at Miriam, then did a double take. "Miriam," he yelled, throwing his arms in the air then grabbing her in a bear hug. He was a Finnish comrade with whom she had worked during the war years. He made sure our wine glasses were topped up almost after each sip.

As a respite from the daily grind of the rat race and the equally stressful evenings of political activity, we began to use our weekends criss-crossing the remoter areas of the Laurentian Mountains in "Bluebird of Happiness" until we found an island on an isolated lake. We bought it for $750 and built a primitive A-frame house and sleeping cabins for Miriam's two sons and my daughter, who was by now spending her weekends with us.

It was an idyllic time, listening to the loons, going to bed by the light of the aurora borealis and breakfasting on fresh-caught brook trout. It was not, however, popular with our local "commissar." When he heard about our bourgeois deviationist tendencies he dressed us down as "enemies of the Party." We were supposed to spend our weekends in voluntary work at the Party youth camp in the mountains, building additions, painting, scrubbing, clearing bush or cleaning latrines. We decided we should at least put in a token appearance and we persuaded Miriam's teen-age son Jeremy to come with us.

The sexes at the camp were segregated into separate work parties. We met only at meals, eaten at long trestle tables. Our particular skills – mine in construction, Miriam's in painting and decorating – were never investigated. Why bother when there were plenty of Stakhanovite youths to do the skilled jobs, like spray-painting everything in sight, including themselves and the kitchen stove. I was given a sharp stick and a sack and assigned to picking up trash. Miriam disappeared into the steamy bowels of the kitchen, where else! We did not see Jeremy again until it was time to leave. He was in an angry mood, having been assigned to share a bed with an elderly, snoring, garlic-addicted comrade who peed into empty beer bottles he kept under the bed.

Another incident served to show us that "bourgeois" proclivities, our absorption with ourselves, with our island retreat and with our developing careers had usurped political priorities. We were at a meeting, more of a party really, to celebrate some little group achievement. Our hostess had baked a chocolate cake for the occasion. When I took the first bite I realized it wasn't just any old chocolate cake. The blended flavours of chocolate, coffee, butter and some subtle liqueur revealed a loving and unstinted hand not to be found in your neighbourhood supermarket. As we munched our way through it the visiting district representative, chairman for the occasion, delivered his verdict: "Well, comrades, won't it be nice when we have socialism. With communal kitchens, women won't have to slave in the kitchen any more."

These were subjective considerations, but there were other factors. In 1953 we were rocked by news of an alleged plot by Jewish doctors to kill Stalin. This was followed almost immediately by media reports of Kremlin infighting, speculation about Stalin's diminishing power and then by his death on March 6. Stalin's successor, Georgi Malenkov, was replaced within weeks by Nikita Kruschev. What was going on? The Cold War temperature continued to plummet thanks to the Korean War and the rise of the North Atlantic Treaty Organization (NATO) and the corresponding Soviet bloc in eastern Europe. The spirit of internationalism seemed more remote than ever. Without it, even the Peace movement took a beating as the world, including the socialist bloc, rearmed.

The domestic Cold War was also well under way. The Party's important trades union base began to disappear as union after union was "purged" of its red leaders. In numbers and in influence the Party was in decline. Unknown to most of us, bitter fights were developing within the Canadian leadership as a growing number of national and provincial committee members challenged the stubbornly-held Stalinist policies of Tim Buck. Doubt and dissension soon began to filter down to the rank and file. Like many others, Miriam and I drifted away from organized participation. We still saw the same people, kept the same friends, but the associations were now more social than political.

The end came in 1956 when Kruschev leaked the news of Stalin's criminal paranoia. The Party quietly and imperceptibly faded away like April snowdrifts, a few diehards remaining frozen in the deepest ditches. Some comrades who could not face the loss of an abiding faith plunged into religion. Others turned their talents to business or the professions. Some, always given to excessive zeal, became as rabid capitalists as they had been doctrinaire Marxists. Still others were never able to find the formula that would let them adjust to the scorned capitalist society without compromising their socialist and humanitarian principles.

As for me, it was like being sprung for the second time. But this time into a life, with all its inevitable ups and downs, of unbelievable happiness, love, excitement and fulfilment.

Epilogue
Looking Back...and Ahead

This book deals with events in the days immediately preceding, during and following the Allied victory over Hitlerism. The social and political climate then was far different from that of today.

The seeds of the Gouzenko affair were sown by the entry of the Soviets in the anti-Nazi alliance following the German invasion of the Soviet Union in 1941. Unfortunately, the affair was judged and passed into history based not within the context of the Second World War but of the ensuing Cold War.

Although forgotten by many today, the coming onside of the Soviets was welcomed enthusiastically in Canada. It injected new hope and energy into the war effort. Suddenly, victory seemed not just possible but certain. The mood in the West was one of joy at being on the threshold of the peaceful One World with security and justice for all, overseen by a strong world body (the future United Nations). We would live to see this world of the future for which we had sacrificed so much.

Part of this welcome to our new ally was the setting up in Canada of the National Council for Canadian-Soviet Friendship under the auspices of such eminent citizens as John David Eaton. Typical of the council's activities was a mass meeting that filled the Montreal Forum to the rafters in a campaign to collect money for medical aid to the Russians. My future wife Miriam – a volunteer worker for the committee – was "mother hen" to the important guests on the speakers' platform. In the row ahead of her sat John McConnell, owner of the Montreal Star. Behind him sat the founder of the Seagram empire, Sam Bronfman. During an impassioned appeal for funds from the speaker, McConnell swivelled in his seat and said to Bronfman, "Fifty?" Bronfman nodded.

Why, the pikers, thought Miriam, just a lousy fifty bucks?

But, of course, they were talking in thousands.

At the same time most Canadians were welcoming the entry of the Soviet Union into the war on the Allied side, an influential segment of society – including some military leaders, politicians, bureaucrats, businessmen and churchmen – remained deeply hostile to socialism in all its forms, particularly Soviet socialism. Under a 1942 agreement, the British provided the Soviets with a wide range of "weapons, devices or processes" with which to fight the war against the common enemy. The Americans were against such an agreement. The Canadians were, at best, ambivalent.

Science by nature is universal and international, sharing information and building incrementally on the discoveries of others all in the interests of human progress. Even the development of atomic energy was achieved step by step by many scientists from many different countries and cultures. But the atom bomb changed all that.

Initially, U.S. President Harry Truman brushed the bomb aside as being just another weapon of mass destruction – like poison gas – that would fall under strict international control. Soon, however, he reversed his position and put the atom bomb program under the strict control of the U.S military with General Leslie Groves as the boss surrounded by compliant scientists. The less compliant – like the distinguished Dr. Robert Oppenheimer – were hounded and humiliated either into submission or out of the program.

Not all scientists in Canada were willing to accept the restrictions imposed on them. Raymond Boyer was one of those charged in the Gouzenko affair. In court, he openly and unapologetically stated that he had felt it his duty to provide an important ally – the Soviet Union – with information that had been promised under the 1942 sharing agreement. His forthright defence during no less than three trials earned him two years in the penitentiary. In a scholarly paper entitled Secrets Between Different Kinds of Friends, Professor Donald Avery of the University of Western Ontario acknowledges that Canadian scientists during the Second World War had to operate under a new set of principles that ran counter to traditional scientific freedom. But he concedes that the popular view of the Russians as gallant ally was a factor in the actions of those like Boyer which should be "considered though not excused." The tragedy, says Avery, is that the gallant ally became a dangerous enemy overnight.

This aspect was ignored by many of those who reviewed an earlier version of this book which was released under the title The Making of a Spy. Instead, events that took place during the Allied war effort were reviewed under the context of the subsequent Cold War. Though most of the reviews were generous, they took their cue from the year-long sensational reporting in the press that followed the Gouzenko defection and the subsequent trials. Most reviewers wrote freely about "treasonable activities," "betraying one's country" and so on. The Montreal Gazette used the word "treason" in a banner headline. But, of course, treason charges were never laid. The charge used was "Breach of the Official Secrets Act." And even that was beefed up by adding conspiracy charges in order to obtain convictions.

Not surprisingly given the many years that had passed, most of the reviewers ignored the fact that the Soviet Union was an ally – not an enemy – without whom the war might never have been won. They were seemingly unaware that a section of the Canadian establishment was so hostile to the Soviets that they were willing to withhold aid in the hope that the Russians would drown in their own blood. And the reviewers often did not understand that the Province of Quebec – which was where I lived and worked at the time – was to a great extent opposed to the war effort. Many church and political leaders in Quebec openly admired the fascist leaders Mussolini, Salazar and Franco. They called de Gaulle a communist and praised and supported Marshal Pétain – the leader of Vichy-ruled France – even after he threw in his lot with the Nazis and congratulated Hitler on his victory over the Canadians at Dieppe. So who were the real betrayers of their country?

The first interest in the earlier version of this book came from a Learned Society of Canada. I was one of the people in Montreal invited to do a reading and participate at a symposium on Socialism. In its coverage of the event the Montreal Gazette quoted me as saying, "As far as I was concerned he [Canadian Communist Party MP Fred Rose] never levelled with me at all…If he had told me exactly what the involvement was that he was promoting me for, if I had know how the Russians were operating – silly little programmed men, you know – I would certainly not have become involved as I did."

And I wouldn't have gone to prison.

But I did become involved. And I did go to prison. And I accept the consequences without bitterness, secure in the belief that I acted – naively, stupidly and admittedly outside the law – in the best interests of winning the war against Nazism.

The Gouzenko affair helped trigger the Cold War. And it speeded up the events that led to the great divide between the Western and Eastern blocs. But in politics, the goals and strategies are always meticulously planned years in advance. Those goals were already in place. Gouzenko's effect was to increase the pace toward globalization, to the transfer of hitherto national democratic decisions into the hands of unaccountable international trading groups, to the rich getting richer and the poor getting poorer, to the withering of social services with all its consequences for the common man – and to a world of war, genocide and crushing poverty in the midst of plenty. My only regret is that I played a part in making it happen so soon.

The Ottawa of 1944, when I was posted there by the army to work on an Army magazine designed to prepare the troops for civilian life, was still a small town in which snow from the streets was removed by the shovelful and loaded into horse-drawn carts. Members of Parliament, cabinet ministers, senior civil servants and powerful men who for the honorary salary of a dollar a year would formulate policy for the government all mingled with the "hoi polloi" in the streets and restaurants. They drove their own cars. And they sat – and often chatted off the record – with soldiers like myself in the Friday evening CNR train to a weekend leave in Montreal. Ottawa was a town in which all shades of political and class attitudes had a voice, in which unions and left-of-center parties were fully integrated in the decision-making process. I sat on a Wartime Information Board committee of people with widely-conflicting views – but we were still able to find enough common ground in the interests of furthering the war effort.

It was in the course of this work that I came to know Paul Martin Senior (the father of the future Liberal Finance Minister and – as I write this – Canada's newest prime minister and head of a minority Liberal government). I found him easy to work with, never standing on ceremony, asking only that you give your best to the job at hand.

My association with Paul Martin inspired me to put whatever skills I had at the service of the public instead of the advertising rat race. The measure of the man can be judged by what he wrote about me in his Memoirs many years after I had been convicted and imprisoned:

> "I came to know Lunan fairly well. Sitting behind me at our morning delegation meetings, he impressed me as an outgoing fellow who performed his work very capably. He had written some speeches for me that were broadcast back to Canada… On the day of his departure – and eve of his arrest – he wrote me a farewell note that mentioned that he had used my name as a reference for a position for which he had applied at the United Nations secretariat."

Martin withheld judgment on the whole affair, even visiting my parents in London to explain subsequent developments in as kind a way as possible.

As I look back on my association with Martin in Ottawa during the closing days of the war and in London following VE-Day, and as I read the daily sniping at his son Paul Martin Junior in the press these days, I cannot think of two people who better personify the differences between these two periods of our history – pre-Gouzenko and post-Gouzenko. In presenting his budget to parliament several years ago, then-finance minister Paul Junior paid an emotional and sincere tribute to his father. But despite the warm words, the son demonstrated none of the passionate commitment to social programs that was the hallmark of his father's years in cabinet.

This is hardly surprising. Paul Senior was born into a relatively poor family of mixed Irish and French background. At one time, they lived in a house with only two bedrooms for the parents and seven children. His father never earned more than $20 a week. At the age of four, Paul Senior was stricken by spinal meningitis which left him with a life-long muscular weakness. Despite the condition, he worked hard throughout his boyhood to pay for his education, toiling in lumber mills and the Ford auto plant in Windsor. He had already established himself as a successful lawyer when, at age 33, he first entered Parliament. But even as a backbencher he fought fearlessly for social legislation – sometimes to the point of being cautioned by the Prime Minister to "watch his words." While he respected and became close friends with high-born members of the Canadian Establishment, he felt they knew or understood absolutely nothing about ordinary people. His final paragraph in Volume One of his Memoirs sums up his political credo:

> "It was clear that my political values and background would dictate the goals that I must strive for in my newest assignment [at the UN General Assembly]. The benefits of medical science should be made universally accessible; families must be protected against unemployment; the elderly must be given adequate old-age pensions; children should receive the assurance of at least the basic necessities of life and an education that did not come from the beneficence of others."

Son Paul shared one thing with his father – childhood illness. He contracted polio at age eight but survived a lengthy recuperation with courage and without any permanent damage. Thanks to his father's hard work and success, he was spared any of the discomforts and indignities of poverty. Paul Senior encouraged his son to establish himself as a businessman before even thinking about a political career. And in 1966, the 28-year-old Paul Junior joined the Montreal-based financial and industrial giant Power Corporation and began his climb up the corporate ladder. A strong head for business and a willingness to execute daring leveraged buyouts soon helped to make him a multi-millionaire. He wouldn't enter Parliament until he was 50. But almost immediately he became one of the brightest stars of the Liberal government. He has been praised for his remarkable performance as Minister of Finance in eliminating the crippling federal budget deficit. In their 1998 book *Paul*

Martin: A Political Biography, authors Robert Chodos, Eric Hamovitch and Rae Murphy note his ability to "adjust his sights" and get the job done. However, they also conclude that his claim to fame rests on "what he reduced, ended or prevented rather than on what he started or created."

As I write this, Paul Martin Junior has assumed his position as Canada's prime minister. He continues to be tight-lipped or ambivalent – even contradictory – about his proposals to deal with the weakening of the country's social safety net, the crisis in the national health care system and social legislation in general. He won't discuss his long-term legislative program or give any specific details about what he has in store for Canadians. And he has resisted all demands to reveal the source of his financial backing. As required by conflict of interest guidelines, he has given up personal control of his business empire. But to whom? To his three sons. He has enjoyed consistent support from Ethics Counsellor Howard Wilson who apparently sees no possible conflict of interest in a minister stepping outside the Cabinet room for a coffee while matters of concern to his family fortune are being discussed.

Amongst the actions of Paul Martin Junior the shipping magnate while still in control of his holdings was the transfer of Canada Steamship Lines vessels to foreign registration with the resulting firing of the unionized Canadian crews. The move was perfectly legal. It might even have made good business sense. But it was hardly consistent with a commitment to fair treatment for loyal Canadian workers – the kind of commitment his father made.

Time cannot stand still. The world must grow and change. In the years that have passed since the optimistic pre-Gouzenko days, the pace of change has accelerated like never before taking us not only to the moon and to great wealth but also to war and great poverty. Rather than benefiting the common man – as we dreamed it would – progress and change has lowered his standard of living. It's the old story of the rich getting richer and the poor, poorer. In the streets where the poor come to protest, the war between rich and poor is now fought by the authorities not just with billy clubs as before but with mace, pepper spray, tear gas and rubber bullets. Sometimes the bullets are real. Peaceful demonstrators become excusable "collateral damage."

So what are we to do?

When I show people this manuscript or tell them what it was like during the years just before and after the Gouzenko defection, they usually react with astonishment or disbelief. Small wonder. In our schools today little attention is being paid to Canadian history. ("Shamefully ignored" in the words of author Pierre Berton).

Politicians – justifiably or not – have come to be looked on by the public as cunning, self-serving, double-speaking opportunists. Surely, the answer is not to write them off as beyond redemption but to convince them – by rubbing their noses in their current sorry state – to re-occupy the high ground. We must use the democratic rights we still have – to vote, to speak up in our communities, to write letters to the press and to the politicians – to show that we count. But to do so, we must first arm ourselves with a knowledge of our own history and the ability to take a critical look at world events, at history in the making.

I hope this book contributes to that cause.

Sources

Inasmuch as this book is autobiographical, memory has been my principal source. However, I approached memory with some degree of skepticism and did my best to place remembered incidents in correct historical context by reading newspaper reports covering the thirty-year period from 1925 to 1955. I found that the newspapers acted as a catalyst to memory. In the darkened library microform reading rooms I was transported into the past. Not just headlines but also unexpected stray items triggered long-forgotten attitudes and refocused the mental astigmatism of decades.

Prior to 1938 these newspapers were mostly British; after 1938, Canadian. These included the Times, Daily Express, Daily Mail and Daily Herald, all of London, The Montreal Star and the Montreal Standard, The Ottawa Citizen, The Financial Post, and the Toronto Star, Toronto Globe and Toronto Globe and Mail. The periodicals consulted included the New Statesman and Nation.

As a stimulus to recreating as much as possible the atmosphere and mind sets of those days, I also read or re-read many of the contemporary books of biography, memoirs, reportage and commentary, plus some that were subsequently published by writers who had observed at close hand or had participated in the events about which I write.

I found travel also to be very evocative. I revisited former homes and stamping grounds, some of which, like 81 Spencer Place, Leeds, I had not seen for sixty-five years. I found that house just as I remembered it – same walls, fences, tatty lawn, even the same cast iron gate. The church and school appeared unchanged. The neighbourhood, however, had become almost exclusively Caribbean.

Bibliography

Part I

Belfrage, Cedric. *Away From It All*. Penguin Books, 1940.

de la Mora, Constancia. *In Place of Splendor*. London: Michael Joseph Ltd., 1940.

Gedye. G.E.R. *Fallen Bastions*. London: Victor Gollancz Ltd., 1939.

Gunther, John. *Inside Europe*. New York & London: Harper & Brothers, 1937.

Henderson, Sir Nevile. *Failure of a Mission*. New York: G.P. Putnam's Sons, 1940.

Orwell, George. *The Road to Wigan Pier*. Penguin Books, 1962.

Reed, Douglas. *Insanity Fair*. London: Jonathan Cape, 1938.

Sheean, Vincent. *Not Peace But a Sword*. New York: Doubleday, Doran & Co., Inc., 1939.

Shirer, William. *The Rise and Fall of the Third Reich*. New York: Simon & Shuster, 1960.

Schusnigg, Kurt von. *Farewell Austria*. London: Cassell, 1938.

Thyssen, Fritz. *I Paid Hitler*. London: Hodder and Stoughton, 1941.

Viscount Rothermere. *Warnings and Predictions*. London: Eyre & Spottiswoode, 1939.

Part 2

Abella, Irving. *None Is Too Many*. Toronto: Lester Publishing, 1991.

Beeching, William C. *Canadian Volunteers, Spain 1936-1939*. University of Regina: Canadian Plains Research Centre, 1939.

Betcherman, Lita-Rose. *The Swastika and the Maple Leaf*. Toronto: Fitzhenry & Whiteside, 1975.

Black, Conrad. *Duplessis*. Toronto: McClelland and Stewart, 1977.

Buck,Tim. *30 years, 1922-1952. The Story of the Communist Movement in Canada*. Toronto: Progress Books, 1952. The People v. Monopoly. Toronto: New Era, 1937.

Canadian War Office Records. *Thirty Canadian V.C.s, 23rd April 1915 to 30th March 1918*. London: Skeffington, 1918.

Carroll, Jock. *The Life and Times of Greg Clark*. Toronto, Doubleday, 1981

Centre de l'Enseignement du Québec. *Histoire du Mouvement Ouvrier au Québec.*

Harvison, Clifford W. *The Horsemen.* London: Macmillan, 1967.

Hilliker, John. *Canada's Department of External Affairs. Vol. 1: The Early Years.* Montreal: McGill-Queen's University Press, 1990.

Histoires des Travailleurs de Beauharnois et Valleyfield. Montréal: Les Éditions Albert Saint-Martin, 1974.

Lacelle, Nicole. *Entretiens avec Madeleine Parent et Lea Roback.* Montréal: Les Éditions du Remue-Ménage, 1988.

Lipton, Charles. *The Trade Union Movement of Canada, 1827-1959.* Montreal: Canadian Social Publications Ltd., 1966.

Livesay, Dorothy. *Right Hand, Left Hand: A True Life of the Thirties.* Erin: Press Porcépic Limited, 1977.

Massey, Vincent. *What's Past is Prologue. The Memoirs of the Rt. Hon. Vincent Massey.* New York: St. Martin's Press, 1984.

Myers, Gustavus. *History of Canadian Wealth.* Chicago: Charles H. Kerr & Company, 1914.

Penner, Norman. *Canadian Communism: The Stalin Years and Beyond.* Agincourt: Methuen, 1988.

Repka, William & Kathleen M. *Dangerous Patriots: Canada's Unknown Prisoners of War.* Vancouver: New Star Books, 1982.

Rose, Fred. *Fascism over Canada.* Toronto: New Era Publishers, 1938.

Rothwell, Robert. *Canada 1900-1945.* Toronto: University of Toronto Press, 1990.

Warner, Philip. *World War II.* Coronet edition, 1990.

Wittke, Carl. *A History of Canada.* Montreal: The Cambridge Society, 1935.

Part 3

Bothwell & Granatstein, editors. *The Gouzenko Transcripts.* Ottawa: Deneau Publishers & Company Limited, 1982.

Cléroux, Richard. *Official Secrets.* Toronto: McGraw-Hill/Ryerson, 1990.

Gaddis, John Lewis. *The United States and the Origins of the Cold War.* New York: Columbia University Press, 1972.

Granatstein, J.L. & Stafford, David. *Spy Wars.* Toronto: Key Porter Books, 1990.

Mackenzie King, W.L. *The Mackenzie King Diaries 1932-1949*. Microfiche, National Library of Canada.

Pickersgill, J.W. *The Mackenzie King Record*. Toronto: University of Toronto Press.

Reuben, William A. *The Atom Spy Hoax*. New York: Action Books, 1955.

Sawatsky, John. *Gouzenko, The Untold Story*. Toronto: Macmillan of Canada, 1984.

Snell, James and Vaughan, Frederick. *The Supreme Court of Canada: History of the Institution*. Toronto: The Osgoode Society, 1985.

Stacey, C.P. *A Very Double Life: The Private World of Mackenzie King*. Toronto: Macmillan of Canada, 1976.

Part 4

(Archambault Report). *Report of the Royal Commission to Investigate the Penal System of Canada*. Ottawa: King's Printer, 1938.

Boyer, Raymond. *Barreaux de Fer: Hommes de Chair*. Montréal: Éditions du Jour, 1972.

Chodos, Robert. Hamovitch, Eric. Murphy, Rae. *Paul Martin: A Political Biography*, J. Lorimer & Co., 1998

Curtis, Dennis et al. *Kingston Penitentiary, The First 150 Years*. Ottawa: Correctional Service of Canada, 1985.

Jackson, Michael. *Prisoners of Isolation*. Toronto: University of Toronto Press, 1982.

Scott, George *MD Inmate*. Montreal: Optimum Publishing International, 1982

Topping, C.W. *Canadian Penal Institutions*. Toronto: Ryerson Press, 1929.

Withrow, Oswald C.T. *Shackling the Transgressor*. Toronto: J. Nelson, 1933.

In General

Blake, George. *No Other Choice, Autobiography*, London: Jonathon Cape, 1990

Chomsky, Noam *Secrets, Lies and Democracy*, Odonian Press, 1994 *Superpowers in Collision: The Cold War*, Penguin Books 1984 *Deterring Democracy*, Hill & Wang, 1992 *For Reasons of State*, Vintage Books, 1973

Cleroux, Richard. *Official Secrets*. Ryerson: McGraw-Hill, 1990

Moss, Norman. *Klaus Fuchs: The Man who Stole the Atomic Bomb.* Grafton Books, 1989

Index

pch